GENDER AND MATERIAL CULTURE

GENDER AND MATERIAL CULTURE

The archaeology of religious women

Roberta Gilchrist

London and New York

First published 1994
by Routledge
11 New Fetter Lane, London EC4P 4EE

Simultaneously published in the USA and Canada
by Routledge
29 West 35th Street, New York, NY 10001

First published in paperback 1997

Typeset in Garamond by
Ponting–Green Publishing Services, Chesham, Bucks
Printed and bound in Great Britain by
Biddles Ltd, Guildford and King's Lynn

British Library Cataloguing in Publication Data
A catalogue record for this book is available from the
British Library

Library of Congress Cataloguing in Publication Data
Gilchrist, Roberta.
Gender and material culture : the archaeology of
religious women/ Roberta Gilchrist.
p.   cm.
Originally published in 1994.
Includes bibliographical references and index.
1. Monasticism and religious orders for women–Great Britain–
History–Middle Ages, 600–1500.   2. Women–Great Britain–History–
Middle Ages, 500–1500.   3. Convents–Great Britain–History.
4. Christian antiquities–Great Britain.   5. Excavations
(Archaeology)–Great Britain.   6. Great Britain–Antiquities.
7. Sex role–Great Britain.   8. Sex role–Religious aspects–
Christianity–History of doctrines–Middle Ages, 600–1500.
9. Great Britain–Religious life and customs.   I. Title.
[BX4220.G7G55   1997]
271'.90041–dc21   96–48007

ISBN 0–415–08903–4 (hbk)
ISBN 0–415–15656–4 (pbk)

CONTENTS

TABLES AND FIGURES

TABLES

FIGURES

PREFACE

The completion of this book marks ten years since I first came to Britain from Canada in order to read archaeology as an undergraduate at York. Like so many others drawn to the subject, the past holds a deep fascination for me. Yet archaeology is more than just the study of the material culture of past societies. Archaeology seems to be all things to all people. The discipline is equally concerned with the arts and sciences, and increasingly strives to engage with current political issues. This diversity attracted me to archaeology, and my own approach to the subject is influenced by its varied strands, so that parts of this book are informed in turn by medieval archaeology and history, social theory, environmental archaeology and art history. These sources and approaches are, however, driven by a central motivation: to understand what it meant to be a man or woman in medieval society.

The driving force behind my research no doubt results from my own politics. I am a product of my own times, so that gender suggests itself to me as a topic of critical importance in any social research. My great affection for medieval monasteries has developed in parallel with my commitment to feminism and equal opportunities in archaeology and universities. While the inclination to study gender has always been clear, the choice of subject for my doctoral thesis, which forms the core of this book, came suddenly. I began with a typically broad topic, and while compiling a preliminary bibliography to consider gender and medieval settlement, realized that male-bias in previous scholarship had been even greater than I had anticipated. Despite the massive number of academic and popular books and articles on monasticism, not a single work had been devoted to the archaeology of religious women. This omission fired my imagination and commitment, both to feminist scholarship and to the archaeology of religious women, so that for some years I have tested the patience of friends, colleagues and family by travelling miles out of my way just to see a single fragment of wall or grave-slab connected with a medieval nunnery.

During my undergraduate and postgraduate years at the University of York, I was fortunate in receiving the encouragement and assistance of many of the city's medieval historians and archaeologists. Particular thanks are due to my doctoral supervisor, Harold Mytum, and to Richard Morris, for providing an apprenticeship in church archaeology, and to colleagues at the Department of Archaeology, the Environmental Archaeology Unit and the Council for British Archaeology, all of whom provided the support which sustained my doctoral research. A wider network of encouragement came from those whose work first drew me to theoretical archaeology: John Barrett, Richard Bradley, Ian Hodder and Alison Wylie. In pursuing the archaeology of medieval nunneries I have met with great generosity from a number of individuals and archaeological units, among them David and Evelyn Baker, the late Maurice Barley, Derek Keene, Margaret Gray, Pauline Stafford, Barney Sloane, and others in archaeology units at the Museum of London, York, Winchester, Humberside and Norfolk. I am grateful to Glyn Coppack for drawing my attention to errors in my earlier transcription of Figure 23.

The process of transforming a doctoral thesis into a book was undertaken while at the Centre of East Anglian Studies, University of East Anglia, whom I joined in 1990. I have benefited from the encouragement of UEA's complement of art historians, and from the Centre's own scholar in residence during 1991–2, historian Dr Marilyn Oliva, from Fordham University, New York. Together with Marilyn, my vision of medieval religious women expanded considerably, and I discovered that truly inter-disciplinary research can be achieved. The spirit of this book owes much to Marilyn's enthusiasm, and to the support and reassurance of Alex West, who never ceases to remind me that I must continue to ask 'why?'. This book is for the enduring friendships of my first ten years in Britain, for my mother who supported my decision to come here, and most especially for Alex.

ACKNOWLEDGEMENTS

Figure 13 has been redrawn from an unpublished plan provided by Professor Martin Biddle. Figures 17 and 18 are reproduced with permission of Laurence Keen, David Sherlock and the Suffolk Institute of Archaeology and History. Figures 22 and 27 are reproduced from figures 124 and 84 in P.L. Everson, C.C. Taylor and C.J. Dunn, *Change and Continuity: Rural Settlement in North-West Lincolnshire,* by permission of the Royal Commission on the Historical Monuments of England. Figures 25 and 26 are reproduced with the kind permission of Anthony Crawshaw. Figures 28 and 44 of excavations at Elstow have been redrawn by David Baker and reproduced here with his kind permission. Figures 29 and 58 are reproduced by permission of the Royal Archaeological Institute. Figure 35 is reproduced by permission of the Society for Medieval Archaeology and courtesy of Exeter Museum Field Archaeology Unit. Figure 59 is reproduced courtesy of Exeter Museum Service. Figure 60 is by permission of the Council for Kentish Archaeology. Figures 72 and 73 are reproduced by permission of Professor Philip Rahtz. Philip Judge drew figures 13, 14, 46, 48 and 55. Special thanks are due to Ted West, who has drawn Figures 1, 38, 62, 63, 65 and 66.

ABBREVIATIONS

Archaeol. Rev. Cambridge	*Archaeological Review from Cambridge*
BVM	Blessed Virgin Mary
HE	*Historia Ecclesiastica*
Medieval Archaeol.	*Medieval Archaeology*
Norfolk Archaeol.	*Norfolk Archaeology*
Records of Bucks	*Records of Buckinghamshire*
VCH	Victoria County Histories

1

THE HANDMAID'S TALE

1.1 INTRODUCTION

This book focuses on the relationship between material culture and the social construction of gender in later medieval English monasticism. Gender, like class, is defined here as an aspect of social structure which is socially created and historically specific, in contrast with the categories of male and female sex which are fixed and biologically determined. The purpose of the present study is twofold: first, to examine how gender works in relation to material culture through a detailed archaeological case study; and second, to introduce the archaeology of medieval religious women, a rich and distinctive monastic tradition which has remained hitherto 'hidden from history'.

In drawing together these two strands I provide in this opening chapter a background to gender archaeology and a review of the relationship between medieval archaeology and social theory, before presenting my own approach to gender and material culture, which focuses particularly on aspects of gender and space. In contrast to most previous gender studies in archaeology, this framework emphasizes the study of gender as power. This is achieved through a comparison of male and female cultural categories, their meanings, and the resultant social expectations placed on men and women in medieval society. The main subject of the case study is the archaeology of medieval women's religious communities, which are compared with the better-studied monasteries for men. Thus gender is studied as an analytical and comparative category. The relationship between institution and individual experience, or structure and subject, is explored through the interaction of gender, ideology and material culture in the construction of gender identity.

A brief historiography of the study of medieval nunneries is presented in Chapter 2, with the aim of exploding androcentric traditions in monastic history and archaeology. The status and social value with which women's communities were perceived by medieval society is examined through long-term changes in female monasticism, including a summary of evidence for religious women in the Saxon landscape, and a comparison of provision for male and female monasteries in later medieval England. Chapters 3 to 6 attempt to balance symbolic and sociological approaches to medieval nunneries with ecological and economic concerns. In Chapter 3 the religious and economic expectations placed on male and female monasteries are examined according to landscape situation and economic production and consumption. Chapter 4 defines the form and function of medieval nunneries, with reference to liturgical roles for men and women and links to forms of secular architecture appropriate to the gentry society with which nunneries were closely allied. In Chapter 5, female religious symbolism is explored through the iconography of nunnery architecture. Chapter 6 is concerned with gender and space in medieval monasteries, with a comparison of the construction of gender and class in relation to space in monasteries and castles. In Chapter 7, forms of alternative female monasticism are outlined, including beguinages, hospitals, anchorages and hermitages, in order to assess the full range of opportunities available to medieval religious women. A concluding chapter summarizes the new perspectives which have been gained by adopting gender as an analytical category in the study of medieval monasticism.

1.2 THE ARCHAEOLOGY OF GENDER

Gender may be seen as the social construction of difference between men and women. Thus it is socially created and historically specific; rather than simply reacting to social structure, gender can stimulate change. Gender archaeology classifies male and female activities, roles, relationships and cultural imagery according to the social and sexual divisions of a given society. It does not just study women; gender archaeology aims at a more comprehensive, humanistic, and sensitive study of the lives of men and women in the past. Because gender archaeology often focuses on the day-to-day playing out of domestic roles, it may offer a more accessible theoretical archaeology, which deals less with abstract processes and more with the intimacies of human lives.

To address gender through archaeology will not necessarily require new data, but rather new questions and new thinking regarding the nature of gender and society. The archaeological study of gender has developed in response to feminist politics and scholarship in the social sciences, particularly in anthropology (H. L. Moore 1988), although the attitudes and constraints of evidence in archaeology resulted in a delayed response of up to two decades (discussed in Wylie 1991; 1992). Like the gender archaeology to which it has contributed, feminism is varied and cannot be defined as a single movement. However, underpinning the diverse schools of feminist thought is a political commitment which, in the disciplines of history and archaeology, challenges us to re-examine our preconceptions about the gender relations of past societies.

The first archaeological studies to address gender issues explicitly emerged from feminist critiques of androcentrism, or male-bias, in archaeological interpretations (Conkey and Spector 1984). Parallel to this feminist critique, the revision began of previous narratives of the past which omitted or stereotyped women's roles. 'Women' formed a topic for revised histories which challenged accepted syntheses which were male-dominated or featured gender-neutral characters (for example, Fell 1984; Ehrenberg 1989). More recently, gender has been approached as a structuring principle primary to all social structures (Barrett 1988; Sørensen 1988), just as classifications based on status, age, culture or ethnicity structure societies.

Alison Wylie (1991: 31–2) has compared the gradual development of gender studies in archaeology with a similar three-stage process of maturement experienced in other disciplines: initial critiques of androcentrism; 'remedial' research focusing on women; and finally broader reconceptualizations of existing subject fields which consider gender with other structuring factors (after Harding 1983). Archaeology has been slow to ascend to this third stage of development in gender studies, in which conceptual approaches are united with archaeological data in providing new and 'engendered' interpretations of the past (now see *Archaeol. Rev. Cambridge* 1988, 7.1; Gero and Conkey (eds) 1991; Seifert (ed.) 1991). This reluctance may stem from two factors which set archaeology apart from other disciplines in the study of gender.

The first concerns the very definition of gender as a socially created and historically varied force. For some time this definition of gender has been resisted in favour of a biological definition of sex, which for an archaeology grounded in empiricism, is more easily quantified as a fixed factor which can be deduced from the sexing of skeletons. This form of biological essentialism has been countered by new attitudes to social structures more generally within archaeology, which have been fostered by post-modernist thought in philosophy and sociology. Processualist and structuralist approaches to the past had emphasized universal tendencies in social formations and the use of material culture. In contrast, post-processual archaeologies have explored the specificity of social structures and the active, variable nature of material culture (for example, Hodder (ed.) 1987a; (ed.) 1987b; Hodder 1990; Shanks and Tilley 1987a; 1987b; J. Thomas 1991; McGuire and Paynter 1991). A new emphasis on individual agency and smaller-scale variability over larger-scale processes, has encouraged the rethinking of definitions of gender in archaeology.

The second impediment to the development of gender archaeology has stemmed from the nature of archaeological interpretation itself. Emphasis on the empirical testing of data according to the hypothetico-deductive approach prevalent in archaeology, which attempts to develop and test hypotheses by data-gathering and analysis, has demanded that a meth-odology must be sought in order to address gender. This attitude assumes that a material manifestation of gender is latent in the archaeological record, and that testing according to the appropriate theorem will unlock gender, making it visible and rendering it amenable to methods of archaeological quantification. In this vein, previous approaches have sought material correlates which are thought to reflect directly the presence of men and women in excavated material. Such correlates might take the form of particular artefacts or tools which when recovered through excavation would suggest the activities of men or women. Where attempted, the identification of artefacts as sexual correlates has been based on implicit assumptions concerning the sexual division of labour, for example that women cook and weave and that men hunt and manufacture tools (D. Clarke 1972; Flannery and Winter 1976); in correlations between objects associated with anthropologically sexed skeletons (Gibbs 1987; Brush 1988); and in observations drawn from ethnohistoric and ethnographic sources (Conkey and Spector 1984; McEwan 1991). The identification of sexual correlates is problematic in a number of ways, particularly because it relies on interpretations of the sexual division of labour which result from personal preconceptions or from anthropology and history often formulated from the perspective of male-bias. In addition, in order that material correlates reflect male or female, an exclusive sexual division of labour must be assumed, when in most cases task-sharing or fluidity in labour can be expected.

Such methods of 'gender attribution' have been challenged recently: 'Why is there a "need" to "find" females and not the same "need" to "find" males who are, by implication, already present, active, and the primary contributors to the archaeological record and the human past?' (Gero and Conkey (eds) 1991: 12). In other words, why should the onus of proof fall upon 'engendered' interpretations rather than on the androcentric histories which they challenge? Joan Gero and Meg Conkey have argued that progress in gender archaeology can be made only by rejecting the attitude that 'testable' data is fundamental to commenting on the past. By adopting gender as an analytical category, it should be possible to proceed from a strongly developed theoretical position (ibid. 20). Abstract concepts of gender should be no more difficult to countenance than approaches to state formation, the emergence of elites, or other issues which characterize more traditional approaches to social archaeology.

Thus recent work in gender archaeology can be seen to challenge accepted assumptions in archaeology which have dominated the discipline, particularly in America, for over two decades. Principally this approach questions the hypothetico-deductive method and the reflectionist attitude that social structure will be mirrored directly in material correlates. The overturning of standard scientific method has been a feature of much feminist research, in particular that of the more radical, 'standpoint' feminists who have questioned the structures within which knowledge is constructed (see Harding 1986). Feminist critiques of scientific method and structures, particularly in its claims to objectivity and the politics of the construction of knowledge, have features in common with branches of post-modernism. Some 'standpoint' feminists would concur with the validity of subjectivity in informing archaeological interpretations, so that studies of women in the past could only be intuitively carried out by female archaeologists, and not by their male colleagues, however sympathetic. Feminists have been invited to explore their subjectivity in relation to archaeology. But despite the taunt that feminism has contributed little to a value-committed, post-processual archaeology (Shanks and Tilley 1987b: 191), feminists have tended to resist the danger of the relativist trap, which, by virtue of the acknowledgement and elevation of subjectivity, sometimes accepts all interpretations as equally valid. Indeed, it is because of its political com-mitment that feminism resists the relativism which would judge its own interpretations to be only equally valid to those androcentric narratives which it seeks to replace. Feminist subjectivity has inspired critique and introduced new topics of analysis, including the nature of personal agency, sexuality and the body. However, few feminists would support a body of theory based on the subjectivity of being a woman, regardless of time or culture.

Gender arrived firmly on the agenda of archaeology as a result of the politicization of women working in the discipline (Gilchrist 1991; Walde and Willows (eds) 1991; Wylie 1992). And their political motivation and subjectivity shares much in common with the 'critical' or 'radical' archae-ology of post-processualism, which has been vilified as relativist (Binford 1989). But despite having been influenced by post-modernism, feminists have reserved the right to choose *between* different versions of the past. In order to refute androcentrism, feminist archaeologists must be able to evaluate archaeological data and their varying interpretations. Despite their reticence regarding the hypothetico-deductive method, feminist archae-ologists must traverse the distance between archaeological hypothesis and data. Thus certain problems remain surrounding the issues of epistemology and method in making the leap of faith towards interpretation.

The emphasis on historical and cultural specificity in feminist and post-processual approaches has led to a crisis in archaeological interpretation more generally, in which the use of cross-cultural analogy has been brought into question. Gero and Conkey have called for a greater scrutiny of ethnographic and ethnohistoric sources for androcentric (and ethnocentric) bias rather than a total rejection of the potential for these sources. The thrust of their argument, however, suggests that the future for gender archaeology does not lie in interpretation through analogy or empirical testing. Instead, conceptual frameworks will provide the basis for 'engendering' archaeology through feminist re-evaluations of anthropological constructs such as kinship, the family, and the household (Gero and Conkey (eds) 1991: 12).

The diversity of feminist and archaeological approaches will lead inevitably to many gender archaeologies. This variety is borne out by contrasting approaches taken in prehistoric and historic studies and in those informed by American or European theoretical traditions. While all gender archaeologists are linked through the common concerns of critique and theory-building, prehistorians will be more concerned with re-evaluating the uses of cross-cultural analogues, while archaeologists of the historic period grapple with the relationship between documentary and archaeological sources.

Many European archaeologists have studied gender as a descriptive category of material culture linked to biological sex, particularly in relation to Anglo-Saxon grave goods (for example Härke's work on masculinity, Härke 1989). More explicit studies have concentrated on the study of gender as a symbolic construction, focusing on studies of space and imagery. At first gender was addressed as an expression of the structuralist categories of male and female as opposed pairs, exploring male/female as dichotomies such as public/private, political/domestic and culture/nature (H. L. Moore 1982; Braithwaite 1982; Sørensen 1987; Gibbs 1987). Binary oppositions imply a universal contradiction between male and female cultural categories, and exclude the possibility of other gender constructions, including trans-sexualism or a third gender, such as the eunuchs of medieval Byzantium, who occupied their own convents (Patlagean 1987: 597) or the Native American *berdache*, individuals who in entering adulthood chose to change the gender ascription of their youth (Whelan 1991: 24). Gender archaeology must remain open to considering any number of 'genders' in past societies.

The influence of contextualism (Hodder (ed.) 1987a) led to gender archaeology which explored the potential meanings derived from archaeological context, often relying on the sexing of skeletons and the assignment of male or female categories to associated artefacts (Gibbs 1987; Therkorn 1987). This approach, like 'gender attribution', assumes that women must be made visible in the archaeological record. My own objection to this framework lies in the premise that women, their behaviour and material culture, can be recognized only as a deviant pattern to a standard which is male. Marxism has had little influence in gender archaeology, possibly due to earlier friction with feminism over its general under-representation of female labour (Hartmann 1982), although the domestic labour debate can be useful in discussing spatial segregation and the division of labour (Gilchrist 1988). In some post-processual archaeology, gender has been integral to studies of power, agency and social change (for example, Barrett 1988; Bender 1989). Studies of women in historical archaeology have begun to re-evaluate social structures such as kinship and power (Dommasnes

1991) and the role of female agency in economic activity, including trade and exchange (Stalsberg 1991).

American approaches to gender archaeology have been more concerned to analyse gender in terms of economic production, leading to the wider deployment of archaeological data, including environmental sources and variability in artefact-patterning. Two recent volumes on gender in pre-historic and historical archaeology have made great progress in dem-onstrating the potential for gender archaeology – and it is interesting to note that these volumes consist of papers which were in effect com-missioned, often asking archaeologists who were initially sceptical to reconsider their own data from a gendered perspective (Gero and Conkey (eds) 1991; Seifert (ed.) 1991). Several of these studies re-examine the role and status of female labour in subsistence, manufacture and social change, and through standard archaeological approaches overturn previous errors and misconceptions (Gero and Conkey (eds) 1991). These studies of gender have successfully examined the issues of female agency, for instance in the emergence of agriculture (Watson and Kennedy 1991), changing gender relations and the definition of the household (Brumfiel 1991; Hastorf 1991). More sophisticated approaches to analysing gender in relation to cultural imagery have rejected earlier claims for binary representations, instead exploring the ideological content of art, whether as pornography or iconography (Conkey 1991). Stronger links to anthropology have encouraged a greater interest in ethnographic and ethnohistoric sources and their applications to understanding a sexual division of labour and its material culture (Spector 1991).

Some 'empirical' feminist approaches to historical archaeology continue to employ methodologies of artefact-patterning in order to 'find' women in the archaeological record (Gibb and King 1991; Seifert 1991); and many studies have continued to employ a reflectionist paradigm in which archaeological correlates or patterns are accepted as reflecting static, descrip-tive categories associated with women and their work. However, others have been influenced by Marxist and post-modernist approaches in examining the active nature of material culture in the historic period, contributing to debates on female agency, differential male and female mobility in con-structing the household (Purser 1991) and women's choices in consumer goods and their role in constructions of 'domesticity' (Wall 1991). 'Engen-dered' approaches, as they have come to be known in American archae-ological parlance, sometimes confront traditional methodologies. Anne Yentsch (1991a) has criticized standard artefact pattern analysis which enumerates artefacts primarily according to a description of their materials (South 1977), and has proposed an analysis according to the functions of pots and the activities which they represent in terms of men's and women's work. Mary Whelan (1991) has overturned traditional approaches to grave goods in a thought-provoking study of Sioux burial in nineteenth-century

Dakota. She considered the biological sex of burial only *after* patterns of association had been drawn on the basis of artefacts. In this manner Whelan identified gender categories which could overlap between men and women, including individuals closely identified with ritual. In addition she considered children a separate category of gender in that they are gen-derless – without the ability to sexually reproduce.

Despite differing approaches, certain definitions of terms have been adhered to since Conkey and Spector's ground-breaking article (1984). *Gender* refers to the socially created distinctions between femininity and masculinity. *Gender ideology* is the social classification of male and female roles and relationships. The resulting *gender relations* inform attitudes and relations between the sexes and are linked to a wider framework of social relationships which structure society. Gender is one of many aspects which construct social identity, including occupation, ethnicity, age, religion, and especially class or social status. Gender cannot be isolated from other social variables, nor should women form a category for study separate from other aspects of social identity. Here an approach is advocated which considers the structures of gender and class, or social rank, through the social institutions by which human reproduction, the social division of labour, property and inheritance were organized.

While gender archaeology enjoys a healthy degree of debate, there is general agreement that no single method or theory of gender exists, or should be sought. An overarching theory would be anathema to studies which define gender as a socially created and historically specific force. Progress lies instead in asking new questions, in refining our understanding of the relationship between gender and material culture, and in exper-imenting with case studies which will unite data with conceptual frameworks.

1.3 'THE HANDMAID'S TALE': ON HISTORY, ARCHAEOLOGY AND SOCIAL THEORY

We may call Eurydice forth from the world of the dead, but we cannot make her answer; and when we turn to look at her we glimpse her only for a moment, before she slips from our grasp and flees. As all historians know, the past is a great darkness, and filled with echoes. Voices may reach us from it; but what they say to us is imbued with the obscurity of the matrix out of which they come; and try as we may, we cannot always decipher them precisely in the clearer light of our own day.

(Margaret Atwood, *The Handmaid's Tale*, 1985: 324).

Since its emergence in the 1950s, the discipline of medieval archaeology has been coined – most often by historians – the 'Handmaiden of History'. In the decades that followed, medieval archaeologists often sought to justify themselves and the independent contribution which archaeology might make to understanding the medieval period, particularly through its greater interest in social theory (Rahtz 1981; 1983; Hodges 1982; 1983). And yet archaeology has continued to be used only to illustrate a version of the medieval past which is recovered through documents. In Margaret Atwood's novel *The Handmaid's Tale*, a futurist distopia is portrayed in which pro-creative women are socialized into acting as handmaids for a governing elite. Like the 'handmaid' of the novel, archaeology has been stripped of its own identity in order to serve a reproductive function – in this case reproducing another discipline's idea of the past. But Atwood's novel also comments on the insecurity of historical facts, interpretation and objectivity in our post-modern age. For feminists like Atwood, to lose faith in the meaning of history would be to lose faith in the possibility of change in the future. What is the relationship between history and medieval archaeology in light of recent social theory?

There can be no doubt that some medieval archaeologists have demon-strated the potential for theoretically informed interpretations. Archaeology of the early medieval period (*c.* 450–1050) has made use of processualist models in evaluating large-scale processes such as the development of towns and long-distance trade (Hodges 1982), and long-term changes in social formations (Mytum 1992). The potential of the *Annales* school has been explored (Hodges 1983), which aims to reconstruct a total history which does not emphasize the significance of particular dates and events. Archaeological data have been analysed according to principles of struc-turalist theory and substantivist economics (Pader 1982; Richards 1987; Driscoll and Nieke (eds) 1988; Samson (ed.) 1991). The greatest impetus for such studies has come from Britain, whereas in Germany the role of theory in medieval archaeology has been criticized as an 'anti-historical tendency' (Fehring 1991: 235).

In contrast, later medieval archaeology (*c.* 1050–1550) has, for the most part, been accorded a secondary role to historical documentation, being used as an illustrative or descriptive companion to historical readings of medieval life (for example, H. Clarke 1984; Steane 1985). The most significant archaeological contributions to medieval studies have been in the fields of landscape studies, environmental archaeology, economic and demographic history. The topic of social archaeology, however, has remained largely unexplored.

The absence of theory in later medieval archaeology may be explained by the limited purpose which it has been set by those who practise archaeology. For example, in relation to monastic studies the following comments have been made:

> monastic archaeology has come of age and permitted an accurate impression of monastic life to be recreated … in our attempts to

understand their [monasteries'] function we have tended to lose sight of their purpose, and very reason for being.... Archaeology can provide the *how* but it *cannot provide the why.*

(Coppack 1990: 30, my italics)

In terms of potentially well-documented units of landscape, such as lay and monastic estates, we should be using the trowel to answer questions which have been posed through recreating their form and development from written sources.... It is by using archaeology as a means to an end rather than an end in itself that it will provide the greatest service for understanding the monastic estate.

(Moorhouse 1989: 67)

Thus archaeology the 'handmaid' is again seen to illustrate, recreate, and reproduce visions of medieval life drawn from written sources. While a multi-disciplinary approach is of course desirable, the general attitude accords archaeology a subserviant role – one which never asks *why* of archaeological data, and thus reaffirms Philip Grierson's contention that 'the spade cannot lie, but it owes this merit in part to the fact it cannot speak' (Grierson 1959: 129). I would argue, however, that it is not a matter of the spade being mute, but rather that we seldom ask it the right questions, or understand its answers.

The problematic partnership of history and archaeology has included both the identification of general aims and the accepted methods for the treatment of sources. Medieval archaeologists themselves have used historical narratives to define excavation objectives and to interpret archaeological material, often searching to attribute names and dates to actions and events observed archaeologically. Some advocate the integration of historical and archaeological sources only at the stage of synthesis, where each discipline acts as an independent source to be cross-checked (Rahtz 1987: 110). A contradictory view suggests that any degree of integration of the two sources leads to circularity of argument, and that a material approach to the past would identify its own 'less sophisticated aims, but more practical intentions' (Reece 1987: 115). Archaeologists remain divided on the issues raised by historical archaeology, but they tend to agree that historical sources should not be used to date or explain material evidence (ibid. 114), and that our understanding of history must move beyond a concentration on persons and events to an appreciation of source criticism.

Later medievalists have integrated written sources and archaeology in thematic enquiries, such as the nature of the medieval countryside (Astill and Grant 1988a). Grenville Astill's work has emphasized a multi-disciplinary approach in which the sources of each discipline are critically evaluated and used to compensate for deficiencies that each encounters alone (ibid. 6). Others have attempted to set up rules for integration through the classification of archaeological and documentary sources. Anders Andrén

10

(1985: 247–8) for instance, distinguished between 'manifest' and 'latent' archaeological data, or deliberately *versus* less consciously disposed material. The sheer size and variety of archaeological and historical sources, however, mitigates against any unifying methodology or paradigm, even if this were to be accepted as desirable.

David Austin has attributed the paucity of theory in medieval archaeology to its dominance by an agenda set by historians (1990: 13), arguing that to make progress archaeologists must set a new agenda 'founded in our own epistemology and data, and use the written record as only one part of a wider suite of evidence, depending on its relevance to our analysis' (ibid. 14). He has attempted one of very few case studies in later medieval archaeology to have drawn from recent social and critical theory (Austin and Thomas 1990). In a contextual study of a settlement in medieval Dartmoor, he examines the signification of material culture according to the use and meaning of space, buildings and landscape to people in the community. In separating agendas, however, crucial documentary evidence and comparative material may sometimes be deliberately ignored. Agendas similar to Austin's have been set within social and feminist history, for example in Barbara Hanawalt's study of community spatial relationships reflected in medieval coroners' rolls (Hanawalt 1986).

Tim Champion has commented that the condition of medieval archaeology results more from political circumstances than constraints of evidence:

> the prevailing tradition of research has been within frameworks of historical explanation, with archaeology seen as subsidiary to history and providing it with illustrative detail, and with little interest in the kind of approach adopted in American historical archaeology … medieval archaeology has very largely been constrained by the prevailing European mode of historical consciousness, with its implicit acceptance of European superiority and its ideologically laden emphasis on descent from the Classical world and on the literary record.
>
> (Champion 1991: 146)

While it is true that American historical archaeology draws upon theory, this may result more from the strong links which all American archaeology shares with anthropology. If anything, much American historical archaeology emphasizes 'European superiority', frequently seeking to establish connections between forms of European material culture and their use and disposition in American settlement contexts (for example, South 1977). More innovative work in American historical archaeology, however, does reject an agenda or framework set by history. Its sources are multi-disciplinary, but its goals are primarily to explore the active nature of material culture without privileging documentary over archaeological evidence (for example, Beaudry *et al.* 1991).

The key to the relationship between archaeology and history lies in the way in which documents should be used in archaeological enquiries. To date, their use in theoretical medieval archaeology has been to provide explanation, particularly in processualist studies which describe large-scale processes and explain changes and motivations according to individuals and events in documents (Hodges 1982). A more productive approach, particularly for later medieval archaeology, would be to establish research agendas linked to the concerns of theoretical and prehistoric archaeology, for example in studies of gender, social change, power, and the dynamics of space and material culture. In this agenda, documents would be used but they would not be privileged to a position in which they provide explanation while archaeological data merely illustrate. Documents and archaeological data are best used as sources of contemporary analogy. They are integrated not to provide illustration or explanation, but to link themes between media. This method of contextual analogy can be used to set up thematic, problem-specific enquiries between disciplines. Moreover, archaeologists might overcome the intimidation which they have suffered over the bulk of documentary evidence. This daunting amount of evidence has hindered the development of theory in medieval archaeology; this is demonstrated by the greater number of theoretical studies in the early medieval period, where relatively smaller numbers and varieties of documents survive.

For all archaeological theorists the tenets of post-processualism, which deny any objectivity, have caused a crisis of inference. Emphasis on contextualism, in which data are evaluated according to social and historical context, has questioned the use of analogy in interpretation. The issue of our own subjectivity has cast doubt on any form of explanation, be it the analogy of ethnographic parallels or the use of extant documents. Prehistorians and medievalists are united in the need to develop dialogues between archaeology and its sources of analogy, particularly because these sources are no more objectively constituted as facts than our own archaeological data. Documents, in their original creation and subsequent transcription and interpretation by historians, are not absolute in their meanings and thus cannot be applied in order to form categoric explanations for archaeology.

For many medieval archaeologists the questions may remain 'Why should I be concerned with post-modernism?' and 'Why should I be interested in archaeological theory?'. The first response results from the way in which archaeologists traditionally employ documents to provide *explanation*. Current debates on the nature of historicism question the objectivity of historical facts and interpretations. Given the subjectivity involved in the study of all historical material, including documents, should archaeologists continue to explain their evidence through the uncritical use of only one source material or agenda? From the joint perspectives of archaeology and history, debates may begin on assessing subjectivity in the interpretation of medieval evidence. Second, more recent approaches in archaeological theory may be better suited to the subtleties of medieval data. The theories of processualism, structuralism and the *Annales* dealt with long-term generalities and universal tendencies. In contrast, post-processual archaeologies emphasize 'context'. Smaller-scale, more specific problems can be addressed through an alternative to the historical agenda, one which is explicitly archaeological in exploring the material world. In particular these debates focus on the connection between material culture, the individual and social structure. Here it may be appropriate to review some aspects of social theory which have been used in archaeology recently, and their relevance to the study of gender, power and medieval material culture.

In common with post-processualism, feminists share an interest in the relationship between material culture as signifying practice, social institutions and individual agency (Davis *et al.* (eds) 1991; Moi (ed.) 1987; Weedon 1987). However, certain sources for post-processualism have been found inadequate for feminist analyses, particularly Marxism, which through its emphasis on capitalist patriarchy considers only one unifying category of 'women' oppressed through domestic labour, and omits to consider the ways in which women are differentiated through class, culture, religion, ethnicity, and so on. Feminists in other disciplines have made considerable use of psychoanalysis, considering the different genesis of masculine and feminine subjectivity. Like gender archaeology informed by structuralism, much of this work has tended to recognize universals, such as the role of motherhood in constructing femininity or the place of warfare and aggression in constructing masculinity. This approach has had little influence in gender archaeology, although some post-processualists appear to have accepted its tenets, especially Michael Shanks, who has called for a 'feminine' archaeology, which would consider issues of subjectivity, emotion, nature, privacy, and the body (Shanks 1992: 132).

More important have been studies of power and discourse analysis in feminism, which like archaeology, has drawn particularly from the works of Michel Foucault (1979), Pierre Bourdieu (1977), Antonio Gramsci (1971), and Anthony Giddens (1984). Two central themes emerge as being of fundamental importance in understanding gender and power. First is the issue that gender is both structural, reinforced by governments, institutions and structures such as the family, and personal to each man or woman. In this respect gender can be viewed as dualistic, but what precisely is the relationship between personal agency and structural determinism? The second issue arises in considering power asymmetry in gender relations (Davis 1991). In particular, to what extent is this achieved through consensus or coercion?

Discourse analysis (Foucault 1979) considers the social construction of femininity and masculinity, for example through classifications of the body, and gender as a relationship structured by power. This approach has been criticized for under-emphasizing the role of individual agency and the ability of social actors to bring about change (Komter 1991), a weakness which is addressed by Giddens's theory of structuration. Structuration considers social systems both to *result from* human action and to organize and *reinforce* human action. This 'duality of structure' (Giddens 1984: 374) considers the interdependence of social structure and human agency, thus power is seen to be enabling as well as constraining. As a conceptual framework it allows consideration of female agency *and* the structural relations of gender.

But why should women as active social agents accept gender relations which oppress them? Are women coerced or are they complicit in their own subordination? In his critique of structuralist approaches, Bourdieu suggested that 'agency', the activities of individual social actors, supported hierarchical systems of classification based on age and sex (Bourdieu 1977). He observed that these agents were not fully aware of the implications of their actions in any wider structural sense, and thus where their actions reproduced structural relations which were against their own best interests, they could be considered to have acquiesced rather than acted by consensus. Their actions were governed by an unconscious 'learned ignorance', or *habitus*, which provides agents with a practical logic and sense of order. In other words, women acting on their own common sense knowledge of the world around them, their *habitus*, would reproduce structural relations and yet possess the freedom which sometimes would lead to opposition and social change.

Gramsci (1971) considered the way in which consensus is developed between dominant and subordinate groups through the gradual social process of hegemony. Subordinate groups, which may sometimes include women, approve dominant values, symbols, and beliefs, which are part of an encoded value system which is maintained through institutional and individual action. In medieval England, monasteries were part of the church and state apparatus for marshalling hegemony, for example by assisting in the cultural domination brought about by the Normans (M. W. Thompson 1991: 135–7). But was hegemony fully pervasive? Common interest groups, such as women of a particular class, may have developed their own shared views which were alternative to the orthodox. In addition to the social divisions imposed by relations of production and consumption, interest groups can be formed on the basis of attitudes toward gender, age, and ethnicity.

In later medieval England gender relations were organized from within the family, a dynastic institution which transmitted property primarily through male lines of inheritance (Goody 1986). Male and female roles were idealized by a religious doctrine which elevated monogamy and the ideals of female chastity and fidelity. Gender identities in any society are maintained by ideology as *habitus*, a common-sense knowledge of how to proceed as a man or woman in one's community. In medieval society hegemony was created through the ideology of a formalized religion which was sexually divisive and misogynistic. Examples of theological treatises and biblical exegesis are thought to have conveyed negative perceptions of women and of female sexuality (Armstrong 1986; McNamara and Wemple 1977).

Knowledge of the formal teachings of the church would have varied according to levels of education and instruction. At a general level Biblical standards established normative gender roles through explicit Pauline teachings on female behaviour (Harris 1984: 47). At a higher social level, and degree of education, theological sermons and treatises depicted female role models like the opposite figures of the Virgin Mary and Eve, and Mary Magdalene and Martha. The gender relations relevant to later medieval monasticism originated with the Patristic writers who formulated a dualistic psychology in which women were hated while virgins were praised (Ruether 1974: 150). The Augustinian view of the Creation equated humanity's maleness with the soul, spirit and intellectuality, whereas woman was the body, carnality and sinfulness. Patristic theology placed woman below man in the natural order 'as flesh must be subject to spirit in the right ordering of nature' ([Augustine] ibid. 156). This theological understanding of woman's natural inferiority was developed in the thirteenth century by Thomas Aquinas, who justified the application of different moral standards for both sexes by isolating the rationale for women's existence only for biological reproduction (Ferrante 1975: 105; McLaughlin 1974: 214). Woman's corporeal nature, associated with physicality and the body, excluded her from the sacramental and teaching function of the priesthood. But virginal monasticism offered the potential for individual spiritual equality. Christianity held the promise of sexual equality in salvation through acceptance of a code of social inferiority and subordination of women within Creation (Warner 1976: 72).

The hegemony of medieval religion conspired to create a *habitus* for women, in which their own desire for spiritual salvation caused them to reproduce the structural gender relations of medieval society through their own agency. And it is particularly through material culture that *habitus* constitutes gender.

1.4 'ENGENDERING' MEDIEVAL MONASTICISM: A THEORY OF GENDER AND MATERIAL CULTURE

The greatest contribution of post-processualism to archaeology is its premise that material culture is *active* in social relations. Far from merely *reflecting* society, material culture can be seen to construct, maintain, control and transform social identities and relations. Post-processualists also propose that meaning constructed through material culture is not fixed or singular. In other words, landscapes, artefacts, monuments or post-depositional sequences have meanings specific to their time and place; these patterns would not necessarily signal the same meanings to all people in a society, nor will they remain static. Archaeological data are seen to have no universal meaning. Rather, they are explored as possessing overlapping, multiple meanings. This plurality of meaning (the polysemy of material culture) allows us to consider meaning specific to common interest groups defined by gender, status or monastic affiliations, a theme explored in the architecture of nunneries and its iconography (see Chapters 4 and 5).

How is material culture linked to social relations? Simone de Beauvoir once commented that 'a woman is not born, but made'. She is made primarily through material culture in defining *habitus*, a common-sense knowledge which is socially constructed with reference to the material world. For instance, children are enculturated by their societies through material culture – buildings and space, the coding of dress, food and social activities. They learn what is perceived to be correct behaviour for a boy or girl. Today children are enculturated through books, television and toys, at its worse guns for boys and little ironing-boards for girls. Similarly in the past children were enculturated by the material world around them, and by observing the interactions and activities of older children, men and women. Working from this learned knowledge, individuals can create change through material culture. Hence the 'duality of structure' links material culture with structure, agency, and the potential for social change. The impact on gender relations is demonstrated by the sexual politics of the late 1960s onwards, in which forms of material culture, particularly clothing and graffiti, were articulate in demanding change.

It is in this way that material culture constructs gender roles and gender identities. It may be recalled that gender refers to the social construction of difference between men and women. *Gender role* refers to culturally specific, normative expectations of men and women; in other words how men and women are *expected* to act. *Gender identity* is the private experience of gender role which expresses an individual's masculinity or femininity; in other words how one perceives oneself as a man or woman. Gender is learned social behaviour associated with each sex. It is not biologically predetermined – a fact confirmed by the existence of transsexualism (Cahill 1987: 83), nor is it universal. Recent research on masculinity, in particular, stresses divergent, inconsistent and contradictory meanings (Segal 1990).

Gender identity is a process of self-classification in which individuals express their own masculinity or femininity through the values which they have learned. This 'symbolic interaction' is made through reference to the material world; it provides the common-sense knowledge of how to proceed as a man or woman in one's society. These symbolic gestures reaffirm one's own gender identity, while constructing, maintaining, and reconstructing structural gender relations (Deegan 1987: 4). The relationship between social expectations, conformity and material culture was made to me most forcefully when I was first offered a 'ladies' glass' when ordering beer in a

Yorkshire pub. The potential for disrupting gender roles through material culture can be seen in the power of dress in representing genders, for example the centrality of cross-dressing in transsexualism, and the 'uniforms' associated with particular groups within gay and lesbian culture. The importance of space in achieving transformations in gender relations has been recognized in feminist approaches to architecture (MATRIX 1984).

Gender as *habitus* is an informing ideology which is communicated and reproduced through a process of socialization or enculturation in which material culture plays an active role. Material culture constructs gender identity and maintains distance between social groups. The subject constitutes her or his own personal identity while at the same time reinforcing the structural relations of society. She or he interprets and acts upon material culture and is complicit in being conditioned by it – in this way consensual gender relations are achieved.

Space as a form of material culture is fundamental in constituting gender. It determines the contexts in which men and women meet; it assists in defining a sexual division of labour; it reproduces attitudes toward sexuality and the body. The archaeological study of space is based on the premise that space and behaviour are mutually dependent. Henrietta Moore, in *Space, Text and Gender*, proposed that space reproduces social order as a metaphoric extension or transformation of societal divisions (1987: 88). In the study of monastic space, group membership and encounter are structured according to divisions between people of secular and religious status, categories which are composed of sub-groups defined by sex and either religious rank or social status.

Moore suggested a conceptualization for space which has proven useful in the study of gender and space in medieval monasticism. She distinguished between the physical *movement* through space (as a mnemonic which informs and reinforces social action) from the activity of *interpreting* spatial orientation (1987: 81). Her work is based on Paul Ricoeur's semantics of language and texts, in which symbols are understood to have primary and secondary meanings produced through interpretation (Moore 1990). Meaning is constructed through a creative process in which the participant observer refers to the myths and metaphors of his/her own culture. The emphasis is on the action and interpretation of individual social actors in an historical context. This framework rejects the ahistorical structuralist approach to spatial analysis and allows the study of male and female agency.

In this study, categories for spatial analysis are based on a distinction between physical movement through space *versus* the action of interpreting space. Movement, examined in Chapter 6, encompasses the study of access to and segregation within monasteries. Active interpretation of space includes the form and function of monastic architecture and the meanings invoked by its producers and observers. This approach owes much to Richard Krautheimer's iconography of medieval architecture (1942), but

17

respects Moore's use of distanciation (after Ricoeur 1981), which concentrates on the relationship between the intention of the producer and the perceived meanings of the cultural product. These themes will be examined in Chapters 4 and 5. Through space, gender identity can be examined in a monastic context through the processes of building commission, construction, embellishment, occupation and maintenance.

1.5 GENDER IDENTITY IN MEDIEVAL NUNNERIES

This study approaches medieval monasticism by adopting gender as an analytical category, exploring the dynamics of gender in relation to material culture and social identity. While informed by a conceptual framework, theories of gender are drawn from and 'tested' against archaeological evidence. A comparative approach is taken to the archaeology of medieval monasteries for men and women. Patterns of similarity and difference drawn from this reassessment of the archaeology of medieval nunneries comment on gender in medieval society. Meaning is given to these patterns according to social theory, archaeology and forms of contextual analogy including documents, art and literature.

The impulse to assert a self-image is a central human characteristic. One's personal identity is formed in reference to social identity, which is related to group membership (Wiessner 1989: 57). Gender identity is the private experience of gender role, through constructions of masculinity and femininity. But how does any personal sense of gender identity reveal itself in a monastic community? Upon entering a monastery, personal identity is structured through two stages: denial of one's previous identity, and construction of an alternative, new sense of self. The taking of monastic vows involves renunciation of personality, sexuality and social status. For example, the Rule of St Benedict comments on the rejection of private property and personal pride upon induction into a community, 'thenceforward he will not have disposition even of his own body' (The Rule Chapter 58, McCann 1952). This process was facilitated through the structuring of selfhood in relation to time, space, ceremony, and material culture; identities were created in relation to sexuality, liturgical roles and power.

The control of sexuality by institutions has been studied by Foucault (1979). Institutions (such as medieval monasteries) discipline an individual's mind, body and emotions according to appropriate hierarchical relations, such as gender, social rank or religious status. Power is exercised though 'force relations' which classify the body. In medieval monasteries this was achieved through the discourse of celibacy, often involving the stripping away of sensuality. Peter Brown (1987: 267–70) has commented on the loss of male sexuality upon taking monastic vows. The tonsure was a symbolic negation of personal sexuality. The celibacy which followed created a public space within the body; celibate priests became accessible to others through the creation of public space where personal sexuality had previously resided. Here it is suggested that when medieval nuns embraced celibacy theirs was more closely linked to a concept of chastity shared with secular women of the upper classes (see pp. 167–9). Their bodies became private spaces. In contrast to the asexuality of celibate priests, nuns committed their virginity to the church as Brides of Christ. Nuns gave up possession of their own bodies; equally, they became private spaces inaccessible to others. Sensuality, by contrast, was sometimes retained. Writings of the female mystics remind us that this could be redirected through meditations on Christ.

Construction of gender identity began with a ceremony in which the postulant donned bridal garments to commit her virginity to Christ. This union was symbolized by the wearing of the nun's finger-ring. Afterwards, the nun's hair, as a symbol of sensuality, was cut, and she adopted the uniform common to each member of her order. Henceforward the nun shared a common identity with her sisters. Individuality was rejected through the renunciation of private property (a vow later compromised by many monastic houses) and the wearing of identical dress. Where jewellery has been recovered from nunneries, this too reflected a common commitment to Christ. A fourteenth- or fifteenth-century bronze strap-end of a woman's girdle, recovered from Blackborough (Norfolk), was inlaid with the inscription *IE XCE* (?Jesus Christ) (Norfolk SMR). Uniformity was reinforced through the ordering of time, as each member of the community observed the strict monastic timetable (*horarium*).

In situations of extreme conformity individuals are thought to differentiate themselves through non-verbal behaviour, such as facial expressions and spatial gestures (Wiessner 1989: 57). While personal gestures most often elude the archaeologist, collective spatial gestures may be indicated through the development of nunnery plans (see Chapter 4, section 3). Particular communities may have constructed collective identities through their dress and the forms taken by their buildings; these group identities may have been individualistic or conformist. For instance, the Yorkshire Cistercian nunneries were not recognized by the order to which they were committed (see below p. 39). However, the nuns expressed their filial allegiance through the wearing of white habits appropriate to the Cistercians (Elkins 1988: 86).

The nun exchanged her former family relationships for the hierarchy of the monastic community. Authority within the house was articulated through spatial delineation in living spaces, seating patterns and liturgical processions. An abbess's personal power was reflected in the crozier which accompanied her burial (as excavations have shown at Winchester, Qualman 1986) and by representations of croziers on grave-slabs, such as the rare example at Romsey (Hants.) (Figure 1).

Figure 1 Abbess's grave-slab, Romsey (Hants.). Both abbots and abbesses used croziers to signal ecclesiastical rank on their coffin lids. Only nunneries of the highest status shared such symbols of monastic power. Illustration by Ted West.

Nuns possessed no recognized liturgical identity, so that no correlate is known for the chalice which accompanied priests' burials and was depicted on their coffin-lids. However, nuns were occasionally recorded as acting as sacristans, for example at Romsey in 1372 (Coldicott 1989: 61); and the Gilbertines regularly acknowledged a female sacristan (Elkins 1988: 141). Eileen Power (1922: 64 n. 6) noted that in lists of inmates of nunneries, some nuns' names were accompanied by the title of 'chaplain', for example at Campsey Ash (Suffolk), Redlingfield (Suffolk), Elstow (Bedfords.), and Barking (Essex). Clearly, certain nuns were recognized as fulfilling a liturgical role within their communities. It is possible that the relatively frequent occurrence at nunneries of grave-slabs showing chalices may refer to female sacristans or chaplains, rather than to male priests.

Gender identity in medieval monasteries was depersonalized. Monastic institutions numbed any private experience of self through the construction of collective identity. In principle, each member of the monastic community had renounced kin relations, which were structured according to age, gender and marriage, in favour of the monastic hierarchy which was articulated through authority and merit. Gender identity was informed by institutional traits, by the collective identity of a common interest group represented by the monastic order and each convent. These institutional traits are introduced in the following chapter, which presents information on the numbers and orders of women's convents in comparison with those of men. Interest groups are examined through filiation (monastic order) and patronage by particular social groups or families.

2

MAPPING WOMEN'S RELIGIOUS COMMUNITIES

2.1 BREAKING ANDROCENTRIC TRADITIONS: AN HISTORIOGRAPHY OF NUNNERIES

The paucity of archaeological scholarship on medieval nunneries is striking, and puzzling, given that monasteries formed the prime interest of the gentleman antiquaries who anticipated the birth of archaeology itself (see Rodwell 1989; Coppack 1990). With a tradition of monastic archaeology which stretches back some three centuries to the publication of Sir William Dugdale's *Monasticon Anglicanum* (1655–73), why have we not previously considered how, or whether, nunneries were different from monasteries for men? It could be that the scantier remains of nunneries were overlooked, while visually more impressive monasteries were incorporated into land-scaped parks of the eighteenth and nineteenth centuries, and served as a focus for the Romantic Movement exemplified by the works of J. M. W. Turner. It could be that the less imposing buildings of nunneries, and their lower rate of survival meant that quite naturally the antiquaries, and the archaeologists who followed, turned their eyes to the more titillating sites of male houses like Fountains and Rievaulx. Or could it be that the attitudes inherent to monastic archaeology have previously precluded the study of women's monasticism? Has this neglect resulted from the politics implicit within monastic archaeology?

It can be no coincidence that the body of scholarship on the history of later medieval religious women has appeared in two waves which cor-responded with political movements. These movements brought about a greater awareness and interest in women's history. In the late nineteenth and early twentieth centuries women historians were first attracted to this topic during the era of suffrage when they were impelled to examine the activities of women in the past (for example, Eckenstein 1896; Bateson 1899; R. Graham 1903; R. M. Clay 1909 and 1914; Power 1922; Bourdillon 1926). For decades these pioneering works remained unsurpassed. Recently, however, a fresh wave of scholarship has emerged, once again side by side with a rekindled interest in women's history (Burton 1979; S. Thompson

1978; 1984; 1991; Elkins 1988; Rubin 1987; Warren 1985), although only now is this work being conducted from an explicitly feminist perspective (Oliva 1994).

For some time male historians of male monasticism claimed that sources for religious women were simply not available or adequate – a claim admirably discounted by the recent proliferation of work on religious women by female historians. Similarly the lack of synthesis of the archaeology of nunneries cannot be explained by absence of primary sources. Nunneries were explored by local antiquaries, for example Nunburnholme (N. Yorks.) (M. C. F. Morris 1907), Goring (Oxfords.) (Stone 1893), Kirklees (W. Yorks.) (Armytage 1908), and Hampole (W. Yorks.) (Whiting 1938), albeit with results which should be viewed cautiously. During the celebrated 'Golden Age' of monastic archaeology nunneries were 'stamp-collected' along with other monasteries. Sir William St John Hope conducted work at Gilbertine Watton (Humbs.) (1901); Sir Harold Brakspear excavated at the Augustinian nunneries of Lacock (Wilts.) (1900), Burnham (Berks., formerly Bucks.) (1903) and Kington St Michael (Wilts.) (1922); Sir Alfred Clapham investigated the Benedictine Abbey of Barking (Essex) (1913), the Dominican nunnery at Dartford (Kent) (1926), and the remains of St Helen's Bishopsgate, London (Reddan and Clapham 1924); and Sir Charles Peers excavated the small nunnery of Little Marlow (Bucks.) (1902). Nunneries have been the subject of excavation fairly frequently within the last thirty years. The larger projects include Elstow (Bedfords.) (Baker 1971; 1989); Polsloe, near Exeter (*Medieval Archaeol.* 23, 1979: 250–1); Nuneaton (Warwicks.) (Andrews *et al* 1981); Denney (Cambs.) (Christie and Coad 1980); Campsey Ash (Suffolk) (Sherlock 1970); Higham (Kent) (Tester 1967) and Davington (Kent) (Tester 1980). More fragmentary excavations in advance of development have included St Mary's, Chester (Rutland 1965); the Minories, London (*Medieval Archaeol.* 31, 1987: 128); St Mary's, Winchester (Qualman 1986); Carrow Priory, Norwich (*Norfolk Archaeol.* 38 1983); Clerkenwell, London (*Medieval Archaeol.* 26, 1982: 194); St Helen's, Bishopsgate, London (*Medieval Archaeol.* 35, 1991: 152); Holywell (Haliwell), London, (*Medieval Archaeol.* 34, 1990: 181); Godstow (Oxfords.) (*Medieval Archaeol.* 5, 1961: 313); Clementhorpe in York (Dobson and Donaghey 1984); Malling (Kent), an unpublished excavation by Martin Biddle; Sopwell (Herts.) (*Medieval Archaeol.* 10, 1966: 177–8); Hinchingbrooke (Hunts.) (*Medieval Archaeol* 12, 1968: 166); Romsey (Hants.) (*Medieval Archaeol.* 18, 1974: 189) and Waterbeach (Cambs.) (Cra'ster 1966).

Clearly archaeological evidence for nunneries exists, and several survive with substantial medieval architectural remains, among them: Lacock (Wilts.); St Radegund's, Cambridge (now Jesus College); Burnham (Berks.) and Malling (Kent), both reinstated as convents. I would suggest that the disinterest shown in the archaeology of nunneries, results not from lack of evidence, but from a misunderstanding which has resulted from their stereotyping. Nunneries are lumped together as being poor, scandalous, passive institutions which were eschewed by medieval patrons. They are not interesting to monastic scholars because they are not considered successful in the world of male monasticism. For example, Christopher Brooke displayed his own prejudices, not those of medieval people, when he wrote of nuns, 'there were a number of reasons, sensible and absurd, for supposing their prayers less efficacious than those of men' – a misconception which has remained within the historical literature (C. N. L. Brooke 1974: 168; Burton 1979). In her book on medieval nunneries, Eileen Power portrayed impoverished houses rocked by female vanity and sexual scandal (1922). However, scholars now agree that Power's sources were biased (S. Thompson 1991; Oliva 1994). She used only published and very late documents from a small number of houses and accepted the Dissolution surveyors' accounts of poverty, mismanagement and scandal, without assessing the possibility that these represented propaganda. Even recent reassessments of the historical evidence for nunneries continue to devalue female religious experience. Sally Thompson emphasizes the passivity of nunneries in their reliance on masculine support in sacramental and administrative functions, as 'an inevitable consequence of the lay status and inferior position of the female sex', and suggests that there were 'few women of spiritual vision or stature following a religious vocation ... or if there were, they have left no trace on the records' (Thompson 1991: 3, 11).

The lower status of religious women has been assumed by historians on the basis that women's monasticism was not well documented. And while archaeologists are generally eager to test and supplement poorly documented phenomena, in this case they have chosen to reproduce stereotypes. Where nunneries appear within monastic studies they are used as examples of poor monasteries (Gilyard-Beer 1958; Coppack 1990). Moreover, they are judged as failures according to the model of male monasticism:

> Prioresses lacked prestige. In a feudal militaristic Anglo-Norman society a Mother Superior was a contradiction in terms.... It was considered that the prayers of women had far less value when offered in intercession to the saints. Nearly all the eighty post-Conquest Benedictine nunneries were small in scale, poorly endowed and lurching from one financial crisis to another, perhaps also beset by scandal.
> (Butler 1989: 3)

In a critical appraisal of this historiography, Marilyn Oliva (1992) has demonstrated that small male houses were equally, if not more, prone to poverty, mismanagement and scandal, and that such stereotypes of nunneries can be refuted when a wider range of documentary sources are considered.

The archaeology of nunneries has remained unwritten because monasteries for women have been judged against standards which are male. In so doing, monastic archaeology has remained a classic example of andro-centric, or male-biased, research, perhaps not surprising in the pre-dominantly male preserves of antiquarianism, and subsequent academic and professional archaeology. Alison Wylie (1991: 38) has included within the definition of androcentrism, blatant bias within the definition of fields of study and the adoption of the male perspective as standard. She has argued that such androcentrism results in 'bad science', which is neither rigorous nor complete. According to the framework of male monasticism, historians and archaeologists have dismissed nunneries as unsuccessful, and hence the story of medieval monasticism has remained incomplete. This book rejects previous judgements and argues instead that nunneries were founded for a different purpose than monasteries for men. It demonstrates that archae-ological classifications based on the male standard are inappropriate and incomplete in considering the different social purpose of nunneries, and the more fluid, informal and varied monasticism for women.

2.2 RELIGIOUS WOMEN IN THE SAXON LANDSCAPE

Long before the monastic geography of later medieval England was established, there were settlements of religious women. In order to appreci-ate the changing status of religious women in the long term, it is useful, first, to define and map their earliest communities. In early medieval England two main initiatives for founding nunneries can be identified. The first institutions were seventh- and eighth-century double houses: communities of men and women living under some sort of monastic rule, with the abbess of the female religious presiding over the whole. Double houses could be settlements containing areas for both men and women, or they could be twin male and female foundations. Out of the tenth-century monastic reform came a very different institution: nunneries which were entirely female. Archaeological sources can amplify considerably our under-standing and enumeration of these two types of institution (Figures 2 and 3), in addition to more conventional sources including saints' lives, charters, chronicles and narratives (Table 1).

The idea of the double house, generally a royal foundation, seems to have originated in Merovingian Gaul (Rigold 1968: 27). Such institutions were founded in England between the end of the sixth and eighth centuries. Hitherto they have been distinguished from other types of community only when a specific written reference to women survives (Table 1). In addition to this form of monastery, a number of double minsters may have existed. The precise difference, if any, between minsters and monasteries at this date is unclear. However, a 'minster' (from *monasterium*) was a royal or magnate church with resident priests attached. Often this may have fulfilled pastoral functions, resembling a college of secular canons. John Blair (1987: 88) has suggested that many seventh- and eighth-century minsters were

Figure 2 Distribution of Saxon double houses. Sources include documents, sculpture and archaeology (Table 1).

mixed communities of nuns, monks and priests. St Frideswide's (Oxford) for example, was a minster which included women. If Blair is correct, our image of the double minster/monastery must expand to include an aspect of parochial ministry. The existence of two types of professed religious women at this time is confirmed by the Penitential of Egbert (766–91). He

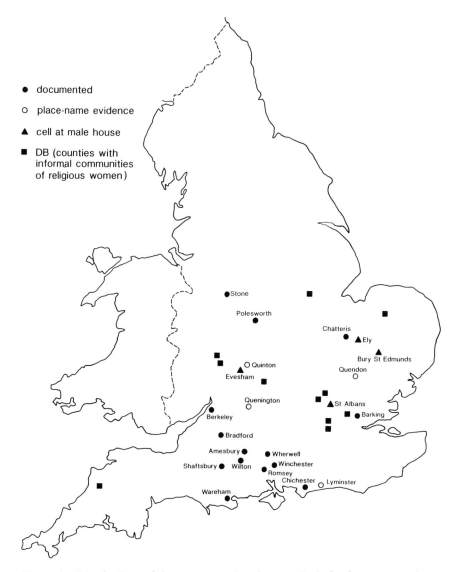

Figure 3 Distribution of Saxon nunneries. Sources include documents, place-names and architecture.

distinguished between religious women according to, 'whether in Orders or not, married or single, virgin or woman, canoness or nun' (Haddan and Stubbs 1964: 417). Contemporary differentiation between *canonica* (woman living under a rule), and *sanctimonialis* (nun), may imply the vocations appropriate to minsters and monasteries.

27

Table 1 Sources for Saxon double houses (seventh to ninth centuries).

Location	Source
Abingdon, Berks.	Helenstow *Chronicon Monasterii de Abingdon*
Bardney, Lincs.	*'Beardaneu', HE* iii. 2
Barking, Essex	*HE* iv. 7 (twin to Chertsey)
Bath, Somerset	charter of Osric 676 (Sawyer 1968: no. 51)
Castor, Northants.	*Vita Mildrethae* (tenth- or eleventh-century)
Chichester, Essex	St Osyth's, *Secgan* (list of saints' resting-places *c.*1031)
Coldingham, Berwicks.	*'Coludesbyrig', HE* iv. 19
Cookham, Berks.	minster given to Abbess Cyntethryth, 798 (Sawyer 1968: no. 1258)
Eastry, Kent	*Vita Mildrethae;* Goscelin's *Vita Mildgithae*
Ely, Cambs.	*HE* iv. 19
Folkestone, Kent	*Vita Mildrethae*
Gloucester	charter of Osric 671 (Sawyer 1968: no. 70)
Hackness, N. Yorks.	*HE* iv. 23
Hartlepool, Cleveland	*'Heruteu', HE* iii. 24
Hoo, Kent	charter of Caedwalla 687 (Sawyer 1968: no. 233)
Leomister, Herefords.	*Vita Milburgae* (late eleventh-century)
Lyminge, Kent	Privilege of Wihtred 697–8 (Sawyer (ed.) 1968: no. 20)
Malmesbury, Wilts.	*HE* v. 18
Minster in Sheppey, Kent	Privilege of Wihtred
Minster in Thanet, Kent	Privilege of Wihtred
Oxford, St Frideswide	*Vita Frideswid*
Peakirk, Northants.	Felix's *Vita Guthlac*
Repton, Derbys.	*Vita Guthlac*
St Albans, Herts.	*Gesta Abbatum*
St Bees, Cumbria	*Vita Bega* (twelfth-century)
Tadcaster, W. Yorks.	*'Kaelcacastir' HE* iv. 23
Wareham, Dorset	Anglo-Saxon Chronicle, 876
Watton, Humbs.	*'Wetadun' HE* v. 3
Weedon, Northants.	*Vita Werburgae*
Wenlock, Shrops.	*Vita Milburgae*
West Dereham, Norfolk	St Wihtburg's, *Liber Eliensis*
Whitby, N. Yorks.	*'Streanaeshalch', HE* iii. 24
Wimborne, Dorset	Anglo-Saxon Chronicle, 718

Possible double houses

Location	Evidence
Brandon, Suffolk	archaeology: timber churches, cemeteries primarily of adult skeletons, religious artefacts (Carr *et al.* 1988)
St Werburgh's, Chester	traditionally thought to have been founded by Æthelflaed after 907
Chichester, Sussex	minster possibly for nuns (Sawyer (ed.) 1968: no. 47)
Crayke, N. Yorks.	*Historia de Sancto Cuthberto* notes the head as 'Geva', a woman's name

Location	Source
Coxwold, N. Yorks.	letter of Pope Paul I, 757–8 (Whitelock (ed.) 1979: 830)
'Dunaemuthe', Yorks.	letter of Pope Paul I
Ebchester, Co. Durham	*Vita Ebbe* (late twelfth-century)
Eltisley, Cambs.	Chronicle of Hugh Candidus (*c.* 1155)
Fladbury (Worcs.)	placename*
Flixborough, Humbs.	archaeology: high incidence of female-associated artefacts (Whitwell 1991)
Hanbury, Worcs.	minster possibly for nuns (Sawyer (ed.) 1968: no. 190)
Hovingham, N. Yorks.	sculpture: female themes; possible twin to Stonegrave
Nazeingbury, Essex	archaeology: skeletal evidence (Huggins 1978); charter of Suebred, 693–709
'Pectanege'	minster given to Abbess Cynethryth, 798 (Sawyer (ed.) 1968: no. 1258)
'Penitanham', ?Worcs.	Oshere to Cuthswith, 693 (Sawyer (ed.) 1968: no. 1258)
Reading, Berks.	traditionally founded by Elfrida
Stonegrave, N. Yorks.	letter of Pope Paul I
Tetbury, Gloucs.	place-name: '*Tettan monasterium*' suggests that land held by Aldhelm (Sawyer (ed.) 1968: nos. 71, 73) was given to Abbess Teta of Wimborne
Thornbury, Binsey, Oxfords.	retreat house of St Frideswide's (Blair 1988)
Wytham, Berks.	retreat house of Helenstow, *Chronicon Abingdon*
Winchcombe, Gloucs.	abbey annals *c.* 1150
Withington, Gloucs.	held by Abbess Aethelburh (Sawyer (ed.) 1968: nos. 1429, 1255)
Wirksworth, Derbys.	sculpture: female themes; associated charter of 835 (Sawyer (ed.) 1968: no. 1624)
Worcester	St Peter's *familia,* possibly a mixed community

Main sources: Bede's *Historia Ecclesiastica* (*HE*); Sawyer (ed.) (1968) *Anglo-Saxon Charters.*

Note: Sir Frank Stenton (1943) noted that women's names were compounded with *burgh* to denote double monasteries at Tetbury and Fladbury, and therefore suggested a number of additional sites for consideration on this basis: Bibury (Gloucs.), Harbury (Warwicks.), Heytesbury (Wilts.), Alderbury (Wilts.), Adderbury (Oxfords.), Bucklebury (Berks.), Queniborough (Leics.), and Alderbury (Shrops.).

A more casual and transient form of religious community for men and women may have been run by lay-people as family monasteries. Our knowledge of these is slight (Bede's *Epistola ad Ecgbertum*). Many monasteries may have alternated between being predominantly male or female institutions. In eighth-century Yorkshire, for example, Stonegrave, Coxwold and *Donaemuthe* passed from the hands of an abbess to an abbot (Whitelock (ed.) 1979 EHD 1: 830).

The list of documented double houses may be increased by additions of houses known from archaeology (Table 1; Figure 2). Impressions of double houses can be occasionally recognized through skeletal remains, artefacts and iconographic sculpture. Excavations at Nazeingbury (Essex) uncovered a cemetery of *c.* 150–200 skeletons associated with two phases of timber churches (Huggins 1978). Radio-carbon determinations upon the skeletons gave date ranges between the seventh and ninth centuries. Skeletal evidence revealed a high number of women (*c.* 84 women to 37 men). It might be argued that investigations at this incompletely excavated cemetery had uncovered a section given over to the burial of a community's women. Two further factors, however, indicate a population made up mainly of celibate women. The women showed no increased mortality around childbearing years, and there was no observed notching of the pre-auricular sulcus of the pelvis which occurs in childbirth. The nature of the religious community excavated at Nazeingbury may be elucidated by a charter of King Suebred (or Swaefred) which survived within a later cartulary of Barking Abbey (Bascombe 1987). Suebred granted land at *Nasingum*:

> Therefore for the salvation of my soul I grant to you *ffymme* my rights in thirty *manentes* of land in *Nasingum* ... with all things appertaining to it, fields, woods, meadows, pastures and fisheries ... for the purpose that you may share in erecting there a house of God.
>
> (trans. Bascombe 1987: 87).

It has been suggested that *ffymme* is a female name (ibid.). The possibility of a female founder, and therefore a double house, is strengthened by the burial of two women within the east end of the earlier timber church – an appropriate position for a founder or first abbess. Suebred's charter can be dated by its attestation by Waldhere, Bishop of London (693–709). This date of *c.* 700 is within the range suggested by radio-carbon dating for the skeleton of the supposed founder at Nazeingbury. Kenneth Bascombe has presented evidence for *Nasingum* having been a cell of Barking. When considered with the topographical evidence identifying this house as Nazeing, the charter corroborates the archaeological evidence for a primarily female monastery.

Recent excavations at Flixborough (Humbs.) have recorded middle Saxon remains, including fourteen timber halls, possibly of a monastic character (Whitwell 1991). Monastic traits include its *vallum* ditch, and interior features linked by metalled paths. The presence of a church or churches is attested by window glass and unused lead cames, possibly produced on site. The literacy of the community is indicated by *styli*, an alphabet ring and an incised lead plaque, bearing a list of five male and two female names, the last followed by the term 'nun'. A group of ten excavated skeletons was predominantly female; the high incidence of female-associated artefacts is reminiscent of assemblages from Saxon Whitby and Barking, documented double houses. Flixborough has yielded keys, combs, rings, strap-ends and a large number of high quality straight pins. The pins were of the sort which were most likely used to fix women's veils (Owen-Crocker 1986:

52). Textile working is suggested by spindle-whorls, pins, loomweights, needles and shears. At Brandon (Suffolk) excavations revealed a middle Saxon settlement with timber churches, cemeteries and religious artefacts, including a richly ornamented plaque depicting St John the Evangelist (Carr *et al.* 1988). Taken together, the information from Brandon suggests an informal community where a mixed monastic population and village were closely connected.

At least two sites, Hovingham (N. Yorks.) and Wirksworth (Derbys.), could be considered as double houses on the strength of their sculpture. Sites yielding sculpture of the eighth or ninth centuries are often termed 'monastic', although only a broad definition of monasticism, including regular, lay or episcopal establishments, may be applicable (Wood 1987: 26). The Hovingham 'frieze', or slab, dated to around 800, is divided vertically into panels. Depicted in the panels are scenes of the Annunciation, the dialogue between Elizabeth and Mary, and the three Marys at the Sepulchre (Figure 4). Such iconography could be appropriate for the casket

Figure 4 The Hovingham slab (N. Yorks.), *c.* 800, represents one side of a slab-built shrine. Depicted from left to right is the Annunciation, the dialogue between Elizabeth and Mary, and the three Marys at the Sepulchre, all themes appropriate for the shrine of a female saint.

or reliquary of a woman, abbess, or female saint (Bailey n. d.). Further credence is lent when Hovingham is considered as a possible twin house with nearby Stonegrave, a monastery less than 3.22 km away which was noted in a letter of Pope Paul I in 757–8, as being formerly under the direction of an abbess (Whitelock 1979 (ed.): 830). At Wirksworth a panel of eighth- or ninth-century sculpture is divided into parallel upper and lower registers, interpreted as male and female – an appropriate opposition for a double house (Jane Hawkes pers. comm.). Eight panels survive in total, with the upper and lower registers dominated by images of Christ and the Virgin, respectively. Wirksworth is not far from the double monastery of Repton. A charter of 835 indicates that Wirksworth was held by Abbess Cynewaru (Sawyer (ed.) 1968: no. 1624).

When mapped (Figure 2) it becomes apparent that the Saxon double house was common outside the better documented regions of Kent and Northumbria, from which Bede drew most of his knowledge. Their absence from the south-west is striking, and presumably reflects an adherence to more eremitic monasticism connected with western Britain. Double houses are expected to occur most densely in areas with close contact with Merovingian France, and indeed this is shown in Kent and Northumbria. The surprising omission, however, is their general absence from East Anglia, a pattern repeated in the paucity of shrines known from lists of saints' resting-places (Rollason 1986). It may be that early East Anglian monasticism was of the more elusive, undocumented type postulated for Nazeingbury, Flixborough and Brandon. If this is the case, our knowledge of it will only be extended gradually through archaeological excavation.

Double houses, like many monasteries for men, are thought to have fallen into disuse during the ninth century. It is unclear whether Viking attack or disintegration of monastic life was the causal factor in most cases, but only a handful of houses appear to have maintained continuity of monastic life, among them Wareham. In the tenth century, southern England enjoyed a monastic revival. During this time, a considerable number of nunneries were established. These were strictly for religious women. In 965 and 975 the *Regularis Concordia*, a standardized monastic rule, was compiled at Winchester. This document contained a section strictly prohibiting men from nunneries, and warning spiritual advisors to take care not to disrupt the regular observances of nuns. Clearly, the character of women's religious communities had changed. Foundations continued to be of royal initiative. Double houses, however, were comprehensively replaced by nunneries (Figure 3).

The majority of late Saxon nunneries were established in Wessex: Shaftesbury, Winchester Nunnaminster, Romsey, Wherwell, Wilton and Amesbury. Smaller numbers are known from Mercia: Polesworth (Warwicks.), Stone (Staffs.) and Berkeley (Gloucs.); nunneries are recorded for Sussex (Chichester), Essex (Barking) and East Anglia (Chatteris, Cambs.). Smaller nunneries may have existed, but few or no references survive them. In 1001 Æthelred gave the vill of Bradford-on-Avon (Wilts.) to the nuns of Shaftesbury (Sawyer 1968: no. 899). Bradford was established as a refuge for the nuns, and for the relics of St Edward of which they were guardians. It was also intended that a small permanent cell of nuns be founded. In discussing the rediscovered Saxon chapel at Bradford, Richard Gem (1978: 110) has suggested that it was the nunnery church. He proposes that its short rectangular body, with *porticus* (lateral chambers) to the east, north and south, appears to be a choir without nave: an appropriate form for a small Saxon nunnery. Its close proximity to the minster church at Bradford would have made priests easily available for the celebration of the nuns' offices.

A nunnery may have existed at Lyminster (Sussex). It was recorded as *Nonneminster* at Domesday although the earliest record of nuns was 1263 (Knowles and Hadcock 1971). Much of the Saxon church survives, constructed in flint with brown sandstone side alternate quoining (Taylor and Taylor 1965, 1: 409–11). The church has the thin, high walls which are held to be typical of Saxon construction (0.76 m thick; 6.09 m high). Its dimensions are unusually long and narrow, but in this respect Lyminster parallels the demolished Saxon nunnery church of Wareham (Dorset). Both churches had naves roughly 19.8 m long, and chancels 15.2 m long. Wareham differed in that its nave appears to have been flanked by rows of lateral chambers (*porticus*) (Taylor and Taylor 1965, 2: 635).

Domesday Book hints at the presence of a considerable number of nunneries which are less formally defined. Communities of religious women were accommodated in the male houses of Evesham, Bury St Edmund's, Ely, and St Albans. At Bury St Edmund's, for example, twenty-eight nuns and poor people were noted who prayed daily for the king (DB Suffolk II fo. 372 R). Æthelswite was given land at Cweney (Cambs.) near Ely, where she practised needlework with her '*puellulae*' (little girls) (*Liber Eliensis*). Such provision for women at these reformed monasteries may indicate that less formal women's communities existed elsewhere. Nuns held land in at least nine counties at Domesday: Gloucestershire (Cwnhild fo. 170 v); Warwickshire (Leofeva fo. 244 R); Worcestershire (Ælfeva fo. 173 v; and Edite fo. 173 v); Essex (Leofhild II fo. 57 v); Lincolnshire (Alswite fo. 337 v; and Cwenthryth fo. 370 v); Somerset (Edith fo. 91 v); Middlesex (Estrild fo. 130 v); Hertfordshire (Eddeva fo. 136 v); and Norfolk (II fo. 26 v). In addition, women and the category of free woman (*libra femina*) held land from the king in alms (*de rege in elemosina*) in Berkshire (Aldeva, Aldrith and Edith, fo. 63 v) and Middlesex (Ælfeva and Edeva, fo. 130 v).

Some women held land but did not necessarily live on it. For example, Edite, a nun, held land at Knightwich (Worcs.) which she returned to a male house. In several cases, however, the holding may suggest an informal religious house for women. The entries for Somerset, for instance, would be appropriate for a monastic house (fo. 91 v):

Edith, a nun (*monialis*) holds 12 acres of land in alms from the king.

She has woodland and pasture, 80 acres. 4 cattle; 4 pigs; 11 sheep. value 5s.

Two nuns (*duae nonnae*) hold 2.5 virgates of land in ?Holnicote in alms from the king. Land for 2 ploughs. Meadow, 5 acres. value 5s.
(Thorn 1980).

Most references to nuns holding land describe the woman as *monial*, a term which, from about the late ninth century, seems to imply a professed nun (Latham 1965). One Lincolnshire nun, Cwenthryth, is termed *monacha* – literally the feminine of monk. Bede's Penitential (731–4) also uses this term for nun (Haddan and Stubbs (eds) 1964: 328). King Æthelred's Laws of 1008 explicitly state that two classes of religious women were known, nuns (OE *mynecena*) and women dedicated to God (*nunnan*) (Whitelock *et al.* 1981: 347; Æthelred 4.1). Somerset DB lists *monialis* and *nunnae* in the same folio, indicating that these perceived classes of religious women are not a product of regional variations in terminology. Barbara Yorke (1989: 108) suggested that Æthelred's Laws were distinguishing between nuns and vowesses, the latter being widows who took vows of chastity in order to avoid the obligation to remarry. These women are not believed to have lived communally, hence the *duae nunnae* of Somerset cast doubt on Yorke's distinction.

The nomenclature of these sources makes two valuable points. First, at least two classes of religious women can be identified, so that corresponding levels of ecclesiastical sites may therefore be expected. Formal communities (for *monialis, monachae, mynecena*) may have been better documented, and consequently known to us, but not necessarily more numerous than the less formal communities of *nunnan*. This category of religious woman may have been predominant in late Saxon England. The term *nunnanhad* is used in Ælfric's Pastoral Letter for Wulfsige III (993–*c.* 995) to denote the nuns' order comparable to the monks' and abbots' orders (Whitelock *et al.* 1981: 205). A *nunne* has previously been defined as a woman who took vows of chastity without entering a community (ibid. 347 n. 4). The holdings of the two Somerset *nonnae*, however, suggest that these women did sometimes live communally.

Second, the naming of religious women within the sources implies communities where none have previously been known to have existed: for example, the house of the *monacha* in Lincolnshire. The Northumbrian Priests' Law (*c.* 1008–23) notes penalties for lying with *nunnan* (Whitelock *et al.* 1981: 466). Communities of religious women seem to have existed even in the north of England, where no real effort toward monastic refoundation had been made.

Additional communities of religious women are implied by place-names recorded in 1086. Especially significant are the elements '*cwene*', women, which should not be confused with *cwēne* (queen), and some occurrences of names containing 'nun'. Nunney (Somerset), DB *Nonin*, may refer either to the island of the nuns, or Nunna's island. Nunwell Park (Isle of Wight) results from DB *Nonoelle*, Nunna's or the nuns' spring. The *'cwene'* element is fossilized in Quendon (Essex), DB *Kuenadana*, the women's valley; Quinton (Warwicks.), DB *Quinentune*, manor of the women; and Quenington (Gloucs.), DB *Quenintone*, the women's tun (Ekwall 1960; J. S. Moore 1982). Particularly strong candidates for nunneries are Quenington and Quinton. Quenington church possesses a pair of unusually fine Norman *tympana*. One of these, the Coronation and Assumption of the Virgin, is iconographically

Figure 5 Quenington church (Gloucs.): the northern tympanum is one of two earliest surviving English depictions of the Coronation of the Virgin (*c.* 1150). This iconography would be appropriate to the nunnery suggested by the place-name 'the women's tun'.

innovative (Figure 5). As only the second earliest rendering of the Coronation to survive in England (Zarnecki 1950), Quenington was graced with sculpture more appropriate to a monastery than an ordinary parish church. The site of the church, in the valley bottom, next to the river, is typical of an early monastery. The Coronation theme would be especially apt for royal religious women (see Chapter 5.4). Quinton was held by thanes at the time of Domesday (DB Gloucester fo. 169 v), but it became a holding of Polesworth Nunnery. Did 'the manor of the women' make Quinton an inspired endowment to this later nunnery?

Together, documents, place-names, sculpture and archaeology present a geography for Saxon monasticism which was characterized by a diversity of vocations and settlements for religious women. In sharp contrast, Anglo-Norman monasticism made little provision for women. The Norman baronial class imprinted a new pattern of monasticism on the English landscape. The first century of Norman settlement saw a wave of new foundations for Benedictines, Cluniacs, and alien priories, the last of which were dependent on a mother house in France. However, only seven or eight nunneries were founded before 1100, mainly in the south-east of England. One purpose for founding Norman monasteries may have been to consolidate the new system of landholding. Whatever the motive, the plantation of nunneries was considered extraneous to it. During previous initiatives to found monasteries, notably during the tenth century, an impetus for establishing nunneries had been realized. In the *Regularis Concordia* the duty to protect and patronize nunneries was recognized as a function of Anglo-Saxon Queenship (Meyer 1977). Nunneries relied upon Saxon royal widows and queens. This precedent would be followed by a small number of Anglo-Norman aristocratic and gentry women, but only after the main monastic landscape had crystallized.

2.3 MEDIEVAL RELIGIOUS FOUNDATIONS FOR WOMEN: NUMBERS, STATUS AND DISTRIBUTION

The small number of Anglo-Norman nunneries noted above may suggest that pious women found places in mixed religious communities. Like the double minsters of the seventh and eighth centuries, certain Anglo-Norman houses were flexible enough to accommodate nuns. Some of the male communities listed at Domesday continued to exist alongside small numbers of nuns. The Benedictine monastery of St Albans, for example, had a group of nuns added by their third abbot, Wulsig (*c.* 940). His successor Wulnoth moved the nuns to the almonry. There they remained until 1140 when they were moved to Sopwell (Knowles and Hadcock 1971: 75). Many of the later Saxon minsters seem to have have included both men and women, in a tradition that was carried through the eleventh century. For a brief time, the delineation of male and female communities may have blurred. When Norman monasteries were founded, it may sometimes have been a case of regularizing existing communities of men and (or) women.

The numbers and institutional traits of medieval English nunneries and monasteries (Figures 6 and 7) shed light on the social and economic expectations placed on communities of religious men and women. Wherever possible, these patterns are compared with those observed for Scotland, Ireland and Wales. English monasteries for men were more numerous. Minimum estimates are 736 monasteries for men, 153 nunneries, 18 double houses, 6 nuns' cells attached to male houses and 4 'quasi-double' houses (Knowles and Hadcock 1971). Nunneries were occupied solely by women, whether nuns, lay-sisters, corrodians (paying guests) or servants. They were

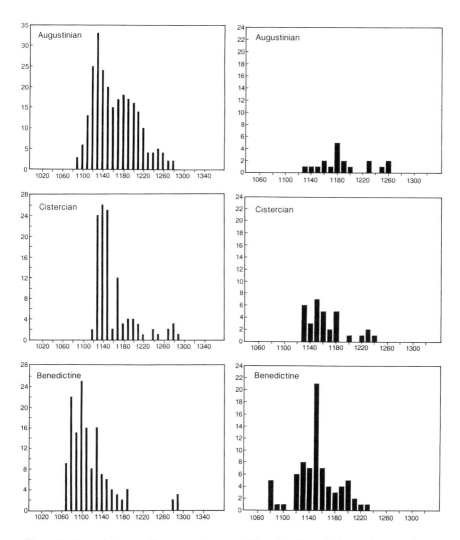

Figure 6 Foundations of monasteries after the Conquest (after R. K. Morris 1979).

Figure 7 Foundations of nunneries after the Conquest (data from Knowles and Hadcock 1971).

presided over by a prioress or abbess. Chaplains, priests, and, more seldom, canons, celebrated services for the nuns in their church. The wealthy Wessex nunneries of Wilton, Winchester, Romsey and Wherwell appear to have had colleges of secular canons attached (ibid.), in an arrangement similar to that observed in larger French nunneries, such as Ronceray and Nyoiseau (Diocese of Angers) (Avril 1989: 38). Mendicant nunneries, such as the Franciscan Minories (London) and Dominican Dartford, provided accommodation for a small group of friars adjacent to the nuns' cloister (Carlin 1987; Clapham 1926). Occasionally chantry priests were later attached to a nunnery through a private foundation, for example at Campsey Ash (Suffolk) in 1347 (Knowles and Hadcock 1971). During their occupation, many nunneries changed the order to which they were committed. Some began as double houses, later to become nunneries. Some, like the ten nunneries of St John of Jerusalem, were short-lived. In their case, the nuns from ten houses were gathered together to form one double preceptory (a monastery of the military orders) at Minchin Buckland (Somerset). When nunneries are considered by order, therefore, some may be counted several times. Up to 119 nunneries claimed at some time to be Benedictine, 34 Cistercian, 4 Cluniac, 10 St John of Jerusalem, 4 Premonstratensian, 1 Dominican and 5 Franciscan (Knowles and Hadcock 1971). Overall, about 150 sites were occupied as later medieval English nunneries.

Along with the nunneries may be considered the later medieval double houses. These were monasteries which housed men and women, but in which the two sexes were segregated. Often the community was made up mainly of religious women, with a smaller number of canons to celebrate divine services, and lay-brothers to carry out manual tasks. These houses can be considered primarily as nunneries; indeed Elkins (1988: xviii) considers the term double house inappropriate. Here, the term is used to distinguish mixed institutions according to their morphological and economic traits. Within this category were 4 houses of the alien order of Fontevrault (dependent monasteries with a mother house in France), 12 Gilbertine double houses and 2 Bridgettine houses, orders which evolved in England and Sweden, respectively. Occasionally, primarily male monasteries were planned with a small community of nuns within the precinct, over which the canons or monks would supervise. This type of double house was rare, and generally these evolved into single sex establishments fairly soon after being founded. Blackborough (Norfolk), Blithbury (Staffs.), Broadholme (Notts.), Harrold (Bedfords.) and Catesby (Northants.) developed into nunneries; Marton (N. Yorks.) became a fully-fledged male institution. In addition, four 'quasi' double houses seem to have existed. These houses are generally known as Cistercian nunneries, although from about 1200 to the mid-fourteenth century they accommodated Premonstratensian canons as well as Cistercian nuns. A small number of alien priories and preceptories may have accommodated individual religious women. A royal nun of Fontevrault appears to have kept her own household at Grove Priory (Bedfords.) in the twelfth century. Perhaps more remarkable is the case of Joan Chaldese, a woman following the Templar rule and possibly residing in their preceptory at Saddlecombe, Sussex (VCH Sussex II 1907: 92). Similar cases have been reported for the French diocese of Limôges, where individual noble women took nuns' vows and installed themselves in monasteries or houses of Fontevrault (Becquet 1989: 69).

Contemplative communities observed the Rule of St Benedict, with additional tracts, notably by St Augustine, St Bernard of Clairvaux and Norbert of Xanten, practised by the reformed orders. Clearly the flexible organization of the Benedictines, in which each house was autonomous, appealed to male and female houses, but represent a greater relative proportion of nunneries. Quantifying Cistercian nunneries is problematic, a matter of definitions, since only two were officially recognized by the order, Tarrant Keynes (Dorset) and Marham (Norfolk) (S. Thompson 1978). The remainder were small, fluid institutions. Their organization was idiosyncratic, often incorporating lay-brothers in their early years and swapping allegiance between Benedictine and Cistercian.

The pattern of founding nunneries in Scotland seems to have been little influenced by those in England. Of only 13 nunneries founded, 7 were Cistercian (53.8 per cent) (Cowan and Easson 1976), whereas Ireland had only 4 Cistercian nunneries (6.4 per cent of the total number of nunneries). Of the four nunneries established in Wales, three were Cistercian and one was Benedictine, Usk (Gwent). Lawrence Butler (1982) noted that royal Welsh favour for the Cistercians may have been a reaction against the Norman penetration of Wales associated with the Benedictines. Welsh Cistercian monasteries were sometimes located at sites with early Christian memorial stones (ibid.) in an effort to assert connections with earlier Celtic monasticism. The Cistercian nunnery at Llanllyr was one of these, where a cross-decorated stone dated to the seventh–ninth centuries, may commemorate an earlier religious community to (Saint?) Madomnuac (Nash-Williams 1950: 26). The most notable discrepancy in the balance of filiation between monasteries and nunneries can be observed for the Augustinians. While the informal structure of the Augustinian Rule might be expected to attract followers among nunneries, only about 24 examples, approximately one-sixth of the total, can be detected. In contrast, over one-third of the monasteries for men were Augustinian. This order frequently included pastoral obligations within its observances, perhaps making it an inappropriate choice for female houses. Nevertheless, affiliation with the Augustinians may on occasion have been deemed acceptable, especially where a nunnery superseded or maintained a community with parochial functions. John Blair (1986) has suggested that the foundation of the

Augustinian nunnery at Goring (Oxfords.) was of this nature. The nuns seemed to have shared the parish church before having their own church and cloister added (c. 1170–90). Blair suggests that the nuns 'may have succeeded some non-regular establishment with parochial functions, the former community of priests being either devolved to chapelries or allowed to coexist with the nuns'. Support for this argument comes from the positioning of the parish church at Goring in relation to the excavated cloister (Stone 1893). The parish church formed the north range of the nunnery cloister, with the nuns' church (attached to the east) projecting beyond the eastern line of the cloister. Lay-brethren were recorded at Goring up to 1304 (Knowles and Hadcock 1971).

The small number of Augustinian nunneries in England forms an interesting comparison with Ireland, where of 62 nunneries, 8 were Augustinian and 43 were Arrouaisian (following the Augustinian Rule). In total, therefore, c. 82 per cent of Ireland's later medieval nunneries followed the Rule of St Augustine. This pattern has been interpreted as the result of a single initiative by St Malachy, who founded many nunneries after a visit to Arrouaise in 1139–40 (Gwynn and Hadcock 1970: 307). It may have been more usual for the Irish nunneries to perform some aspect of pastoral work.

Few nunneries of the mendicant orders were established in England (five Franciscan; one Dominican). Friaries – communities of male mendicants – were generally established with an evangelical mission in mind. About 189 friaries existed in medieval England. Due to Pauline prohibitions against women preaching and the greater degree of enclosure expected of religious women (see Chapter 6), few mendicant nunneries were founded. Despite the work of early Franciscan and Dominican nuns in preaching and education (Brooke and Brooke 1978; Leclercq 1984: 12), by the time of the English foundations the mendicant nuns were strictly enclosed. Religious women did, however, support an initial wave of male mendicancy. The nunneries of Clementhorpe (York), Moxby (N. Yorks.) and Markyate (Herts.) bolstered new friaries with gifts of food (Martin 1937: 7). The English mendicant nunneries had little or no function of practical or charitable ministering. In Ireland, the situation developed along very different lines. The general lack of formally established nunneries is thought to have been compensated for by the activities of the Tertiaries, or Third Order of Franciscans. These were unenclosed mendicants whose vocation lay in missionary service (Neel 1989: 321). Ireland and Scotland were similar to England in having few houses of mendicant nuns. Ireland had four Franciscan nunneries; Scotland had two Franciscan and one Dominican (Gwynn and Hadcock 1970; Cowan and Easson 1976).

When comparing the number of monastic foundations by decade (Figures 6 and 7), it is evident that the timing differed between monasteries for men and for women. Enthusiasm for the establishment of Benedictine

40

monasteries for men peaked between 1080–1110. Benedictine nunneries reached their height of foundation much later, in the years either side of 1160. A similar discrepancy can be observed for the Augustinians, whose male houses reached a climax in foundations c. 1130–40; female houses achieved theirs c. 1180. Cistercian monasteries for men were most successfully founded c. 1130–50; similarly, the 'unofficial' Cistercian nunneries were founded mainly in the decades c. 1130 and c. 1160. Those nunneries recognized by the order, however, were founded considerably later. Tarrant Keynes was founded sometime before 1199. Marham was established before 1249. Both nunneries were formally incorporated into the order only by 1250 (S. Thompson 1984: 251).

The overall pattern in the founding of nunneries is one of time-lag, or a delayed response. This trend must be mainly a product of choices made by patrons. The earlier tendency for setting up male houses may be based in economic and political motivations. The greater political power of a male house would render it a better ally for a Norman baron. The productive aspects of rural monasteries for men, especially where land reclamation was initiated, made them a better financial prospect. Those who could afford to set new trends in religious foundations opted for male institutions. The establishment of a nunnery was seldom an innovation in pious benefaction. Where aristocratic women patrons felt inclined to initiate new types of religious community, they too directed their efforts toward male foundations. Joan Fossard, for example, founded the first of the three English Grandmontine monasteries (at Grosmont, N. Yorks.) in 1204 (Graham and Clapham 1924: 171). Ela, Countess of Salisbury, founded Hinton (Somerset), the second English Carthusian monastery, in 1227. The first Trinitarian house in England was founded by Margaret de Moddenham, Abbess of Malling, in 1224 at Moatenden (Kent). Queen Maud (first wife of Henry I) founded St Giles' leper hospital, initially for men, at Holborn (Middlesex) in 1101, making it the third Norman hospital to have been established (R. M. Clay 1909: 71). Patrons felt compelled to found nunneries only a generation after new fashions in endowment had been forged for male communities. Nunneries were founded in a second, delayed wave of endowment, a situation very much a product of the social identity of their founders (see below).

Often it has been said that later medieval English nunneries were poor (S. Thompson 1991; Power 1922). Many parallels for this poverty can, of course, be cited for male houses, especially the smaller cells, retreat houses and hermitages. Was there any significant difference in the prosperity of male and female houses? Levels of wealth between male and female communities may be compared through a fiscal assessment, or estimate of size (number of inmates). The most convenient guide to a monastery's financial status comes from the *Valor Ecclesiasticus* (1535), which, while sometimes a less reliable source than the later records of the Court of

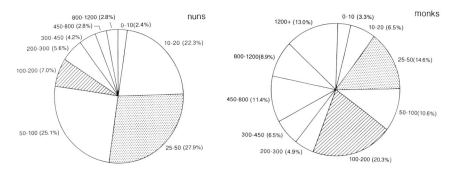

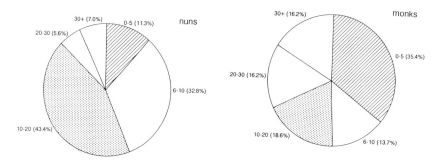

Figure 8 The financial value (above) and numbers of inmates (below) in Benedictine Houses in 1535 (data from Knowles and Hadcock 1971).

Augmentations, is an easier source for broad comparisons. A reliable census of inmates is more problematic, since the Dissolution produced three sets of totals. The most trustworthy of these was taken 1534–5, when monasteries subscribed to the king's supremacy. From that time until the general Dissolution, numbers of inmates may have been reduced by up to 25 per cent (Knowles 1955: 257). In some ways more useful are the poll taxes of 1377, 1379 and 1380–1. Here wealth and numbers of inmates are presented for Benedictine nunneries and male houses, using the best figures available for each house (Knowles and Hadcock 1971). Benedictines have been chosen for providing the largest sample of nunneries (n = 71) with which to compare monasteries for men (n = 123). For each criterion considered as affecting male and female houses, statistical significance has been corroborated by means of a chi-square test (Gilchrist 1990). These tests

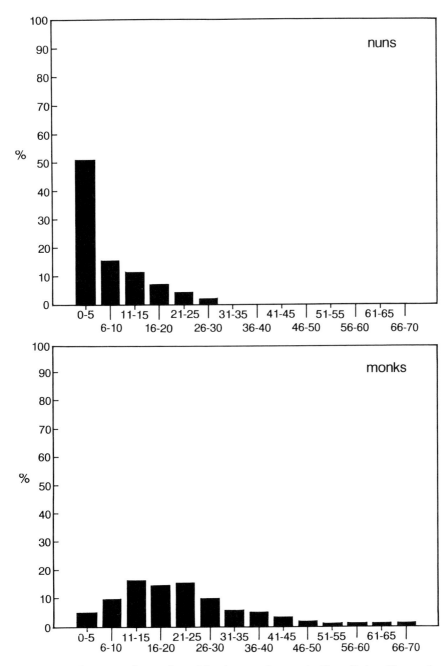

Figure 9 The approximate financial value per inmate in Benedictine Houses in 1535 (data from Knowles and Hadcock 1971).

confirm that there is significant evidence for an association between the sex of a monastery's inmates, and the relative proportion of values at the Dissolution; numbers of inmates per house; and wealth per inmate. When wealth is considered alone (Figure 8), it is indeed apparent that there was a greater number of wealthy male Benedictine houses. Monasteries for men show a greater spread of wealth, whereas nunneries are valued mainly between £10–£100. It may be noted, however, that the male houses have a greater percentage valued under £10. Figure 8 illustrates that there was a greater number of large monasteries for men (30+ inmates). Again, a greater spread of values can be observed for the male houses, whereas the nunneries had mainly between five and twenty inmates. The unexpected finding is that, in comparison with nunneries (n =8; 11.3 per cent), a greater relative proportion of Benedictine male houses had under five inmates (n = 44; 35.7 per cent).

The most revealing comparison is made when value and number of inmates are considered together. Figure 9 charts the approximate value per individual inmate for each house in the sample. The real poverty of the nunneries cannot be disputed. The histogram produced for nunneries is a positive skew, with numbers of houses decreasing as value per inmate increases. Just over 50 per cent of the nunneries can be estimated at under £5 per inmate; no nunnery achieves a score over £30. The monasteries for men, in contrast, have highest scores between £10 and £25, with houses well represented up to £50 per inmate. The disparity in standards of living suggested by these figures is illustrated by the circumstances surrounding the foundation of the nunnery at Thetford (Norfolk). A monastic cell was established on the site by the abbey of Bury St Edmunds, but when the endowment was found insufficient to support three monks, the abbot transferred a group of nuns from Lyng (Norfolk), establishing a priory for women by c. 1160. A site considered inadequate for three monks was supporting at least twenty-six nuns in the thirteenth century (Knowles and Hadcock 1971: 267).

The relative status of monastic houses has been measured frequently by the dimensions of certain of their buildings (Cook 1961; Robinson 1980). The cloister garth is the indicator most often used, although more likely to reflect the developed status of the house is the total length of the church. When the dimensions of nunnery buildings are considered, cloister areas range mainly from c. 200–330 sq. m (n = 13); with the majority under c. 550 m (Gilchrist 1990). No meaningful comparison can be made between the nunneries and the large Cistercian, Benedictine or Cluniac male houses. A more appropriate scale for comparison is with the orders of canons, particularly the Augustinians. Only four Augustinian monasteries fall within the range of cloister areas up to 330 m^2, but a larger number are known to fall within the category up to c. 550 m^2 (Robinson 1980). The mean for total length of nunnery churches is 49.9 m (Table 2), although over half are under 31 m (n = 32). Several of the smaller canons' churches were of a length close to the mean for nunnery churches (ibid.). Nunnery buildings were not, then, built to a scale below that known for male houses, but equivalent to the smallest, modestly constructed Augustinian monastery. Indeed at Chester the nunnery church was the smallest of any of the town's religious houses (S. W. Ward 1990: 224).

Table 2 Length of nunnery churches.

Nunnery	Length of church (m)
Barking, Essex	102.9
Romsey, Hants.	78
Shaftesbury, Dorset	76.2
Nuneaton, Warwicks.	70.5
Elstow, Bedfords.	64
Watton, Humbs.	61
Carrow, Norwich	61
Malling, Kent	60.8
St Radegund's, Cambridge	57.7
Lacock, Wilts.	43.6
Brewood, Shrops.	40
Polsloe, Exeter	39
Davington, Kent	38
Ickleton, Cambs.	37.5
Bishopsgate, London	36.6
Ellerton, N. Yorks.	?35.8
Dartford, Kent	?31
Denney, Cambs.	31
Burnham, Berks.	29.2
Wykeham, N. Yorks.	27.4
Easebourne, Sussex	25.9
Kirklees, W. Yorks.	24.4
Little Marlow, Bucks.	23.7
Cornworthy, Devon	21.3
Chester	20.5
Pinley, Warwicks.	19.5
Guyzance, Northumb.	18.6
Littlemore, Oxfords.	18.6
Baysdale, Yorks.	18.3
Thicket, Yorks.	18.3
Wilberforce, N. Yorks.	18.3
Aconbury, Herefords.	17
Nunkeeling, Humbs.	14

Sources: extant buildings, ground plans recovered through excavation, and descriptions of the Dissolution surveyors (W. Brown 1886).

Nunneries were founded throughout England, yet in certain areas they were more common. Figure 10 shows that in the north of England they

Figure 10 Distribution of later medieval nunneries (based on Knowles and Hadcock 1971).

tend toward the east coast, and are almost absent from the west coast. Concentrations of nunneries occur in the south-east (around London and in Kent), East Anglia, the West Midlands, Lincolnshire, Yorkshire and Hampshire. They are largely absent from the south-west of England. Gilbertine double houses and 'quasi-double houses' hug the eastern coast

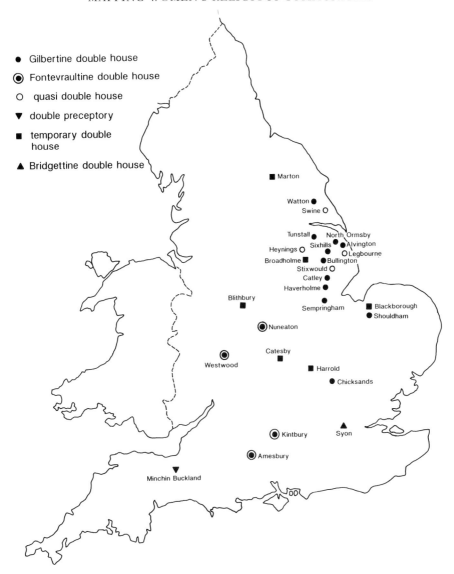

● Gilbertine double house
◉ Fontevraultine double house
○ quasi double house
▼ double preceptory
■ temporary double house
▲ Bridgettine double house

■ Marton
Watton ●
Swine ○
Tunstall ● North Ormsby
Sixhills ● ● Alvington
Heynings ○
Broadholme ■ ● Bullington
Stixwould ○
Catley ●
Haverholme ●
Blithbury
■
Sempringham ● ■ Blackborough
● Shouldham
◉ Nuneaton
Catesby
◉ ■
Westwood
■ Harrold
● Chicksands
▲
◉ Kintbury Syon
◉ Amesbury
▼
Minchin Buckland

Figure 11 Distribution of later medieval double houses (based on Knowles and Hadcock 1971).

of England (Figure 11). In comparison with the distribution of male Benedictine, Cistercian and mendicant houses, there is a marked tendency for nunneries to cluster in certain regions, beyond the concentrations to be expected in areas of greater population. Clustering is particularly prevalent towards the east coast. This phenomenon is paralleled by the Scottish

47

nunneries. Nine of Scotland's thirteen nunneries are sited toward the east coast, and two on the south-west coast. Clusters are apparent in the Berwick and Lothian regions.

One explanation for the relatively dense occurrence of nunneries in certain areas may be their relatively late dates of foundation. Competition between male houses for large tracts of land may have left only certain areas amenable to new monastic foundations, for example the Yorkshire Dales and areas of the midlands. This assumes, however, that nunneries were established with the same aims as other monasteries: an assumption which will be questioned throughout this study. Rather than reflecting competition for land, the distribution of nunneries may relate to their social function.

The clustering of nunneries may have respected earlier traditions in female piety. Nunneries in Hampshire, Wiltshire and Dorset are mainly refoundations of the tenth-century royal nunneries of Wessex. Some nunneries may have evoked nostalgic memories of Saxon double houses (see Chapter 5, section 3). One concentration can be attributed to locally based support for the order of Gilbertines. St Gilbert of Sempringham (Lincs.) established the only monastic order to have originated in England. All but one of the Gilbertine double houses were founded during Gilbert's lifetime. Their distribution may reflect the popular support he received from his baronial peers within the locality.

David Robinson (1980: 45–6) has noted that, like the nunneries, small Augustinian houses were founded fairly late (after 1100) and have a tendency to cluster in some regions (notably East Anglia). The patterns for both categories of site signal a change of preferences in monastic ben-efaction. During the twelfth century it became appropriate for small local landowners to endow their own religious houses. Previously this had been the privilege of the episcopal and baronial classes. Lower gentry had made unremarkable gifts to powerful abbeys. Weary of appearing unattractive suitors, the minor landowners established a rank of monastery over which they would wield greater influence. The clusters, therefore, may denote a number of religious houses founded at a similar social level. Figure 12 shows the distribution of nunneries according to their status at the Dissolution. Houses valued over £200 cluster in southern England (Wessex and the south-east). Nunneries valued between £100–200 have a wider occurrence, taking in isolated examples in the south-west, midlands and East Anglia. More likely to occur in close association are those valued under £50–100, accounting for virtually all the northern English nunneries. In these regions it was possible for minor gentry to establish a greater number of more modest religious houses.

Monasteries were founded for a plethora of motives – both pious and political. An individual might endow a religious house as a form of spiritual insurance, as penance, or as a substitute for crusade or pilgrimage. A sense

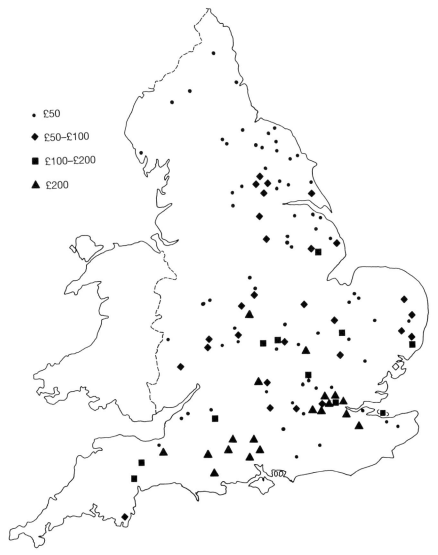

Figure 12 Status of nunneries at the Dissolution (data from Knowles and Hadcock 1971).

of piety could be heightened by one's own illness and impending death, or by the death of a loved one, sometimes resulting in a form of commemorative monastic foundation. Monasteries were founded as chantries: for perpetual prayer devoted to the benefactor. Chantry chapels were sometimes added later to nunnery churches, for example at Campsey Ash (Sherlock 1970:

49

121), St Helen's, Bishopsgate (London), Haliwell (Shoreditch, London), Barking and Lacock (Cook 1947: 25–6). Land may have been given to monastic houses as a financial investment. In this way marginal land, especially in Lincolnshire, was reclaimed, cleared, drained and enclosed by monasteries (Owen 1981: 57). In England, founding a monastic house was a method of laying claim to insecure or threatened estates (Burton 1986: 35). This can occasionally be demonstrated as a motive in the founding of nunneries, for example Keldholme (N. Yorks.) (Rushton 1965). But who founded nunneries, and why?

The distribution of nunneries, their more modest endowments, and their late foundation dates relative to monasteries suggest that the majority were established by a different social group to those associated with male houses. Recent historical research has suggested that often nunneries were established by women, in many cases on land which had formed part of a wife's marriage dowry (S. Thompson 1991: 177). Previously this connection was overlooked where foundations were considered to be the joint initiative of a husband and wife, masking the primary role of the woman as founder. This situation appears to hold true for both aristocratic foundations, for instance those founded by widows at Godstow, Elstow, Lacock and Marham, among others, and the smaller gentry foundations typical of the majority of Yorkshire and East Anglian nunneries. These smaller houses appear to have been founded by, and for, the gentry. As Oliva's study of 542 nuns from the Diocese of Norwich reveals, 64 per cent of the nuns were representative of the lower gentry (Oliva 1990). These nunneries were closely linked to gentry of their locality, people concerned with local parish and village affairs and local family ties.

2.4 AN ARCHAEOLOGY OF PATRONAGE

Nunneries clustered because of the motivations and social links which joined their founders. In some areas the process of establishing small nunneries became a family concern. This can best be demonstrated with reference to a group of Yorkshire nunneries, established by the families of de Arches and de St Quintin. Nunkeeling (Humbs.) was founded 1143–53 by Agnes de Arches (Burton 1979), the widow of Herbert de St Quintin. Between 1147 and 1153 the de Arches established a nunnery at Nun Monkton (N. Yorks.) (ibid.). Meanwhile, the nunnery of Nun Appleton (N. Yorks.) was set up by Alice de St Quintin and her husband Eustace de Mercia. Alice's son-in-law was founding Bullington (Lincs.) at roughly the same time (1148–54) (Elkins 1988: 94). It has also been suggested that Keldholme (N. Yorks.) and Rosedale (N. Yorks.) shared founders in the Stuteville family, although the Rosedale foundation is disputed (Burton 1979: 9).

The concerns of founding families could, therefore, result in the clustering of nunneries to certain regions. The motives involved in setting up the nunneries were also, at times, rooted in family ties. At Nun Monkton, the founder's daughter became the first prioress (Burton 1979: 20). At Marrick (N. Yorks.) the daughters of the founder, Roger de Aske, entered the nunnery (Tillotson 1989: 4), and at Wykeham (N. Yorks.), Lacock (Wilts.), Aconbury (Herefords.) and Clerkenwell (London) the founder's grand-daughter entered (S. Thompson 1991: 181). Some nunneries remained under a family's influence beyond their early years. At Minchin Barrow (Somerset) the patron's permission remained necessary for the election of the prioress. In 1316, a member of the founding family of de Gournay was elected prioress – even though she was not, at the time, a professed nun (Hugo 1867: 11). At Shouldham (Norfolk) in the fourteenth century, and Esholt (W. Yorks.) in the fifteenth, there were close associations with female members of the families Beauchamp and Ward, respectively (Tillotson 1989: 4).

At a higher social level, particular families, or dynasties, were responsible for introducing women's religious orders into England. The Fontevraultine houses in England can be traced to the individual interests of Eleanor of Aquitaine. After her marriage to Henry II, he founded houses of Fontevraultine nuns at Westwood (Worcs.) and Amesbury (Wilts.). Henry's steward, Robert of Leicester, founded Nuneaton (Warwicks.). Plantagenet associations with Amesbury remained strong. The wife of Henry III and the daughter of Edward I both entered the house (Boase 1971). A similar process can be traced for the Franciscan nuns. The first formal English house of the Minories (1293–4; at Aldgate, London) was established by Blanche, Queen of Navarre. Blanche was a relative of Blessed Isabella sister of Louis IX and the original patron of the order (Bourdillon 1926). Denney (Cambs.) was founded by Mary de St Pol, Countess of Pembroke, who was related to the foundresses of both nearby Waterbeach, which was set up in 1294 and superseded by Denney by 1342–51, and the Minories. The Duke of Clarence established Bruisyard (Suffolk) in 1364–7 for his mother-in-law, Maud, who was a granddaughter of the foundress of the London Minories.

In addition to their distribution, aspects of patronage may have affected the material culture of nunneries. Where a male house was founded, especially within the Cistercian order, the patron's role was limited to supplying land and starting endowments (Brooke 1986: 11). Evidence suggests that for some Yorkshire houses, notably Meaux, Kirkstall and Roche, the monks selected the precise location of the monastery within a general area offered by the founder (Burton 1986: 35). Since nunneries were affiliated to monastic orders on a much more casual basis, the role of patron may have been more fundamental in determining the location and architectural form of the house. It is sometimes possible to recognize the impact of an individual patron's taste on the architecture of a male house.

The influence of Roger Bigod at Tintern is a case in point (Coldstream 1986: 157).

A similar case might be constructed for only one nunnery. Around 1090, Gundulf, the first Norman Bishop of Rochester, founded a Benedictine nunnery at West Malling (Kent). During rebuilding in the 1960s, part of the site became available for excavation. From Martin Biddle's plan of the excavated church (unpubl.), it seems that the church began as a long, narrow, aisleless cruciform layout (Figure 13). Projecting from the original

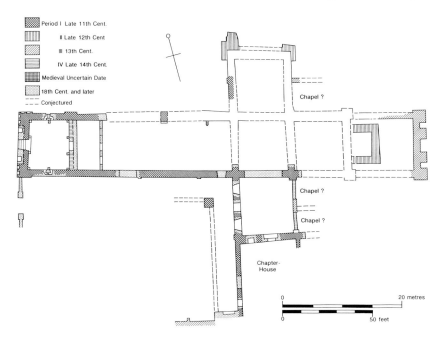

Figure 13   Plan of the church at West Malling (Kent). The excavated eastern end had a small square chamber projecting from it, possibly emulating the design of the Norman plan of Rochester Cathedral, the see of Malling's founder, Gundulf. Based on an unpublished plan by Martin Biddle. Crown copyright preserved.

east end was a smaller square chamber. It has been suggested (Newman 1969: 602) that the design of the first church was modelled on the Norman plan of Rochester Cathedral, the seat of Malling's founder. Unfortunately, the footings of the east end were robbed, so that its relationship with the square projection is uncertain. Biddle has suggested the chamber is a secondary construction, possibly of the twelfth century. It is uncertain, therefore, whether the founder was himself responsible for the unusual configuration of Malling's east end, or whether a later building campaign emphasized a connection to the nunnery's founder and bishop's see.

Founders concerned with promoting a particular order may have ensured that the design of a nunnery followed filial guidelines. Nuneaton (Warwicks.) mirrors the mother church of Fontevrault in layout. Fontevrault church was completed *c.* 1150 in the Angevin style. Its wide unaisled nave met the crossing tower of a cruciform church (Boase 1971). Similarly, Nuneaton was built as an unaisled cruciform church with crossing tower. Much of the church was rebuilt in the thirteenth century, and again by Brakspear in the nineteenth. Enough survives, however, to indicate that the arrangements were dissimilar to those established for the English double houses of the Gilbertines, or standard nunnery churches (see Chapter 4, section 1).

Excavation of the church of the Minories in London has revealed that it possessed an unusual semi-octagonal east end (R. Ellis 1985). The Franciscans displayed no filial control over the design of friary churches. Their characteristic traits were limited to a long preaching nave divided from the friars' choir by a walking place. The closest analogy for the Minories church, however, is Winchelsea Franciscan Friary (Sussex), founded about thirty years previously. When Blanche of Navarre established her Franciscan nunnery, she may have looked for architectural prototypes from within the order. Excavations at Denney (Cambs.) (Christie and Coad 1980) have shown that the Countess of Pembroke altered the arrangements of an existing monastery, first founded for Benedictine monks (1159) and sub-sequently modified for use by the Knights Templar (1170–1308), and finally purchased by the Countess in 1324, who instituted an open court cloister typical of Franciscan architecture (Figure 14). The nuns' refectory seems to have incorporated the pulpit required in mendicant dining practices, from which readings would take place. Above the north doorway is a blocked aperture which corresponds with a north annex shown on an eighteenth-century engraving by Buck (Poster and Sherlock 1987: 79), and interpreted as a possible pulpit and gallery.

Similarities might be expected between nunneries founded within the same family, for example those of the de Arches in Yorkshire. The landscape situations of Nun Monkton, to the north-west of York, and Nun Appleton, to the south-west, are markedly similar. Both are fairly inac-cessible, approached by long roads which lead to no other settlement. Both nunneries are sited on slight rises, surrounded by flat, low-lying marshy land, and adjoining rivers; Nunkeeling (N. Humbs.) was perched above the marshy surrounds of Holderness. Much of the church of Nun Monkton survives as a parish church in use. Like many nunnery churches, it is an aisleless parallelogram. It possesses fabric of exceptional quality for a Yorkshire nunnery (Figure 15). The west front consists of a fine doorway of five orders, flanked by double niches to either side, decorated by waterleaf capitals. Above are three long, Early English lancets, incorporating dog-tooth ornament. The west tower rises above the top of the west gable, but is included within the west bay of the nave. The entire church is constructed in fine limestone ashlar. The west front was apparently executed

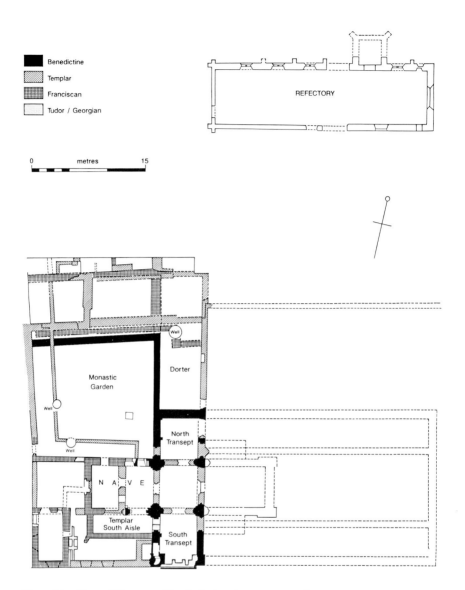

Figure 14 Plan of Denney (Cambs.) showing extant and excavated buildings. The monastery was founded for Benedictine monks, who were later replaced by Knights Templar. The Countess of Pembroke purchased the site in 1324 in order to establish a Franciscan Nunnery. She modified the south transept and nave for her own lodging and arranged the nunnery around an open court cloister which was preferred in Franciscan planning (after Christie and Coad 1980).

54

Figure 15 West front of Nun Monkton church (N. Yorks.): lower stage *c.*1170, topped by a phase of *c.*1220–40. The quality of work and materials were matched at Nun Appleton and Nunkeeling. All were founded by the Yorkshire family of de Arches.

55

in at least two phases: the lower stage *c.* 1170, topped by a phase of *c.* 1220–40. Recent excavations at Nun Appleton (W. Yorks. Archaeology Service 1988, unpubl.) have revealed foundations of stone buildings to the north and east of the seventeenth-century house. The monastic cemetery was located in association with a possible church. This east–west orientated structure had substantial foundations of large, finely-tooled limestone blocks. Fragments of worked stone recovered include keeled capitals and a water-holding base *in situ* (*c.* 1180–1200). The excavated structures and quality of finish are comparable to the fabric at Nun Monkton. While the region possessed a number of sources for limestone (Senior 1989: fig. 1), these were seldom exploited for building nunneries. Most, for example, Wilberfoss and Arthington, were constructed largely in timber. An engraving of Nunkeeling made in 1784 (Figure 16) shows the parochial church before it was rebuilt. It is not clear whether this was the remainder of a crossing and aisled nave, or the original east end of the church. The late, moulded capitals of the northern arcade were reincorporated into the rebuilt (and now ruined) church. The quality of work at Nun Monkton, Nun Appleton and Nunkeeling, and their topographical similarity may be linked to their familial tie.

Links to a particular patron or benefactor are often fragmentary. In excavated material this is most frequently represented through heraldic devices on ceramic tiles, for example those of the Uffords at Campsey Ash (Suffolk) (Figure 17) (Sherlock 1970: 133). The Augustinian nunneries of Goring (Oxfords.) and Burnham (Berks.) have both yielded tiles bearing the arms of Richard of Cornwall, the founder of Burnham who installed nuns from Goring to Burnham. Extant stained glass is rare, but at St Helen's, Bishopsgate, a group of fifteenth-century roundels survived until recent bomb blasts in the City of London (1992–3); these included those of the merchant Sir John Crosby and his wife, and the Grocer's company. Bishopsgate boasted unusual patronage for a nunnery: it was supported by London's merchants, mayors and guilds.

Monastic patrons had the privilege of burial within the monastery to which they were affiliated: a custom with direct archaeological implications. Families were frequently buried at a particular house, with any transferral of the chosen place of burial being viewed as an act of disaffection. Excavations in the church at Campsey Ash produced a high quality fourteenth-century Purbeck marble tomb (Figure 18) (Sherlock 1970). Its stylistic date may support a connection to the Earls of Ufford, known patrons of the house. At the Minories, excavations of the church uncovered a tomb known to be that of Anne Mowbray (R. Ellis 1985). Grave-slabs, coffins and tombs excavated from nunneries seldom provide the inscriptions necessary to identify individuals commemorated as nuns, although exceptions are the coffin lid at Romsey of Abbess Joan Icthe (d. 1349) and the Scottish nunnery of Elcho (Perths.), where a portion of grave-slab has a

Figure 16 Nunkeeling church (Humbs.) in the eighteenth century. This engraving of 1784 shows the church before rebuilding. The features may represent the crossing and aisled nave or the original east end of the church. The moulded capitals were reincorporated in the rebuilt (and now ruined) parish church (from Poulson 1840).

Figure 17 Ceramic tile from Campsey Ash (Suffolk). The cross engrailed with a fleur-de-lis indicates the arms of the Ufford family. The initials 'BM' refer to the Virgin, *Beata Maria*. Reproduced with the permission of Laurence Keen and the Suffolk Institute of Archaeology and History.

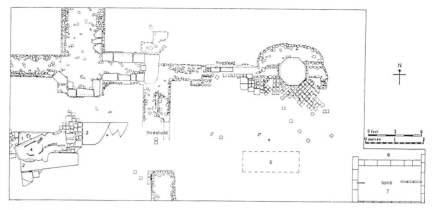

Figure 18 Excavations at Campsey Ash (Suffolk). Private chapels were suggested within the south aisle of the choir of the church on the basis of a number of internal thresholds and burials. The easternmost area contained a marble tomb with brick chamber, possibly linked to the Ufford family (from Sherlock 1971). Reproduced with the permission of David Sherlock and the Suffolk Institute of Archaeology and History.

band lettered 'ICHONUNO', presumably identifying a nun of the house (Reid and Lye 1988). Excavations at the church of a French nunnery, Fontenelle in Mainge, produced several funerary monuments with inscriptions, including an abbess and female patrons (Beaussart and Maliet 1983). A considerable number of priests' slabs, with chalice depicted, survive (for example at Marrick, N. Yorks., and Brewood, Shrops.), and a priest's grave with chalice has been excavated at Carrow, positioned at the east end of the church before the altar steps (*Norfolk Archaeol.* 38, 1983).

It has been suggested elsewhere that female religious patrons would have preferred burial in a nunnery, rather than in a male community (Hirst and Wright 1983: 62). The skeletal population of a nunnery church and cemetery may represent any combination of individuals who were nuns, lay-sisters, servants, patrons, children attending a nunnery school, and relatives of the nuns. Burials from within the church of St Mary's, Winchester showed fairly equal proportions of male (n = 8) and female (n = 11) (S. Brown 1986). The cemetery area of Clementhorpe, York, produced 139 adult skeletons of which 67 per cent were female (n = 89) and 33 per cent were male (n = 43) (Dawes n. d.). Because the Clementhorpe assemblage derives from the cemetery, it might be expected to represent a more diverse social group than the sample from St Mary's Church, containing, for example, female servants of the nunnery. Both sites have higher proportions of males than might be expected, in contrast to smaller, predominantly female groups excavated from Chester (S. W. Ward 1990: 22) and Carrow (*Norfolk Archaeol.* 38, 1983), and provide comparisons with the predominantly male assemblages from male religious institutions. Examples of the latter include

Bordesley Abbey, Halton Abbey, and the friaries of the Oxford Dominicans, Oxford Franciscans and Guildford Dominicans, where the ratio of men to women was roughly 5:1 (Lambrick 1985: 203). Proportions of children at Winchester and Clementhorpe were low, 20 per cent and 15 per cent, respectively, to be expected in a monastic assemblage. Some degree of spatial distinction between social groups may be suggested for both sites. At Winchester, female skeletons in elaborate chalk and limestone coffins were situated towards the east end. An abbess, buried with crozier, was located in the south aisle. Male graves occurred in the north aisle in a neat north–south row. A similar spatial pattern may be suggested for Carrow Priory (Norwich), where twelve burials were excavated, including a priest in the chancel, a child buried in the graveyard, and ten adult women buried in the choir and side chapels. Burials at Clementhorpe took place in coffins, or shrouds, and in two cases stone cists were used. The large group from Clementhorpe is said to fit into two zones: one ordered and one disordered (Dawes n. d.). The more ordered area may represent burial within the nunnery church, possibly corresponding with areas of the nave, aisles and chapels. A larger proportion of male and children's graves occur in the disordered area, whereas the ordered area contained ten skulls with bands of bronze staining, which it has been suggested may have been caused by the headdress fastening worn by a nun. A similar pattern is suggested at Romsey (Hants.) where a small group of male burials was excavated just within the southern boundary of the precinct (*Medieval Archaeol.* 35, 1991: 158).

Within nunneries it seems that more equal proportions of male and female patrons were accepted for burial, although certain areas were designated only for the burial of women (possibly nuns). These spatial distinctions, in addition to the observed differences between groups buried in a church and cemetery, may be further elaborated with reference to funerary monuments in extant nunnery churches. Several churches became fully parochial at the Dissolution. Some of these retained the nuns' church. St Helen's, Bishopsgate, possesses funerary monuments of the nuns' and parish churches *in situ*. In the nuns' church are medieval brasses of priests (Nicholas Wotton 1482; John Breux *c.*1500; see Figure 19); a lady in heraldic mantle with cross, *c.*1535; and a full length armoured effigy of John Leventhorpe, 1510. While priests and individuals were buried and commemorated in the nuns' church, married couples were remembered in chapels of the parish church (for example, Thomas and Margaret Williams, 1495; civilian and wife, *c.*1450; see Figure 20). Extant wills occasionally record a testator's chosen place of burial within a nunnery church. Most often chapels are cited, although a chaplain of Wherwell requested burial in the nave (Coldicott 1989: 107). Three testators associated with Clementhorpe requested burial before the altar of the Blessed Virgin Mary, situated in the nuns' choir (Dobson and Donaghey 1984: 23); another

Figure 19 Funerary brass of Nicholas Wotton, St Helen's Bishopsgate, London: 'Pray for the soul of Nicholas Wotton once Rector of this church and Bachelor of Law who died on the seventh day of April in the year 1482. On whose soul may God have mercy. Amen.' It was common for priests to be commemorated within the nuns' church.

Figure 20 Funerary brass of Thomas and Margaret Williams, St Helen's Bishopsgate, London: 'Here lies Thomas Williams, gentleman, and Margaret his wife. The said Thomas died on the sixteenth day of January 1495 and the said Margaret died ... On whose souls may God have mercy. Amen.' Married couples were commemorated within the parish church.

chose to be buried in the cloister of the nunnery near the grave of her sister.

2.5 CONCLUSIONS: COMMON INTEREST GROUPS IN THE MEDIEVAL NUNNERY

In summary, certain tendencies have been observed in the provision made for religious women, and in the institutional character of nunneries. Nunneries were relatively rare in later medieval England, being outnumbered by monasteries for men and friaries by six to one. Saxon and Anglo-Norman religious provision may have tolerated a greater degree of informality, including a greater variety of communities for religious women and a more flexible approach to mixed communities.

The filiation of nunneries was insecure. Filial preferences differed from male houses especially with regard to the Augustinians, whose pastoral obligations may have been considered inappropriate to nunneries because women could not act as priests. The largely Benedictine identity of English nunneries contrasts with the smaller nunnery populations of Scotland and Wales, which were predominantly Cistercian; and Ireland, where most nunneries followed the Rule of St Augustine. The fashion for founding English nunneries peaked about a generation after their male counterparts. This was largely due to the social and economic identity of nunneries and their founders. In certain regions, especially Yorkshire, East Anglia and the Midlands, nunneries proliferated where lesser gentry had opportunities to establish modest religious houses. These nunneries, when considered according to the numbers of inmates that each house was responsible to support, were substantially poorer than monasteries for men. It is usually not apparent whether founders and benefactors of nunneries imprinted their own personal tastes on the architecture of the house, although links can be made between secular and religious architecture of the same social status (see Chapter 4). Patterns in the distribution and date of nunnery foundations reflect their links to founder of the same common interest group: primarily the local gentry.

Burial within female monasteries was more open to a mixed, widely representative group than that of monasteries. This may reflect a wider range of social connections and interest groups associated with nunneries than with monasteries. Where evidence exists, it seems that funerary arrangements were the reverse of those operating within monasteries for men – adult women were buried in the east end of the church, with mixed burials in the nave, and more equal proportions of male burials in the cemetery outside. Burial at nunneries was less socially and sexually exclusive than that at male religious institutions, although this pattern must be tested further against skeletal populations currently being studied from Elstow (Bedfords.) and Usk (Gwent). Lay support for nunneries came from particular common interest groups: specific families, gentry, and women representing all levels of society. Benefaction of medieval religious houses observed no clear boundaries according to the sex of either patron or inmates. In their endowments, however, patrons made clear the different expectations placed on religious men and women. The following chapter puts forward the social and economic role of nunneries according to their landscape situations, levels of productivity and patterns of consumption.

3

NUNNERIES IN THE MEDIEVAL LANDSCAPE

3.1 GENDER IDENTITIES AND THE MONASTIC LANDSCAPE

The landscape may be studied as a form of communal use of space. People invest their physical territory with social and symbolic meanings particular to the values of their own society. Landscape situation and management were integral to the gender identities of male and female religious communities, and resulted from the different expectations placed on monastic men and women. Monastic landscapes were invested frequently with very specific religious meanings, so that more austere landscapes were associated with the more eremitic hermitages and Cistercian monasteries. But what meanings can be perceived if we take as our starting-point a comparison between male and female communities, their landscapes, spatial relationships to other settlements, and patterns of economic management?

M. W. Thompson has commented on the occurrence of monasteries in relation to castles (1991: 135–7). In the eleventh and twelfth centuries the Norman barons who laid claim to England established castles with an attendant monastery, which would provide status, chaplains, and strengthen the process of cultural domination. While Thompson has proposed a strong correlation between castles and monasteries for men, no such association exists for the female houses. Nunneries established near castles were founded sometime later and by different baronial families, at Usk (Gwent), Chester, and Bungay (Suffolk). Only at Castle Hedingham (Essex) did the castle and nunnery share their origins in the same family, although the de Veres began the castle keep *c.* 1140 and the earliest reference to the nunnery is from 1191. In contrast to monasteries then, nunneries do not appear to have been founded in conjunction with castles in order to express domination over a surrounding region.

It has been noted that of the *c.* 150 nunneries in England and Wales only 25 may be termed in any sense urban (Butler 1987: 168). Few of these were within the heart of towns; the minority which were so tended to be pre-Conquest nunneries of Wessex that had attracted commerce and settlement, like Shaftesbury, Romsey, Wimborne, Wilton and Amesbury. Post-Conquest foundations were mainly suburban, either on the fringes of towns or further out in the surrounding fields. Exceptions included nunneries in the more vulnerable towns of the Welsh border, including Usk and Chester, where in the latter case the nunnery was founded within the demesne of the castle.

The location of a nunnery in relation to a medieval town is sometimes indicated by early maps, for example John Speed's *The Theatre of the Empire of Great Britaine* (1611–12). Urban nunneries were generally on the outer limits of settlement, at least as such limits stood at the end of the Middle Ages. Nunneries at Norwich (Carrow), Stamford, Cambridge and Derby are among those which occupied such positions. Speed showed the nunnery of St Sepulchre, Canterbury, located on the Dover road to the south-east of the town. Its situation was not uncommon, according to Speed about 270 paces from the city gate: just beyond the urban fringe. Clementhorpe (York) was to the south of the medieval city, contained in a bend of the River Ouse. Nunneries within city walls were rare. A similar detachment was observed in the siting of Scandinavian nunneries. For instance St Peter's Lund, (modern Sweden) was located at the western perimeter of the medieval town. At Roskilde (Denmark) the Cistercian Frauekloster was at the southern limit of the town, and the Franciscan nunnery of St Clare stood at its north-west periphery.

Within their suburban context, nunneries maintained a further sense of separation. Thetford was contained within a loop of the river to the south of the town walls, and St Radegund's, Cambridge, was founded within a bend of the River Cam to the north of the town. In the thirteenth century St Radegund's remained the least populated parish in Cambridge (Rubin 1987: 107). Such severance could have social implications. Taxation lists from fifteenth-century Winchester indicate that St Mary's Abbey provided a haven for a large community of women who 'were employed by nuns or were attracted to that quarter of the city, where Colebrook Street itself houses a topographically enclosed community on three sides of the abbey, by piety or in search of security' (Keene 1985: 388). More common were the extramural nunneries sited in fields beyond the town (*de la pré*), such as Derby Kings Mead, Polsloe (near Exeter), Northampton de la Pré and St Mary de Pré (St Albans). The London nunneries were located in open fields on the margins of settlement. The Minories was founded on the site of a Roman cemetery (Collins 1961); Clerkenwell shared an ecclesiastical enclave with St John's (Hospitallers) and the Charterhouse. Godstow was sited in the Port Meadow to the north-west of Oxford. Whistones was in the northern suburbs of Worcester with the manor of Ladies Aston (Knowles and Hadcock 1953: 227). The nunnery at Bristol was placed on St Michael's Hill, by the side of the road running north out of the city.

Urban nunneries retained their separateness despite the growth of towns.

Suburban and extramural nunneries were often on the rivers and roads which formed main routes of communication into towns. They were distinct, yet dependent on the nexus of the market. Their placement outside the protection of the city walls may seem surprising, for superficially this could be thought to be the most vulnerable location for a house of religious women. But the tendency for nunneries to distance themselves from towns had precedents.

In France the earliest recorded nunneries, more accurately described as sixth-century double houses, were suburban. Caesarius's foundation at Arles was moved from its original position in the suburbs to within the walls; similarly St Salaberga's moved from outside Langres to within Laon (MGH: *Scriptorum Rerum Merovingicarum* 3: 467; 5: 56–7). It has been assumed that these nunneries were relocated to provide greater physical protection (Schulenberg 1989). Similar uprooting may have occurred at early English houses. There is some disagreement, for example, over the original location of the nunnery at Bath. It is generally assumed that the seventh-century house lay inside the walls near the later site of St Peter's. But an alternative siting has been postulated outside the walls, in the area of the unenclosed Roman settlement. Although Barry Cunliffe (1984: 348) has dismissed the alternative site as less likely, such a location would parallel the first positions of sixth-century Merovingian nunneries.

With the acceleration of urban growth in the ninth and tenth centuries the process of relocation was reversed, with nunneries seeking greater security in the isolation of the fields beyond towns. This process is demonstrated by the late Saxon nunnery at Chichester. This brief and little known foundation was displaced in 1075 when the cathedral moved from Selsey to Chichester (VCH Sussex 2 1907: 47). Urban growth and male clericalism left little opportunity for the isolation required by women's religious communities. More conducive surroundings might have been found in the medieval countryside.

3.2 IN A WILDERNESS

It seemed to [the first prioress] that Brian de Retteville's choice of site had been unrealistically too close to the mind of Saint Benedict – since it was a nunnery he had founded. Men with their inexhaustible interest in themselves may do well enough in a wilderness, but the shallower egoism of women demands some nourishment from the outer world.

(Sylvia Townsend Warner, *The Corner that Held Them*, 1948: 8).

In her novel, Sylvia Townsend Warner described life in a small medieval nunnery. Her imagined house was perched on a slight rise amidst fenland, tucked in the loop of a river – a prospect uncannily close to the majority of rural nunneries. Many were at home in waterlands, sited at the highest points of marshes (Minster in Sheppey, Kent; Barking, Essex; Swine and Nunkeeling, Humbs., before the eighteenth- and nineteenth-century draining of Holderness) or fenland (Crabhouse, Norfolk, before reclamation in the thirteenth century; Denney and Waterbeach, Cambs.). Likewise, the double houses of the Gilbertines were set in the Lincolnshire fens or the uplands bordering the fens. Houses like Denney, on the fen edge, and Little Marlow (Bucks.), atop a sandy rise in marshy land, conveyed the impression of an island. Frequently nunneries were surrounded partially by rivers given to flooding. When viewed from their long, isolated approaches (for example, Nun Monkton) these flooded places were islands. Some nunneries were placed on tongues of higher land in flood meadows (for example, Godstow, Oxfords.; Yedingham, N. Yorks.; Lyminster, Sussex; Kington St Michael, Wilts.). Others, such as Moxby (N. Yorks.), used natural or diverted water courses to form two or three sides of the precinct.

Isolation was sometimes achieved in the desolate surroundings of the moors, for example at Handale, Baysdale, Arden, Thicket and Rosedale (N. Yorks.). Hill-top nunneries asserted their own type of insularity. Minchin Barrow (Somerset) was on the crest of a hill above a valley; Shaftesbury (Dorset) commands lofty views over the downs. The Welsh nunnery of Llanllugan (Powys) was set on a high river cliff overlooking the Rhiw streams.

Occasionally nunneries occupy classic monastic sites. Minchin Buckland (Somerset), Brewood (Shrops.), Orford (Lincs.), and Marrick (N. Yorks.) (Figure 21) for example, are set in the sides of river valleys. Flat sites lying on river valley bottoms include Catesby (Northants.), Wykeham (N. Yorks.) and Burnham (Berks). These flat sites were often moated, providing drainage of lowland sites underlain by clay, and precinct boundaries that offered symbolic and limited defensive merits. A considerable number of nunneries were moated – possibly a reflection of their social origins within the gentry. Moat construction expanded 1150–1200 when many of these nunneries were founded (for example, Cook Hill, Worcs., Sinningthwaite, N. Yorks., and Pinley, Warwicks.), and peaked 1200–1325 (Le Patourel and Roberts 1978: 46), taking in moated foundations such as Bruisyard, Flixton (both Suffolk) and Waterbeach (Cambs.). The labour expenditure required in moat construction made them an aristocratic symbol to which the gentry increasingly aspired (Dyer 1989: 107).

Medieval nunneries were liminal places – located at the physical and psychological margins of society. To a degree their prospects resemble the places craved by early medieval ascetics. In Britain the solitude and penitence of desert eremiticism was translated into surroundings of marsh, fen and moor. The ascetic tradition had always included women, metaphorically in the lives of Mary of Egypt and Pelagia, and the apocryphal life of Mary Magdalene; materially in the Saxon hermitages of the women Pega (Peakirk,

Figure 21 Marrick (N. Yorks.) occupies a classic landscape situation for a medieval monastery; set in the side of a gently sloping valley in Swaledale, it was provided with shelter, good drainage and water sources.

Cambs.), whose eighth-century fenland hermitage is recorded in Felix's *Life of Guthlac* (Colgrave 1985), and Modwen (Andressey Island, River Trent), whose ninth-century chapel and well to St Andrew are noted in the *Vitae Modwenae* (–1151) (BM Royal MS. 15 B. IV). Were the later medieval nunneries sited in recollection of such asceticism? Or, as recent feminist interpretations suppose, in order to protect the virginity of their inmates (Schulenberg 1984; 1989: 285)? In actuality this treasured chastity was normally left undefended. Only Shaftesbury (Dorset) applied for a licence to crenellate their church and belfry (Coulson 1982: 94). Moats and walls were seldom built to defensive specifications. Border nunneries, like Ellerton (N. Yorks.) and Holystone (Northumb.) were sacked and burnt. Previously, where the marginal nature of nunneries has been observed, it has been explained as an error of judgement or with reference to economic constraints. For example, Sally Thompson (1984: 133) states simply that '[nuns] were ... less fortunate in their choice of sites than their brothers'. The nuns occasionally complained of their lot. In 1411 Easebourne (Sussex) cited 'the sterility of the lands, meadows and other property of the priory, which is situated in a solitary, waste and thorny place' (Power 1922: 177).

It is likely that patrons determined the situation of nunneries, according to an accepted social norm. Monasteries for men were sometimes endowed with marshy, inhospitable holdings. Where this happened, in contrast to the nunneries, male houses initiated programmes of land reclamation. At Osney Abbey (Oxfords.), for example, the outer court area was reclaimed from marsh in the twelfth century, and the initially constricted precinct was developed by drainage of lands (Sharpe 1985). English nunneries do not appear to have practised land reclamation. Where flooding of the site could not be tolerated, it was periodically abandoned (for example, Crabhouse), or, less often, transferred to a new site (for example, Waterbeach to Denney). Similar marginal sites were chosen for French nunneries, although excavations at Coyroux (Limousin) have revealed a more active approach to site management. Successive sequences of terracing and flooding absorbed most of the nunnery's resources (Bond and Maines 1988: 800; Barrière 1984).

Certain orders provided explicit statutes requiring the isolation of nun-neries. In 1216 the Cistercian general chapter laid down that a nunnery must be at least six leagues from a male abbey and ten from another nunnery (D. H. Williams 1975: 155). But the Cistercian statutes were largely irrelevant to conditions in England, as those nunneries which had fashioned themselves according to Cistercian principles had already been founded in isolation. In France and Ireland, to the contrary, Cistercian nunneries had sprung up beside male houses (Berman 1988: 44; Stalley 1987: 45–6). Unofficial twin houses were established at Mellifont and Jerpoint. In 1228 the monks were warned by Stephen of Lexington to remove the nuns, 'for as long as they remain next to the abbey, we shall place the whole monastery under interdict' (ibid.). It is likely that the nuns at these houses had churches separate from the monks. At Jerpoint a rectangular structure *c.* 182 m north of the abbey church, assumed to be a *capella ante portas*, a chapel at the gate (ibid.: 247), may originally have served this function. At the Irish religious complex of Clonmacnois (Offaly), the small, twelfth-century nuns' church was outside the main enclosure and reached by causeway. In 1137 the General Chapter of the Premonstratensians, originally an order of double houses, decreed the separation of men's and women's houses (Bolton 1983: 84). In England the unofficial twin houses had already disbanded. For example, the cell of nuns beside Benedictine St Albans had been removed to Sopwell by 1140. The nuns from Augustinian Marton had moved to nearby Moxby (N. Yorks.) by *c.*1167–80. Joint houses of St John of Jerusalem, the Hospitallers, continued to be founded, for example Countess Maud's Norfolk foundations at Carbrook Parva (–1180: sisters) and Car-brook Magna (1182: knights). Hospitals served by sisters were established near Hospitaller preceptories: a possible extant hospital chapel survives associated with Clanfield (Oxfords.) (Blair 1985: 213). Shortly after 1180 the sisters from all English Hospitaller houses were removed to Minchin Buckland (Somerset). Once established, the spatial and administrative relationship of nunneries to male houses generally remained remote. Most often their contact was competitive, with the nunneries engaged in litigation to retain advowsons appropriated by monasteries for men (Graves 1984: 220–2; Nichols 1984: 242–3).

Although nunneries remained distant from castles, towns and monasteries for men, they often had close topographical and social links to villages. Occasionally an early nunnery began life in isolation, only to attract village settlement to it. Chatteris (Cambs.) is an example. Some of the northern nunneries appear to have been planned in conjunction with, or incorporating, villages. Nun Monkton village lay with the apex of the green at the gate of the nunnery precinct. Nunkeeling (Humbs.) was established immediately to the south of an existing village. Field survey has recognized a village street and tofts to the south of the precinct at Stainfield (Lincs.) (Everson 1989). To the east of the precinct of Orford (Lincs.) stretches a single-sided village settlement (ibid.) (Figure 22). Both sites were established in river valleys, in a classic monastic situation, but were endowed with a vill and parish church.

Many rural nunneries were sited at the periphery of a village. This enabled the nunnery to share its church with a parochial congregation (Chapter 4, section 1), and provided a source of labour for the nunnery. In addition to hiring in occasional labour for a harvest or shearing, nunneries like Minster in Sheppey (Kent), Nun Cotham (Lincs.), and Polesworth (Warwicks.) employed whole villages (Power 1922: 159). These villages were not entirely agricultural. Weavers, tailors, a wright and a smith were taxed at Nun Monkton in 1334 (Beresford and St Joseph 1979: 11).

3.3 THE NUNNERY ESTATE

Like any monastery, nunneries were in possession of parcels of land and holdings which made up their estate. Ideally, a monastic estate was composed of both upland and lowland components, resulting in a balanced and integrated variety of agricultural activities. Like any secular manor, the nunnery estate was an administrative unit, and not necessarily a cohesive areal entity. But its constituency was more secure than that of a secular estate, since transferral through marriage and inheritance was not an issue (Moorhouse 1989).

Monastic estates included the 'home farm' adjacent to the religious house, and more distant holdings which could include granges, fisheries, mineral workings and mills. In general, a grange may be defined as a consolidated block of monastic demesne land, varying from $c.30$ ha to $c.2000$ ha or more in size, organized as an estate farm. Granges often served specialized functions. These included: agrarian farms, bercaries (sheep farms), vaccaries (cattle ranches), horse studs and industrial complexes (mining and iron-workings). A well-planned and managed monastic estate would include several types of out-station or outlying grange, in addition to the home farm. Together the granges provided food and raw

Figure 22   Survey of Orford Priory (Lincs.). Orford is situated in the side of a river valley. Survey has shown that the nunnery precinct was planned in conjunction with a single-sided village. C RCHME Crown copyright.

materials consumed by the religious house, and produced surpluses for sale as profit. From its appearance in the twelfth century, the monastic estate system aimed to enable at least the self-sufficiency of rural monasteries. Norton Priory (Cheshire), for example, was self-sufficient in most foodstuffs, water, fuel (wood) and building materials (clay, marl, sand, stone). Materials sought from beyond the area immediately adjacent to the manor included lime, slate, lead and iron (Greene 1989: 60–2). Nunneries were similarly equipped, if on a smaller scale. Quarries were held by Marrick, and Kirklees (W. Yorks.) at Stone House. Esholt (W. Yorks.) leased out its quarries at Stone Top from 1360–1440 (Stephen Moorhouse pers. comm.).

The monastic estate can be studied according to the composition of its holdings, the process and sequence of their acquisition and strategies of subsequent management (Platt 1969; Moorhouse 1989; Biddick 1989). Outlying holdings and specialist granges generated records of management by the monastic landlord. The home farm generated little documentation, since transfers to the monastic kitchen or cellar could go unrecorded. Its proximity to the religious nucleus, however, allows easier identification on the ground. Thus, the home farm can often be best studied archaeologically. Sources for the nunnery estate, therefore, must include a document-based assessment of outlying holdings, and archaeological survey of extant outer court areas.

The low survival of documents associated with nunneries (S. Thompson 1984) has hindered assessments of their economy. The major synthesis was provided by Eileen Power (1922); more detailed studies of individual nunneries and regions have appeared more recently. Hitherto, historians have in general examined nunnery estates as components within the overall income of the nunnery (temporalities), with little emphasis on the actual make up and workings of the landscape.

Power used two main sources: *Valor Ecclesiasticus*, and account rolls of several individual houses. These sources are strongly biased in two ways. First, the account rolls and *Valor* are dated from the fourteenth to sixteenth centuries respectively, so that nunnery estates were studied only in their latterday form. Hence, their primary nature and early development were neglected. Second, the survival of documents corresponds roughly to the status of the nunnery (Thompson 1984: 140). This means that those nunneries with extant account rolls tend to be the small minority of wealthy communities (for example Syon, Barking and Catesby). From the 100 nunneries surveyed in *Valor*, Power observed that the geographical spread of a nunnery's holdings had a direct relation to its status; and that although 22 nunneries owned urban property, about 90 per cent of the assessed value of urban property controlled by nunneries was held by the London houses. In order to balance Power's analysis, more recent approaches have studied extant cartularies and early endowments.

The largest monastic landholders tended to be pre-Conquest foundations (Butler 1987: 167). Nunneries were no exception. Holdings of these abbeys were recorded as manors in Domesday Book. Wherwell's (Hants.) possessions were all within a ten kilometre radius of the abbey (Coldicott 1989: 27). This distribution reflects an initial endowment of consolidated blocks of land. St Mary's, Winchester and Romsey (Hants.), in comparison, had more scattered holdings, possibly acquired piecemeal. Chatteris (Cambs.) held lands in Suffolk, Cambridgeshire and Hertfordshire in 1086. Few new holdings were added in the next two hundred years, and virtually none subsequently (VCH Cambs. 2 1948). Wealthy southern nunneries held large arable farms, often at a considerable distance from the house itself. These were productive units in addition to serving as collection points for renders. Linked with Shaftesbury, for example, are the stone-built tithe barn and grange at Bradford-on-Avon (Wilts.), and the manor and grange of Tisbury, which includes a great barn, an external and internal gatehouse and the original domestic range (Platt 1969). Smaller nunneries may have commanded one or more less specialized granges. Grace Dieu (Leics.), for example, held Merril Grange, within the original lordship of Belton that was granted to the house. The 1539 inventory of Merril suggests a mixed arable and pastoral economy. The grange itself housed cattle, pigs and horses, and provided storage for barley, peas, oats and hay (Hartley 1987: 10). Nunneries sometimes had satellites held as rectories. Yedingham (N. Yorks.) held the church at Sinnington, where an adjacent, and still extant, stone-built hall served as collection and staging point to the nunnery.

For the majority of nunneries initial endowments were by any standard small. Barking, a Benedictine nunnery of exceptional wealth, held thirteen manors (Power 1922: 563). Peterborough Abbey, which might be considered its male equivalent, held twenty-seven. Urban nunneries such as Clementhorpe were recipients of grants of small, scattered parcels of land (Dobson and Donaghey 1984: 14). These were difficult to manage, and offered only low financial yields. Northern rural nunneries generally had concentrated local estates. These were acquired soon after the foundation of the house, representing limited donations from the founder's family (Burton 1979: 11). As a result their most substantial holdings were worked as home farms. Marrick, for example, worked the majority of its holdings as home farms at Marrick and Stainmore. A vaccary at Owlands was added by an early grant (Tillotson 1989: 9, 11). The Yorkshire nunneries were most commonly granted 'pasture land' in twelfth-century charters (Burton 1979: 13). These houses relied heavily upon sheep-farming. Such overspecialization must have brought about the nunneries' reliance on marketed foodstuffs. Revenues came from advowsons and rights of multure (Burton 1979: 15); mills were granted in addition to those at the home farm.

Yorkshire nunneries were characterized by their concentrated holdings, their specialization in wool, and the fossilization of their possessions early in the history of each house. In contrast, Yorkshire's monasteries for men were more active in instigating their own long-term programmes of land acquisition (Moorhouse 1989). Their estates were widely dispersed and divided into upland and lowland components. Animal husbandry was more diverse. Bolton, for example, had bercaries, vaccaries and produced pigs. Jervaulx was famous for its horse stud-farms. Mineral-rich land was sought for mining and industrial workings, such as Fountains's water-powered bloomery at Bradley (Walton 1931). Permanent iron-working complexes were run by Fountains, Rievaulx, Byland, Selby and Kirkstead (Moorhouse 1981). Coal-mining was linked to several houses in South Yorkshire and Nottinghamshire (for example, Beauvale Charterhouse).

Certain midland and northern nunneries may have been exceptions to the pattern because of the status of their founders and the original composition of the house. Stixwould (Lincs.) was founded 1129–35 by the widow Lucy, Countess of Chester, a noblewoman tenant-in-chief (Graves 1984: 217). Its extant cartulary and twelfth- and thirteenth-century documents suggest that Stixwould maintained a well-balanced economy of eight granges, involving arable farming, livestock, salt production and fisheries (ibid. 224). This integrated economy may reflect the original endowment of Stixwould as a 'quasi' double house. In common with lesser northern nunneries, Stixwould was granted land by patrons connected to the founder, and within two generations of the foundation of the nunnery. Likewise, the wealthy nunnery of Denney (Cambs.) received its grants in a short period. Between 1342 and 1416 this Franciscan nunnery received four manors. After this time land grants ceased (Bourdillon 1926: 29).

Female houses seldom participated in the active acquisition of lands. Their estates were composed largely of twelfth-century land grants. Male houses continued to consolidate their holdings into the thirteenth century. From the early fourteenth century many monasteries began to withdraw from direct farming of their estates. Later, labour shortages were countered by leasing entire granges to lay-tenants. Many male houses selectively retained arable granges to use as retreat houses. Nunneries leased out all granges and mills other than the home farm (Power 1922: 100, 107 n. 1).

3.4 HOME FARMS AND OUTER COURTS

The nunnery consisted of the precinct, made up of an inner area of claustral buildings (see Chapter 4) and an outer court for subsidiary structures. In addition, rural nunneries had associated agricultural settlements known as the home farm. The home farm of a nunnery is likely to have been represented by a number of appurtenances, outlying features near the outer court, so that the two entities are not always easily distinguished. Entry to the outer court was marked by a gatehouse, such as the extant fifteenth-century examples at Canonsleigh and Cornworthy (Devon). Some, like Malling (Kent) and Polesworth (Warwicks.), contained the usual separate entry arches for carts and pedestrians. Chapels were sometimes contained above (for example, the chapel of the Holy Rood at Barking, Essex), or projecting from the main gatehouse (for example, Malling). These were for the use of secular visitors or the priests of the nunnery. Upper chambers were appropriate places for priests or confessors; the gatehouse to the west of the church at Minster in Sheppey (Kent) is recorded as having served this function (Walcott 1868: 301). A single gatehouse appears to have been favoured over the inner and outer gatehouses provided for Cistercian male houses. Almonries, which commonly occur at the gates of monasteries for men, are rarely associated with nunneries. An exception may be Wilton (Wilts.), where a fourteenth-century section of walling known as 'the Almonry' survives to the west of the present house (Pevsner 1975: 585). Hospitals were occasionally maintained outside the precinct, for example across from the abbey gate at Wilton and Barking (Essex). The precise spatial relationships between hospitals and precincts at Castle Hedingham (Essex), Aconbury (Herefords.), and Wherwell (Hants.) are unknown (see Chapter 7, section 2 for a discussion of hospitals).

The outer court housed guests and servants, and some smaller nunneries, like Flixton (Suffolk) appear to have had permanent secular residents in the outer court (Oliva 1994). Extant buildings sometimes confirm the domestic nature of outer courts, for example those at Redlingfield (Suffolk) and Blackborough (Norfolk). Both sites retain substantial buildings of flint and carstone, respectively, and ashlar limestone dressings; both have pointed arches in the base of the building consistent with features to accommodate a drain. These buildings are situated some distance from the likely positions of the nuns' cloisters and most likely represent residential accommodation in the outer court. Recorded in visitations at Godstow (Oxfords.) were the steward, bailiff, rent collector and gatekeeper (Ganz 1972: 152). Subsidiary structures integral to the nunnery were placed in the outer or inner court. Excavations at Kirklees (W. Yorks.) uncovered a stone-built range with the foundations of a circular oven, possibly a brewhouse and bakehouse (Armytage 1908) (see Figure 42). A late sixteenth-century plan of Marrick (N. Yorks.) shows outbuildings surrounding three sides of the cloister (Figure 23). While the plan itself refers to post-Dissolution use of the nunnery, the outbuildings may have retained some of their original functions. To the west were stables, a pigsty, dovecote, kennel and kilns; a southern block contained a bakehouse, milk-house, storehouse and workroom. An early seventeenth-century plan of Chester (Figure 24) shows arrangements in an urban nunnery. Despite pressures on space which may have existed within the castle demesne and town walls, Benedictine Chester was provided with a cloister and two courts. Few of the buildings shown on the plan were labelled. However, doorways were marked, so that functions can be attributed according to access to the nuns' cloister. A walled space to the east of the church, communicating with the dormitory, may have been a private garden for the convent. A large court to the west of the church was probably a guest court, with entry through a gatehouse at the western entrance to the precinct. An eastern entry led to a passage north of the church and to two chambers in the guest court possibly for

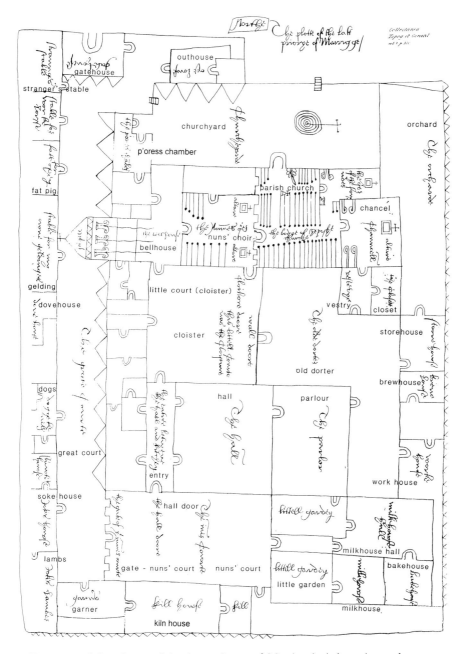

Figure 23 'The plotte of the late priorye of Marrigge'. A late sixteenth-century plan of Marrick (N. Yorks.) refers to the post-Dissolution use of the priory buildings, but shows the medieval position of buildings surrounding three sides of the cloister (transcribed from *Collectanea Topographica et Geneaologica* 5 (1838)).

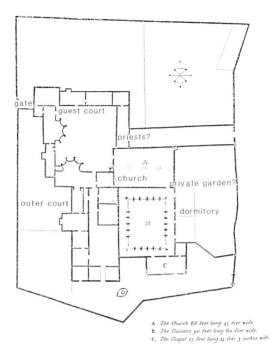

A. *The Church 66 feet long 45 feet wide.*
B. *The Cloisters 90 feet long 60 feet wide.*
C. *The Chapel 23 feet long 24 feet 3 inches wide.*

Figure 24   An early seventeenth-century plan of Chester Nunnery. A walled space to the east of the church may have been a private garden for the nuns; the court to the west is likely to have been reserved for guests, with entry through a gatehouse towards the west. Engraved for D. and S. Lysons's *Magna Britannia* II. ii (1810) from Randle Holmes MSS (Harl. 2073), British Museum.

priests. A smaller court west of the nuns' cloister may have accommodated subsidiary structures.

In principle the monastic home farm enabled the self-sufficiency of the religious community, producing meat, bread, beer, vegetables and dairy produce (milk, eggs, cheese and poultry). From extant accounts, Eileen Power surmised that only fish and spices needed to be bought in (1922: 119). 'Spices' included imported foodstuffs like dried fruit (currants, dates, figs, prunes, raisins), almonds and rice (Dyer 1989: 62). Accounts of the Dissolution surveyors sometimes list components of the home farm. These often include barns, outbuildings, dovecotes, orchards, gardens, closes, pasture, meadows and mills. Occasionally the outbuildings of nunneries survive. Medieval barns are extant at Malling (Kent) and Barrow Gurney (Somerset), with fragments at Minchin Buckland (Somerset). Wealthier nunneries commanded additional features, for example the vineyard planted at Wherwell (Hants.) (Coldicott 1989: 80). The extent of the area and features associated with the nunnery can be elucidated archaeologically.

Sources for the study of this area include aerial photography, field survey and excavation of monastic outer courts.

Aerial photography

Aerial photographs can assist in precisely locating monastic sites, and sometimes give an indication of the range of associated features. Nunburnholme (N. Yorks.), for example, can be identified beyond the eastern edge of the present village (Figure 25). A light covering of snow reveals a large rectangular enclosure (an outer court?) with ridge and furrow cultivation to the north, and a mass of small buildings platforms to the south. A smaller square enclosure to the south-west may represent the nuns' cloister. Aerial photography can be useful in identifying the boundaries of nunneries. Grace Dieu, for example, lay at the foot of a north-facing slope. Its north and west sides were bounded by a brook (Knowles and St Joseph 1952). The area of earthworks extends approximately 350 m east–west × 200 m north–south. Earthworks and cropmarks sometimes reveal appurtenances, especially fishponds and mills, and associated features, including house platforms and field-systems. Precise dating of these features is seldom achieved without excavations.

Certain features are more likely to be contemporary with medieval nunneries. Arable farming at Rosedale (N. Yorks.) is suggested by a field of ridge and furrow cultivation to the immediate south-east of the nunnery precinct; a block of fields showing ridge and furrow is associated with Nun Appleton (N. Yorks.). Small fishponds are sometimes associated with nunneries, for example Aconbury (Herefords.), Bruisyard (Suffolk), Denney (Cambs.) and Grace Dieu (Leics.).

More prominent features are often associated with double houses. Fishponds can be observed at Sempringham, Haverholme, Alvingham (all Lincs.), Nuneaton (Warwicks.) and Catley (Lincs.). Cropmarks observed at Shouldham (Norfolk) reveal fishponds within the ditched enclosure (Edwards 1989). Minchin Buckland (Somerset), arranged as a double preceptory of the Hospitallers, canalized and diverted a stream for three terraced fishponds (Burrow 1985). The 'quasi' double house of Swine (Humbs.) has a series of fishponds to the west of the extant church, and a row of narrow rectangular platforms to the north-west (Figure 26). Swine operated a turbary for producing peat-blocks. Its estate appears to have been equipped with a park-mount – a form of lookout associated with deer parks and secular estates – constructed in peat and clay between the thirteenth and fifteenth centuries (Varley 1973: 144–6). The precinct area of Gilbertine Bullington (Lincs.) is similar to that of many nunneries, approximately 213 m east–west × 260 m north–south (Hadcock 1937). Some of the walls of the supposed nuns' cloister can be discerned on aerial photographs. A 30 m strip contained within the southern precinct boundary

Figure 25 Nunburnholme (N. Yorks.) under covering of snow. A large rectangular enclosure is bounded by ridge and furrow cultivation to the north, and a mass of smaller buildings to the south. To the south-west, a smaller square enclosure may be the cloister. Photograph courtesy of Anthony Crawshaw.

Figure 26 To the west of Swine church (N. Humbs.) earthworks indicate fishponds, with a row of narrow rectangular platforms further north. Photograph courtesy of Anthony Crawshaw.

is thought to represent the area of the canons' cloister (ibid.). Along the eastern precinct boundary is a series of enclosures, perhaps garths; larger enclosures, possibly for stock, are to the west of the precinct. Fishponds lay within the north-west angle of the precinct, and the remains of structures are indicated about 55 m to the north of the cloisters. To the east of the precinct is a moated enclosure.

Field survey

More detailed evidence is provided by field survey of surviving earthworks. Most easily defined are those precincts bounded by moats, including Flixton (Suffolk), Bruisyard (Suffolk), and Waterbeach (Cambs.). The rectangular moat at Sinningthwaite (190 m × 225 m) contains two inner enclosures, tucked into the north-east and south-east corners. These were distinct from the claustral buildings in the centre of the moat, one of which survives. The original entrance to the complex is not clear; several small ponds join the moat around its perimeter.

Comprehensive field survey has been undertaken only at very few nunneries, although recently the RCHME has included a number in its survey programme. Earthworks at Moxby (N. Yorks.) are likely to represent outer court features. Three major components have been identified: a series of irregular compounds, a moated enclosure and one side of a mill dam. The overlapping compounds were enclosed by low banks; one has a funnelled entrance possibly used in stock control. The mill is associated with features representing a complex system of sluices and bypass channels (Mackay and Swan 1989). Survey at Stainfield, Orford and Heynings (Lincs.) (Everson 1989) suggested precincts on a larger scale than the moated sites listed above, approximately 400 m × 250 m, 240 m × 300 m and 180 m × 290 m, respectively. As noted above, Orford and Stainfield were established with planned villages, the latter overlying ridge and furrow cultivation and encroached upon by later, post-medieval emparking and garden features (Figure 27). The earthworks representing the Cistercian nunnery at Heynings have been located at a more isolated spot in keeping with Cistercian expectations, at some three kilometres' distance from the village of Knaith previously assumed to be the site of the nunnery (ibid. 145).

Little comparative material exists for double houses. Surveyed earthworks to the east of the church at Nuneaton (Warwicks.) appear to be divided by a low ridge running east–west (Andrews et al. 1981: 60–2). To the south of the ridge are flat rectangular areas (c. 25 sq m), with hollows, possibly fishponds, to the south. These areas may represent enclosures or garths associated with outbuildings.

Survey at Marton (N. Yorks.) provides an example of a short-lived double house, which developed into a monastery for men (Mackay and

Figure 27 Survey of Stainfield Priory (Lincs.). Stainfield Nunnery was endowed with a vill and parish church and established with a planned village. The priory was superimposed upon ridge and furrow cultivation and encroached upon by later, post-medieval emparking and gardens. C RCHME Crown copyright.

Swan 1989: fig. 1). The area of the precinct (170 m × 250 m) is comparable to those of nunneries, but the density of earthwork features is much greater. Here the River Foss was harnessed for a mill complex to the north-west of the precinct, and a mass of ponds ran in a north–south line to its west. Within the northern boundary of the precinct is a series of enclosures.

Projecting beyond the southern boundary of the canons' precinct at Marton is a moated enclosure, *c.* 50 m × 15 m, set high into the side of the valley. Monastic moats might be used as fishponds or to enclose particular features, such as gardens or orchards (C. J. Bond 1993). At Marton, the moated area was separate from the spur of land on which the canons' cloister was situated, but near a point where the two areas may have been linked by a ford or causeway. In the north-east corner of the moated enclosure is a building platform with stone rubble foundations. This small self-contained area may have been provided as the nuns' enclosure. It would have been inaccessible from the outer court, approached only by a bridge or causeway from the canons' precinct. The moated area apparently fell into disuse during monastic occupation of the site (ibid.). It is suggested here that this secluded, self-contained enclosure would have provided ideal accommodation for the nuns, who were removed to Moxby, 2.8 km south, between 1165 and 80 (Elkins 1988: 118). Moated enclosures associated with other nunneries and double houses may have accommodated specific elements within the community, such as the lay-religious, or servants. Examples include Sinningthwaite, Bullington, and Nunkeeling (Humbs.), where a moated area survives to the south of the cloister.

Excavation

The value of archaeological investigations in outer court areas has been recognized only in recent years. Hence, few nunnery outer courts have been studied. Nevertheless, when patched together their findings represent domestic, service and light industrial activity. The precise function of excavated structures and their location in relation to the cloister, especially where urban sites are concerned, is sometimes difficult to determine. At St Mary's, Clerkenwell, London, a range of substantial timber buildings was excavated to the north of the cloister, one of which was initially industrial before changing function to provide accommodation. This timber complex was demolished before the end of the twelfth century. Subsequent outer court development included a stone building which formed an extension to the east range, and a kitchen forming part of the north range, with a metalled yard surface between (Sloane 1991). An excavated two-cell building at the Minories, London, is thought to have been located in an area to the west of the south range of the cloister. A flagstone floor sealed a hearth, stone base and lead water pipe. It has been suggested that this structure functioned as a laundry (MOLAS 1986 archive).

The dynamic character of outer court areas is to some extent demonstrated by excavations at Godstow (Oxfords.) and Elstow (Bedfords). A group of outbuildings to the north of the cloisters at Godstow underwent three major periods of development (*Medieval Archaeol.* 5, 1961: 313).

Two timber buildings, possibly relating to initial phases of the nunnery's occupation, were constructed in a ditched area. These were replaced by stone structures with a series of gravel floors and floodsilts. A subsequent rearrangement introduced a long stone building on a new alignment, and a substantial enclosure wall containing a row of narrow buildings. At Elstow, stone outbuildings stretched from the dormitory of the nuns' cloister to a possible jettied structure toward the stream (Figure 28). Only the excavated stable might be described as an agricultural building. Service buildings are suggested by drains, sloping stone floors, water tanks and wells. Others certainly had a domestic purpose, indicated by hearths and latrines (Baker and Baker 1989: 267). The functions of these buildings may have changed over time; by the later phases Elstow's outbuildings were taking on a domestic appearance.

Very little industrial production has been recognized at nunneries. Elstow's outbuildings produced copper alloy trimmings (ibid.). Near the excavated structures at Clerkenwell, a kiln was discovered. Intruding into the plough horizons at the Minories was a large circular bell-casting pit (*Medieval Archaeol.* 31, 1987: 128), and excavations on the boundary of St Helen's, Bishopsgate, London, recovered extensive dumps of waste possibly linked to bell-founding (*Medieval Archaeol.* 35, 1991: 152). Little evidence exists for the production of pottery and tiles. A rare example is the Scottish Cistercian nunnery at North Berwick, where an excavated kiln yielded ornamented relief tiles (Richardson 1928).

Production may have been on a greater scale in the outer courts of double houses. Stone buildings to the south of the cloisters at Haverholme (Lincs.) yielded spindle-whorls, bone bodkins and bobbins, possibly representing weaving and bone-working (Jones 1963). Tile kilns associated with Haverholme and Shouldham (Norfolk) have been excavated (Smallwood 1978). To the south of the cloister at Nuneaton a possible malthouse/brewhouse was excavated (Andrews *et al.* 1981: 64). Here, a mortar-lined sunken vat emptied from a chute through an iron pipe in the wall. This structure was not dissimilar to those from male monastic sites. Its location was, however, unusually near the cloisters (ibid.).

The features which occur at nunnery home farms (for example, fishponds, stock enclosures, arable fields) and outer courts (timber and stone buildings, vats) are within the range of components associated with male monasteries and secular settlements. But the scale of economic activity which they represent appears to have been insignificant. This remains true even when the components of nunneries are compared with those of fairly modest male counterparts. Field survey at Bordesley Abbey, for example, revealed a precinct area approximately twice that expected for nunneries. The area of the precinct, and the diversity of activities conducted within it, was increased by redirecting the course of the river (Aston and Munton 1976). Large-scale land management and reclamation has not, to date, been

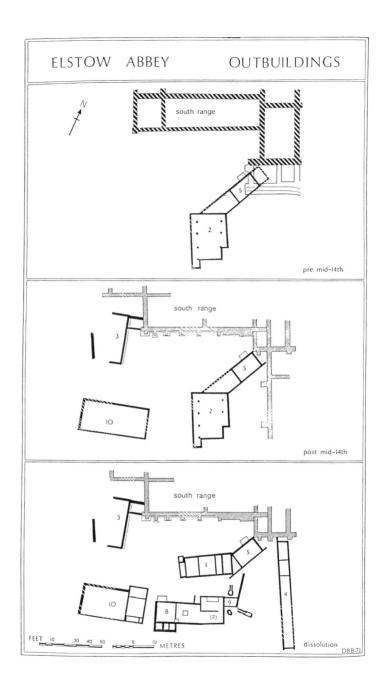

Figure 28 Outbuildings at Elstow (Bedfords.). Multi-period stone outbuildings were excavated to the south of the cloister. By the later phases of occupation, some were domestic buildings, indicated by hearths and latrines and the presence of domestic artefacts, others were service buildings with drains and water tanks. Plan courtesy of David Baker.

84

demonstrated for nunneries. Excavations in monastic outer courts (for example, Thornholme Priory (Lincs.) and Grove Priory (Bedfords.)) have yielded evidence for a greater range of functions and density of features, with more emphasis on frequent renewal and site reorganization (Coppack 1989; Baker and Baker 1989). Within nunneries, by contrast, the outer court was characterized partly by domestic occupation. In comparison to male houses, the nunnery was compact. The outer court areas at Nuneaton and Elstow were unusually close to the claustral buildings. A greater variety of features and activities can be put forward for double houses, such as Shouldham, Bullington and Haverholme. Perhaps appropriately, their scales of production were between those recognized for male and female houses.

3.5 PRODUCTION, CONSUMPTION AND LABOUR IN MEDIEVAL NUNNERIES

From her knowledge of monastic economies, Power supposed that nunneries, like their male equivalents, produced foodstuffs sufficient to feed the community – in addition to a surplus for sale as profit (1922: 109). In her chosen example of Catesby (Northants.), however, the accounts of 1414–15 indicate that profits were made from the sale of wool pells and timber (ibid. 111). Food crops, which included wheat, barley, oats and peas, were stored, consumed, given in alms and kept for seed (ibid. 109). Catesby did not produce surplus food for sale, despite its relatively well-endowed status (initially a house of nuns and canons). The account rolls of Catesby (1414–15) record incoming animals and grain from the home farm (ibid. 333). Additional purchases included beef, eggs, oil, salt fish, pepper, salt, saffron, fat and garlic. Power assumed that the home farm achieved self-sufficiency at least in vegetables, but such small expenditures may not have appeared in accounts (Dyer 1988a: 31). Documents confirm that there were vegetable gardens at Marrick, Sinningthwaite (N. Yorks.), Stainfield, Nun Cotham (Lincs.) (Tillotson 1989: 15–16) and Keldholme (N. Yorks.) (Elkins 1988: 93). Where nunneries held fishponds their projected yields would not have met the needs of the house, with the exception, perhaps, of Clerkenwell (C. K. Currie pers. comm.). Hence, it must be concluded that even self-sufficiency cannot always be assumed, and production of surplus can seldom be demonstrated.

Levels of production must have altered dramatically from the first centuries of a nunnery's occupation to the period reviewed in Power's study. During the thirteenth century monasteries increasingly complained of debt (Dyer 1989: 93). The 'structural indebtedness' of larger abbeys, like Peterborough, was combated by increased scales of production (Biddick 1989: 51). Management of the nunnery estate was contingent upon factors such as the availability of labour. The nuns themselves did little or no manual labour. Periodically they may have assisted in reaping and binding sheaves during the harvest (Power 1922: 382). Perhaps up to the fourteenth century, nunneries worked their own demesne lands. During this time many nunneries included lay-brethren within their community who would have worked the estates with tenurial and hired labour. This home labour force dissolved when the tendency to lease out estates increased. Few nunneries would have enjoyed the privilege of free labour afforded by villeinage. As labour shortages loomed, production gave way to cash economies. Increased circulation of coinage and reliability of local markets (Astill and Grant 1988b: 228) led to a greater proportion of food being bought. By about 1400 it was not uncommon for lay and monastic manors to rely on market commodities (Dyer 1988b: 25), although smaller gentry with only one manor may have remained self-sufficient (Dyer 1989: 68). Despite their largely gentry status, the economic and labour restrictions placed on nunneries appear to have precipitated market-dominated management. Archaeological evidence suggests that nunnery home farms were not capable of feeding the community; outer court areas took on an increasingly domestic character. Nunneries had shifted from small-scale production to an emphasis on cash income from temporalities and spiritualities. To a great extent internal production appears to have been replaced by marketed foodstuffs. Indeed, the inmates of certain nunneries, including Stamford (Lincs.) and St Mary de Pré (Herts.) were expected to purchase their own meat and vegetables with an allowance from the common coffers. The house provided only beer and bread (Power 1922: 382).

Our knowledge of nunnery economies is still impressionistic. For instance, it is difficult to gauge the extent to which nunneries participated in trade. Saxon double houses were often sited on coasts or the heads of waterways in order to benefit from trade and tolls (Yorke 1989: 103). But what commercial role was expected of post-Conquest nunneries? Some held urban properties, sold wool and received imported pottery – activities generally supervised by male bailiffs or stewards, and overseen by the prioress or abbess. The nuns themselves may have marketed embroideries, although Power noted that references to sales in accounts were surprisingly rare (1922: 257). Occasionally commissions for needlework were received, for example by the Cistercian nuns of Wintney (Hants.) in 1265 (Coldicott 1989: 83). Excavation may yield additional evidence, like that recorded at Wienhausen in Germany, where thimbles, scissors, spindles and small-weaving frames were discovered beneath the floor of the nuns' chapel (Moessner 1987: 164–5). On the whole, however, commercial enterprise on the part of nunneries appears limited, and may reflect the passive economic role deemed appropriate to religious women. Nuns had been prohibited from engaging in commerce from the time of their earliest rule, contained in the sixth-century writings of Caesarius of Arles (McNamara and Wemple 1977: 96).

The predominant economic role for nunneries was therefore one of a

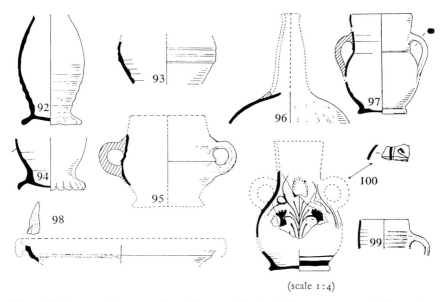

(scale 1:4)

Figure 29 Imported pottery from Denney (Cambs.). Pottery excavated from the medieval garden to the north of the nave may represent a group deposited as a single dump of domestic refuse. Included were jugs, cups and drinking-pots in Raeren stoneware (nos. 92–6), a double-handed cup in 'Cistercian Ware' (no. 97), a plate or bowl in Beauvais slip-ware (no. 98), and sherds from an altar vase in South Netherlands maioloica with underglaze decoration in yellow and blue (nos. 99–100) (Christie and Coad 1980). Reproduced by permission of the Royal Archaeological Institute.

consumer. Excavated sites have yielded substantial proportions of imported pottery (Figure 29), for instance at Waterbeach (Cra'aster 1966), Denney (Christie and Coad 1980) (both Cambs.) and Polsloe, Exeter, where 25 per cent of the total assemblage recovered largely from kitchen/refectory areas was made up of imports. It has been noted that secular sites in Exeter produced lower percentages of imports in comparison to Polsloe (*c.* 20 per cent), whereas sixteenth-century pottery from male monastic houses was made up of *c.* 40 per cent imports (Allan 1984: 104). At Nuneaton (Warwicks.) the assemblage was dominated by table ware, in preference to storage and cooking vessels (Andrews *et al.* 1981). The importing of foodstuffs is attested by excavated environmental material. At Denney, latrine deposits were associated with the converted south transept, which seems to have served as the foundress's (and later abbess's) lodgings (see Figure 14) (Christie and Coad 1980: 155). The remains of elderberry, blackberry, figs and grapes were recovered, of which the latter two are likely to have been purchased as 'spices'. Although the excavators suggested that this was not 'the sort of diet likely to have been provided for the nuns', the abbey of Barking is known to have supplemented its lenten fare with large quantities of figs (Power 1922: 566). The composition of the deposit from Denney matches the soft fruit assemblages typical of medieval castles and high status sites, including the Palace of King's Langley (Herts.), Barnard's Castle (Durham), Norwich Castle and Dryslwyn Castle (Dyfed). The Minoresses, in common with other wealthy nunneries, enjoyed an aristocratic diet. Excavations at St Mary's Nunnery, Winchester, produced animal bones representing farmed and wild game (rabbit, fallow and roe deer), twenty types of fish and twenty-six species of birds (Coldicott 1989: 77–8). While diversity in fish and bird species is recognized as an aspect of urban monastic diet, St Mary's had access to rare species including sturgeon, porpoise, crane and whooper swan.

Perhaps more representative of the majority of nunneries is the excavated site of Polsloe, near Exeter (Devon), where fifteenth- and sixteenth-century deposits containing bird and fish bones were dominated by domestic fowl, goose, ling, conger eel and hake (Bruce Levitan, pers. comm.). Considerations of monastic diet have often led archaeologists to scrutinize excavated human skeletons and animal bone assemblages for indications of diet which are in accord with the ideals expressed in monastic rules. Yet given the fluctuations in the population and observances of any single house, a more fruitful approach may be to consider patterns of food acquisition, preparation and disposal. Possibly due to their rigorous standards of sanitation, few excavated monasteries have yielded more than a few hundred fragments of animal bone. Excavations at Polsloe, by contrast, produced about 10,000 animal bones, most of which related to sixteenth-century monastic occupation (Levitan 1989: 168). The size of the assemblage compares favourably with those studied from male houses, including Austin Leicester (Mellor and Pearce 1981), Gilbertine York (O'Connor 1993) and Dominican Beverley (Gilchrist 1989). When proportions of species are compared between monastic sites, regional patterns become apparent. For northern monasteries the importance of sheep as a dietary source increased over time (York, Beverley, Pontefract); other monasteries saw increased consumption of beef (Oxford Dominicans, Leicester, Polsloe). More significant patterns can be observed for a monastery within its own urban setting. When compared to secular sites in Exeter (Exe Bridge), Polsloe's increase in beef to mutton may be unusual (Levitan 1987). This disparity between monastic and secular sites contrasts with the assemblages from York and Beverley, where monasteries shared the town's market sources from the fifteenth or sixteenth centuries (O'Connor 1993). The discrepancies in proportions of species between Polsloe and Exe Bridge may have been due to sample bias; but further differences in proportions of skeletal elements present could have resulted from the domestic nature of Polsloe, in comparison to the industrial character of Exe Bridge (Levitan 1987: 73). Bruce Levitan (1989) suggests that Polsloe Nunnery bought in whole and/or halved carcasses, with much secondary butchery conducted at the priory. At the male houses of Gilbertine York and Dominican Beverley, in contrast, partially dressed carcasses were procured from the towns' markets. Polsloe's siting outside Exeter, in a position typical of nunneries, may have encouraged processes of food acquisition which differed from those that operated at urban male houses. However, the necessity for secondary butchery on Polsloe's meat also has interesting implications for the labour requirements of the nunnery. The boning and jointing of carcasses required a variety of specialist butcher's tools. The length of apprenticeship and the expensive tool-kit necessary to become a butcher, made butchering one of the few medieval trades exclusively associated with men (H. Graham 1992). Polsloe's suburban position and food requirements, therefore, obliged the nunnery to maintain male servants. Indeed, Power noted the tendency for nunneries to employ male cooks (1922: 150).

Polsloe differs from urban male communities in one further aspect: the deposition of food waste. Bone assemblages recovered from Gilbertine York and Dominican Beverley, for example, represent a brief period immediately before and after the dissolution of the house. Polsloe's bone deposits, on the other hand, have been assigned the greater date range of 1500–30. Bone from the male houses was retrieved from areas beyond the cloister – near the kitchen or little cloister. Bone from Polsloe was recovered from kitchen and garden areas, but also from the cloister garth and buildings such as the dormitory. It may be suggested that female religious experienced a greater degree of enclosure than their male counterparts (see below pp. 152, 167–9). Could it be that this resulted in less regular clearance of domestic waste, and lower standards of sanitation? This theme will be explored further with relation to latrines in male and female houses (see pp. 125–6).

Comparison of the *vitae* of medieval male and female saints has led Caroline Walker Bynum to suggest that female spirituality was strongly linked to food practices (1987: 84). At an institutional level, food asceticism may have been a factor in supplying nunneries. Archaeological and documentary sources suggest that the richer nunneries enjoyed an aristocratic diet of imported fruits and rare birds and fish. Smaller nunneries, like Marrick (N. Yorks.), observed a diet closer, perhaps, to that of better-off peasantry (Tillotson 1989: 16). Although their precise meat intake is unknown, these nunneries consumed the bread, vegetables and beer associated with peasant fare (Dyer 1983). Only the few very wealthy nunneries received quantities of wine and spices proportional to those recorded for Selby Abbey (Tillotson 1988) and Battle Abbey (Searle 1974). Bynum suggested that the sin of gluttony was more likely to occur in monasteries for men due to their greater wealth (1987: 80). A study of the cellarer's accounts from Christ Church, Canterbury, referred to the potential health risks suffered by the monastery's over-indulgence (Hatcher 1986: 34). The lower status nunnery diet may have been a product of its economic position, or the ascetic vocation of the inhabitants, or both. Together the sources for economic production in medieval nunneries indicate that the nuns did not possess the means by which to achieve self-sufficiency, a major tenet of monasticism.

3.6 CONCLUSIONS: ISOLATION AND DEPENDENCE

Nunneries were set in liminal places, with regard to both the natural landscape and the topography of towns. Their economic aspirations were never great – programmes of land reclamation and acquisition were most often beyond their resources. It seems unlikely that nunneries were expected to reach levels of economic self-sufficiency, or to produce surplus for sale as profit. Their estates were generally either constricted, and therefore over-specialized, or made up of small, scattered parcels, resulting in low financial returns. The nunnery home farm and outer court was compact, with little evidence for industry or storage facilities. Double houses fared slightly better. They enjoyed well-balanced initial endowments and a greater range of economic activities.

When the isolation of nunneries is considered beside their apparent economic passivity, a dichotomy may be perceived. Communities of religious women were placed in vulnerable surroundings, but without the means by which to achieve their autonomy. The opposite was true of rural hermitages and male communities which were expected to be self-sufficient. Hence, nunneries were liminal, yet dependent. They were supported through cash rents from temporalities, spiritualities, dowries and benefactions. Frequently they appealed to secular and ecclesiastical authorities to alleviate their poverty. To some extent the dichotomy affected the placement of nunneries. Their dependence on others for both labour and the saying of religious services led to the juxtaposition of nunneries with parish churches and villages.

An eremitic vocation for women is suggested by the locations of nunneries. Godstow was established after its founder, Lady Ediva, spent a period in solitary retreat in which a vision prompted her to set up the nunnery (Clark 1905: 26). Some nunneries developed from their own eremitical origins. Nunneries which began life as cells may have closely resembled hermitages, such as Henwood (Warwicks.), Cambridge, Flamstead (Herts.) and Bretford (Warwicks., which later passed to Kenilworth), and possibly Armathwaite (Cumbria) and Delapré (Northants.) (S. Thompson 1991: 28). In the twelfth century, four groups of female hermits – unenclosed religious women – were recorded. In each case these small groups were regularised into nunneries by the heads of male houses. The *duae sanctae mulieres* near St Albans had a nunnery built for them at Sopwell (Herts.) by Abbot Geoffrey (*c.* 1135) (Warren 1984: 200). The same abbey encouraged the regularization of the women followers of Christina of Markyate (Herts.) in 1145 (ibid.). Kilburn Priory (Middlesex) began as a hermitage owned by Westminster Abbey. The three women at Kilburn were given a male warden, and refounded as a priory by 1139. Later in the twelfth century, a community grew up at Crabhouse (Norfolk) around the hermit Lena. They were granted a hermitage by the prior of Ranham; Crabhouse was established as a priory *c.* 1180 (ibid.). Groups of religious women gathered spontaneously to form communities at Ankerwyke (Bucks.) and Limebrook (Herefords.) (S. Thompson 1984: 141) and were duly formalized.

Ann Warren (1984: 201) noted that references to women hermits (*virago*; *ancilla domini*) had ceased by the end of the twelfth century. Male clerics encouraged female hermits to accept a communal lifestyle. For male hermitages, a more organic evolution was recorded. Charismatic hermits often attracted a following, so that eventually an institutional framework emerged with the adoption of a rule and order (Leyser 1984: 3).

The leap from community of women hermits to nunnery was accelerated by ecclesiastical intervention. Warren suggested that female communities were regularized in order to eliminate the danger of women living unprotected, solitary lives. I would suggest that the lifestyle of the hermit was considered inappropriate for English religious women. The isolated surroundings chosen by hermits necessitated their self-sufficiency. They adhered to principles of manual labour – clearing land, building and farming to support themselves (Leyser 1984: 57–8). Economic independence and physical labour for women hermits were removed by their enclosure as nuns.

An ideal emerged for nunneries in which isolation was coupled with dependence on institutional structures for labour, religious services, market commodities and cash gifts. It is this paradox of isolation and dependence which sets nunneries apart in the study of medieval monastic settlement. While male houses were active in reshaping landscapes, and thus constantly renegotiating their economic, political and religious identities, religious women seldom had the opportunity to physically restructure landscapes. Instead their relationship to landscape was conceptually renegotiated: the marginality of women's communities was given meaning through an eremitic vocation. The next chapters explore the extent to which the form, function and meanings of nunnery buildings are distinctive when compared with the standards of male monasticism.

4

IN THE CLOISTER

4.1 STANDARD PLANS

Monastic studies have tended to emphasize the degree of uniformity in monastic planning, and it has been assumed that standard arrangements outweighed regional variations or subtle preferences expressed by particular monastic orders (for example, Coppack 1990). To a great extent the layout of nunnery buildings was arranged to this standard monastic plan. However, characteristics emerge as distinctive of nunneries when gender is considered in the analysis of monastic architecture. These traits are consistent for nunneries across monastic orders, but vary according to status, and certain regional patterns are apparent in the plan of the church (see p. 104), the placement of the sacristy (see p. 111) and the positioning of the cloister (see pp. 131–2).

Nunneries observed the standard monastic layout in which a central complex of buildings was grouped around a cloister. The cloister provided a community with maximum seclusion, accessibility between principal structures, and order. The cloister plan is formed by three ranges of buildings which together form a U-shape which abuts the church (Horn and Born 1979). The enclosure thus formed is the cloister yard which is composed of an open garth, flanked by alleys which run concentrically within and provide access to the ranges. This format originated with Carolingian monasteries, if not earlier in Merovingian examples such as Chelles.

It is not clear when the cloister began to dominate English monastic planning. Excavation of middle Saxon double houses (seventh to ninth centuries) indicates that their arrangement was less formal than later monasteries, yet distinguished from contemporary secular settlement by a greater emphasis on regular refuse disposal and the delineation of formal areas and spaces. At Whitby (N. Yorks.) stone structures were arranged around the edges of blank linear features, perhaps paths, in a roughly rectilinear pattern (Cramp 1976; Rahtz 1976). At Hartlepool (Cleveland) a number of earthfast timber buildings to the north of the later medieval church appear to have been monastic cells, with different functional areas of the monastery defined by formal empty spaces which served as boundaries (Daniels 1989). At Barking (Essex) a number of timber buildings were grouped together which served partially industrial functions; one was characterized by a fine plaster finish (MacGowan 1987). Late Saxon nunneries may have been planned more formally. Excavation of the tenth-century Nunnaminster (Winchester) suggested an apsed stone church aligned in orthodox east–west fashion (Qualman 1986). Post-Conquest eleventh-century foundations, such at Malling (Kent), observed a cloister plan (see Figure 13).

Later medieval nunneries generally centred on a single cloister. Double houses required domestic buildings which ensured sexual segregation, yielding a variety of different arrangements. The Gilbertines favoured two discrete cloisters for each house, with the nuns' cloister abutting either side of the main conventual church. The canons' cloister was some distance away. It had its own chapel and was divided from the nuns' cloister by a wall and ditch. At Watton (Humbs.) this boundary was traversed by the window house: a structure approached by passages from each of the cloisters, which provided communication via a small turning window (Figure 30) (St John Hope 1901).

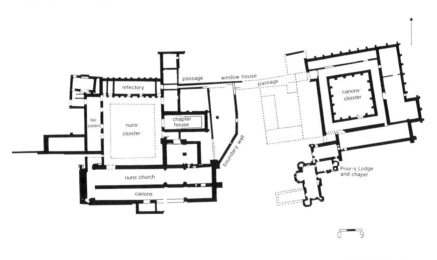

(after St John Hope 1901)

Figure 30 Excavations at Watton (Humbs.): a Gilbertine double house. The double houses of the Gilbertines provided two separate cloisters. The nuns' cloister was located to the north of the main conventual church; that of the canons was situated to the east, together with the prior's lodging and chapel. In order to ensure sexual segregation the cloisters were divided by a boundary wall and ditch, with communication through a turning hatch in the window house. The church was divided into two parallel aisles by a median wall which prevented visual communication between the nuns and canons. After St John Hope 1901.

At Nuneaton (Warwicks.), of the order of Fontevrault, the nuns' cloister was to the south of the church. Detailed contour, auger and geophysical survey has revealed several possible positions for a monks' cloister (Andrews *et al.* 1981: 62). The most likely position may be an enclosed area to the south-east of the nuns' cloister, where the drain of the nuns' latrine could have been used by a second group of domestic buildings. At Amesbury (Wilts.), of the same order, the nuns occupied a standard self-contained cloister to the north of the supposed prioress's lodge, which stood until the mid-seventeenth century. The canons were accommodated in buildings adjoining the parish church, some 275 m south of the nuns' cloister. Their lodgings appear to have been to the north of the chancel, with access to the north transept by a pentice along the nave (RCHME 1987: 235).

Details of male accommodation for the 'quasi' double houses are not yet clear. At Minchin Buckland (Somerset), a double preceptory of the Knights Hospitaller, the preceptor's house, lodgings and dovecote are documented to the north of the nuns' church (Larking (ed.) 1857: 18–19). It seems that smaller groups of monks or lay-brothers attending a nunnery were provided with informal lodgings, possibly within moated enclosures (see above pp. 80–2). The Bridgettines, who founded two English houses in the fifteenth century, rarely placed their buildings around a cloister (Gilyard-Beer 1958: 44; Nyberg 1965: 11). Buildings of the nuns and canons were placed on opposite sides of the church of the convent. Of the buildings of the English Bridgettines only an undercroft of a single medieval building survives at Syon (Middlesex) (RCHME 1937: 86).

Siting of a monastic cloister took into account general topographical factors such as level and drainage, in addition to considering sources of water-supply (see Chapter 5, section 1). Nunnery cloisters were often placed in relation to the parish church. Occasionally the two were entirely separate, such as Barking (Essex). More often a nunnery church was shared by a parochial congregation, thus affecting the monastic layout. An extreme example is Godstow (Oxfords.), where the shared church was placed outside the nunnery enclosure to the north (Ganz 1972). At Goring (Oxfords.) and Clerkenwell (London) the cloister itself abutted the parochial nave in a reversal of the usual arrangement (Stone 1893; MOLAS 1987 archive).

The various groups accommodated within double houses – nuns, canons, lay-sisters, lay-brothers – made the spatial relationship to the parish church more complex. Within one precinct it was possible to have three churches. At Watton (Humbs.), separate churches were provided for the nuns and canons (Figure 30); the parish church stood to the south. Monastic and parochial churchyards overlapped at Gilbertine Alvingham (Lincs.). This grouping of churches resembles the 'families' of churches typical of early medieval monasteries (Taylor 1978: 1020–1). Such sites possessed two, three or more small churches, often built on a single axis. Dedicated to different saints, such churches may have fulfilled separate functions: for example as cemetery chapel, baptistery and shrine(s). Alternatively, each member of the family of churches may have been used by a specific group within the monastery. At the double house of Nivelles (Belgium), for example, the three or four churches may have been required for segregation of male and female religious, lay and secular groups. Families of churches at later medieval double houses represent a continuation of this tradition.

4.2 FORM AND FUNCTION OF NUNNERY BUILDINGS

Cloister dimensions varied according to the land and building resources available to a nunnery, with most clustering within the range 15–20 sq. m (Gilchrist 1990). The central space of the cloister, the garth, was kept clear of structures, and was used instead as a garden or cemetery. In many cases cloisters may have been simple pentices, passages formed by a lean-to roof constructed against the walls of the ranges, including Marham (Norfolk) and Campsey Ash (Suffolk). The south wall of the church at Aconbury (Herefords.) retains corbels for the upright and angle supports of a pentice (Figure 31). Freestanding stone cloisters survive at Lacock (Wilts.) (Figure 32) and St Radegund's, Cambridge, where the cambered open timber roofs of c. 1500 survive largely intact (RCHME 1959: 86); and fragments from cloister arcades have been noted at Stixwould (Lincs.) and Marrick (N. Yorks.). As a measure of economy many nunneries, such as Grace Dieu (Leics.), placed cloister alleys as passages within the main walls of buildings, with the upper rooms projecting over, in an arrangement which was rare for monasteries for men, but common in the poorer friaries. Cloister alleys did not contain the study carrels which are associated with male houses. They were simply walkways which sometimes served as places of burial for monastic inmates and patrons (for example Higham, Kent) (Tester 1967).

The cloister and ranges might be built in stone, rubble, cob or timber, with the exception of the church, which was invariably stone-built. In contrast to standards known for male houses, timber or half-timber claustral buildings on stone foundations seem to have been fairly common, and may be suggested at Brewood (Shrops.), Ellerton (N. Yorks.), Arthington (W. Yorks.), and Wilberfoss (N. Yorks.), confirmed at the last site by the accounts of the Dissolution surveyors. Later additions may have used newly available materials, such as Cook Hill's (Worcs.) half-timber ranges cased with brick. Nunneries which were particularly poor or in regions with little stone are more likely to have built in cob. Excavations at Fosse Nunnery (Lincs.) indicated structural use of earth walls (Barley 1964), and a survey of the site of Crabhouse (Norfolk) taken in 1557 describes walls of earth and brick, noting that only the steeple of the demolished church had 'walls of stone' (Dashwood 1859).

The church was generally placed as the north range with the cloister to the south, in the standard arrangement, although a considerable number of

Figure 31 The south wall of the church at Aconbury (Herefords.) retains corbels which supported a pentice roof to cover the cloister walks. The blocked doorway at the upper storey of the west end of the church originally provided access into a gallery from the west range of the nunnery.

Figure 32 The free-standing cloister at Lacock (Wilts.), largely rebuilt in the fifteenth century, formed the basis of the later house built by Sir William Sharington in the 1540s.

nunneries placed the church as the south range with the cloister to the north (see Chapter 5, section 1). Nunnery churches were rarely planned with the same degree of ornamentation or complexity as the churches of their male counterparts. Even the larger churches, like Carrow, appear to have operated only at ground-storey level, with no evidence for access to upper-level galleries or wall-passages typical of both male monastic houses and the wealthier nunneries founded before the Conquest, in particular Romsey (Hants.) (Figure 33). In plan, nunnery churches were either cruciform or parallelogram, with the latter type by far the most numerous (61.7 per cent of known examples; Table 3). Frequently, nuns' churches were narrow aisleless rectangles; because nuns could not perform masses, there was little demand for additional altars to be housed in side chapels. In appearance these churches are unusually tall and thin, often with west towers. Some, including Irish Cistercian nunnery churches, were also fairly long (Stalley 1986: 133). Liturgical arrangements, the formalized rituals of the church, were simple within the parallelograms; Dissolution surveys of the Yorkshire nunneries suggest that in addition to the high altar there were two altars in the choir and one in the nave (W. Brown 1886: 200). Excavations at Lacock (Wilts.) revealed no structural division between presbytery, choir and nave (Figure 34) (Brakspear 1900). At Polsloe, near Exeter, a single screen divided the church into aisleless eastern and western sections (Figure 35) (*Medieval Archaeol.* 23, 1979: 250–1). Similarly, extant remains at Guyzance (Northumb.) suggest a parallelogram bisected by a stone wall into equal western and eastern parts.

Arrangements within cruciform churches were less predictable. The location of the choir might be in the eastern arm, crossing or first bay of the nave, according to local preference. The cruciform church at Little Marlow (Bucks.) was bisected by a pulpitum screen which crossed the nave in line with the west wall of the north transept (Figure 36) (Peers 1902: 319). At Shaftesbury (Dorset) the choir and nuns' stalls were placed in the eastern bay of the nave until the fourteenth century (RCHME Dorset 4, 1972: 59). The return stalls backed against the pulpitum, which crossed the nave between the first pair of piers. The rood screen stood between the second pair of piers with a rood altar against the west face.

Further subdivision is likely to have been provided by hanging cloths and tapestries, such as those described in the inventory from Minster in Sheppey (Kent) (Walcott 1868: 290–1), in addition to portable screens and painted reredos, like the surviving example from Romsey (Hants.), which would have been placed behind the altar. Areas within the church were sometimes delineated by patterns in ceramic tile floors, shown in excavations at Campsey Ash (Suffolk) (see Figure 18) (Sherlock 1970). These may have been enhanced by corresponding schemes in wall-painting, stained glass and misericords. Carved misericords, the undersides of hinged choir stall seats, survive from Swine (Humbs.), St Helen's, Bishopsgate (London) and

Figure 33 Romsey (Hants.): church interior. Romsey was exceptional among nunneries for the status and scale of its church. Its east end consists of a square-ended choir with ambulatory carried round it, with chapels projecting eastward. In the nave the main arcade and triforium were combined, providing upper-level galleries and wall-passages.

Table 3 Shapes of groundplans of nunnery churches.

Cruciform	Parallelogram
Barking, Essex	Aconbury, Herefords.
Brewood, Shrops.	Bishopsgate, London
Bungay, Suffolk	Burnham, Berks.
Cambridge, Cambs.	Campsey Ash, Suffolk
Carrow Norwich, Norfolk	Chester, Cheshire
Denney, Cambs.	Dartford, Kent
Elstow, Bedfords.	Delapré, Northants.
Goring, Oxfords.	Easebourne, Sussex
Ickleton, Cambs.	Ellerton, N. Yorks.
Malling, Kent	Flixton, Suffolk
Nuneaton, Warwicks.	Guyzance, Northumb.
Polesworth, Warwicks.	Higham, Kent
Romsey, Hants	Kington St Michael, Wilts.
Shaftesbury, Dorset	Kirklees, W. Yorks.
Shouldham, Norfolk	Lacock, Wilts.
Swine, Humbs.	Little Marlow, Bucks.
Thetford, Norfolk	Littlemore, Oxfords.
Winchester, Hants.	Marham, Norfolk
	Marrick, N. Yorks.
	Minster in Sheppey, Kent
	Nun Monkton, N. Yorks.
	Polsloe, Exeter, Devon
	Redlingfield, Suffolk
	Sempringham, Lincs.
	Sopwell, Herts.
	Watton, Humbs.
	Wix, Essex
	Wroxall, Warwicks.
	Wykeham, N. Yorks.

Sources: extant buildings, excavations, antiquarian plans and the accounts of the Dissolution surveyors (W. Brown 1886; Hazlewood 1894).

Farewell (Staffs.). Within parallelograms the nuns' choir and stalls would be expected in the eastern arm of the church. Occasionally, additional liturgical features survive in fragments of ruined walls, for example aumbries, sedilia and piscinae at Marrick (N. Yorks.) and an Easter Sepulchre at Burnham (Berks.). Earthenware vessels have been recorded from the choirs of St Radegund's, Cambridge (Gray 1898: 66) and Farewell (illustrated by R. Green, 1747, *Gentleman's Magazine* 4: 59), presumably placed in an effort to increase resonance for the singing of the nuns' offices (K. Harrison 1968). However, there was no uniformity of liturgy in English nunneries (Chadd 1986: 309) and their observances appear to have resembled parish churches more closely than male monastic churches.

Where monasteries shared their churches with parochial congregations, it was common for the monastic eastern church to be separated from the

Figure 34 Lacock (Wilts.). A typical nunnery plan with parallelogram church (and later Lady Chapel) and cloister to the north. After Brakspear 1900.

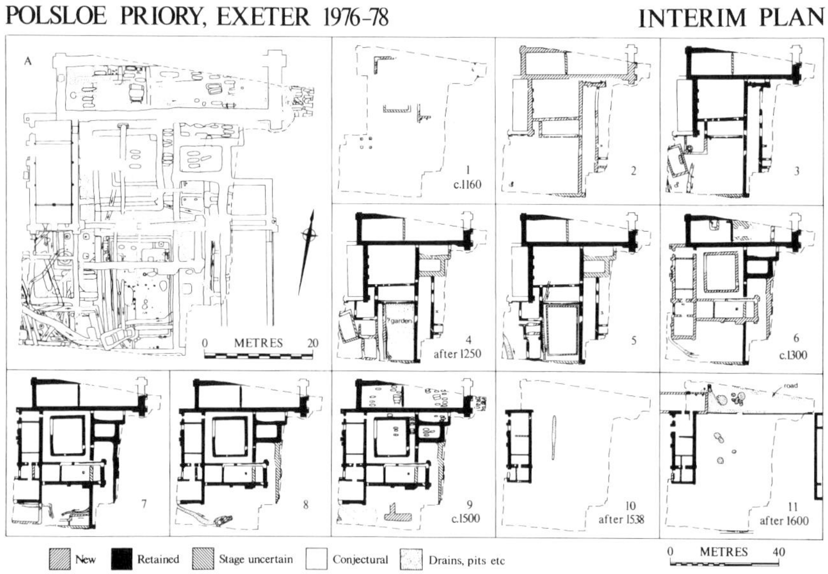

POLSLOE PRIORY, EXETER 1976-78   INTERIM PLAN

Figure 35 Excavations at Polsloe, near Exeter. The aisleless parallelogram church and nunnery buildings were ranged around a courtyard from *c.*1160, but only developed into a cloister with walkways *c.*1300. Reproduced by permission of the Society for Medieval Archaeology and courtesy of Exeter Museum Archaeological Field Unit.

100

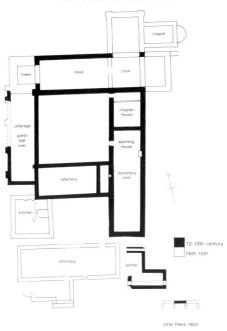

(after Peers 1902)

Figure 36 Excavations at Little Marlow (Bucks.). Excavations showed a cruciform church with west tower, and high quality guest accommodation in the west range; a kitchen was located to serve the refectory and guest house. The east range was partitioned to form a chapter-house and parlour; the latrine block to the south was a simple L-shape with single drain. After Peers 1902.

western parochial nave. Cruciform churches were sometimes split into two parts by a crossing tower, for example at Polesworth (Warwicks.) and Usk (Gwent) where parochial naves are extant (Figure 37). Parallelograms were divided by screens and use of ornamentation. At Nun Monkton (N. Yorks.) the junction of the nave and choir is marked by a corbel in the form of a female head (Figure 38), the only anthropomorphic example of the series. At this point the nave and choir are marked also by distinctions in fabric. The windows of the choir are distinguished from those in the nave by subtle differences in proportion and scale. Those in the choir are marked by three attached shafts, rising from corbels, with annulets. Decoration in the double arch within the wall-passage consists of well-spaced nailhead. In the nave the nailhead is coarser, and the foliage capitals of the choir are replaced by bell-capitals. In the choir, the moulded stringcourse is continued from the outer wall into the window at the springing point of the arch. These distinctions may mark a break in the fabric caused by a pause in the work, or the fabric may be a single programme which correlated architectural detail with the ritual divisions of the church.

The standard monastic arrangement was occasionally reversed in nunnery churches, so that the parish was accommodated in the eastern part of the church and the nuns occupied the west end. This was fairly common in continental nunneries, particularly with German Cistercian houses (Gilyard-Beer 1958: 19), and consistent with practices observed in Crusader Palestine, for example at Bethany (Pringle 1986: 356). At Haliwell (Shoreditch, London), the nuns' choir was positioned in the western part of their church, with the 'great choir' to the east. A late sixteenth-century plan of Marrick (N. Yorks.) indicates a western nuns' choir (see Figure 23). Similar traditions

Figure 37 Usk church (Gwent). After the Dissolution the western part of the church was retained for the parish. In the eastern face of the original crossing-tower may be seen the roof line of the demolished eastern arm, and the blocked archway to the nuns' church. The blocked archway to the north transept is also visible, against which a modern structure abuts.

Figure 38 A corbel in the form of a female head, flanked by two birds, possibly doves, marks the junction of the nave and choir at Nun Monkton (N.Yorks.). The dove may represent the Holy Ghost of the Annunciation or, issuing from a nun's mouth or hovering above her head, suggests the soul rising to heaven and refers to Scholastica, sister of St Benedict, to whom the dove appeared in a vision. Such figural sculpture seems to have been used to indicate important social and ritual distinctions, in this case with iconography pertinent to a Benedictine nunnery. Illustration by Ted West.

are recorded for Davington (Kent) (Tester 1980), Nunkeeling (Humbs.) and Swine (Humbs.). The two latter nunneries originally included a male component within their population; possibly the brethren occupied the eastern part of the church, which transferred to parochial control upon their removal, although at Swine the parish may have taken over the eastern nuns' church at the Dissolution (Coppack 1990: 151). Eighteenth-century drawings of Swine show that the church was originally cruciform, with a Romanesque crossing arch marking the entrance to the western nuns' church (Figure 39). Subsequent demolition of the western annexe and transepts has given the parish church the appearance of a parallelogram with a western tower.

Like the nunnery church at Marrick, the cruciform church at the double house of Nuneaton (Warwicks.), of the order of Fontevrault, was transected laterally with the western part serving the convent. Amesbury (Wilts.) provided separate cruciform churches for the nuns and monks. The monks shared their church with the parish, which occupied an autonomous south aisle built in the fifteenth century (RCHME 1987). The Bridgettines had a

Figure 39 Swine church in the eighteenth century. This engraving of 1784 shows the demolition of the western annexe and transepts. The originally cruciform church of Swine (N. Humbs.), now survives as a parallelogram with west tower. From Poulson 1840.

single church with segregation achieved by split-level worship. The canons served altars at the groundfloor level and the nuns occupied first-floor galleries (Gilyard-Beer 1958: 44). The Gilbertines preferred parallelogram churches split longitudinally by a median wall into two wide aisles. At Watton (Humbs.) the nuns occupied the north aisle, adjacent to their cloister (Figure 30). Their nightstair was indicated by buttresses in the north-east angle of the presbytery (St John Hope 1901). The nuns sat in the east end of the north aisle, and the lay-sisters were seated in the west end, with access from their quarters in the west range of the nuns' cloister. When the canons attended the main conventual church, they entered the south aisle. They were able to pass pax and holy water to the sisters by a turning window in the median wall. Study of the Institutes of the Gilbertine order suggests that the arrangement of the nuns' church precluded them from witnessing the elevation of the host (Elkins 1988: 141).

Mainly in southern and eastern England similar parallel aisle divisions segregated nuns from parishioners. The resulting symmetrical arrangement is indicated at St Helen's, Bishopsgate (London) (Figure 40), Haliwell, Shoreditch (London), Minster in Sheppey (Kent), Higham (Kent), Easebourne (Sussex), Ickleton (Cambs.) (Figure 41) and Wroxall (Warwicks.) (VCH Warwicks. 3 1945: 216). The two churches were separated by a

Figure 40 St Helen's, Bishopsgate, London. The church of the nunnery is to the north (left) and adjoined the nunnery cloister to the north of the church. The parish church occupied the south aisle (right). These 'parallel aisle churches' shared a west front. The nuns' church was given a new west door in the fifteenth century.

screened arcade. At Minster the nuns' church is distinguished by a hood mould to the north side of the arcade. Chantry chapels were built onto the parochial aisle, such as the Chapel of the Holy Ghost at Bishopsgate, a perpetual chantry founded by Adam Franceys in 1371 (Cook 1947: 25). If arrangements within the parallel aisle churches were similar to those followed by the Gilbertines, the nuns may have been denied witness to the moment of transubstantiation, when the bread and wine is thought to become the body and blood of Christ, possibly resulting in a downgrading of the quality of their religious experience.

Occasionally, the establishment of chantries at nunnery churches resulted in a proliferation of chapels, such as the aisle chapels at Carrow (Norfolk) and Chester, where thirteen chapels are listed in a processional of *c.* 1425 (Legg 1899). Nunneries were favoured infrequently as the recipients of chantries, however, since the saying of the masses required the employment of an additional priest. Where chantries were founded, a separate chapel was not always constructed. At Barking, masses were sung at existing altars (Cook 1947: 26). Chantries could be established partly to alleviate the poverty of nunneries. In 1369 a chantry was founded in the church of St Sepulchre, Canterbury, which provided the nuns with their only daily mass (ibid.).

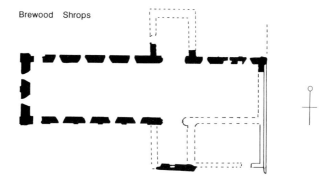

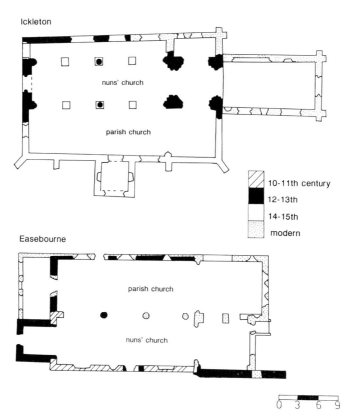

Figure 41 Plans of nunnery churches. Easebourne (Sussex) and Ickleton (Cambs.), show the arrangement of parallel aisle churches. At Brewood (Shrops.), the cruciform church had a sacristy added between the angle of the chancel and the transept. Both Ickleton and Brewood had cloisters positioned to the north of the church. After Weaver 1987, Radford 1967, and VCH 1907.

106

The prioress sometimes had exclusive use of an apartment adjoining the church. A watching-closet is noted in the Dissolution survey of Nunkeeling, and at Wilberfoss, located above the chapter house (W. Brown 1886: 200). This function was suggested for a small timber adjunct excavated to the north of the church at Kirklees (W. Yorks.) (Figure 42) (Armytage 1908). But such apartments may be easily confused with anchorholds, from which a recluse would have viewed the altar through a squint (see Chapter 7, section 3).

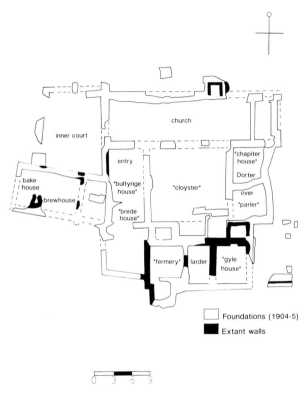

Figure 42 Excavations at Kirklees (W. Yorks.). The refectory was later subdivided in order to serve domestic functions, and a cross-wing with oven was added to the west range. Functions were attributed to rooms by the excavator on the basis of the Dissolution surveyor's account. After Armytage 1908.

Secular female lodgers were frequently noted in the accounts of bishops' visitations to nunneries. Where there was no parish church, these occasional visitors or corrodians (permanent paying guests) required their own place within the church. Long-staying guests would expect to attend services, and to witness the elevation of the host. Yet they were prohibited from sitting in the nuns' choir (Power 1922: 404). Compromise was found by constructing viewing galleries for seculars at one end of the church. At

Figure 43   A blocked doorway from the east range of the nunnery at Burnham (Berks.) provided access into a gallery over the nuns' choir.

Burnham, entrance to an east gallery is marked by an upper-storey doorway in the southern wall of the east range (Figure 43), and at Cambridge a gallery survives in the north transept. At both sites, entry to the gallery would have been through the nuns' dormitory in the east range. It has been suggested that at Minster in Sheppey seven square recesses in the upper part of the east wall of the nuns' choir are remnants of a gallery (Cave-Brown 1897: 152). At Lacock the west bay of the church may have been filled by a gallery carried by a screen, inserted where quoins of the vaulting-shaft were cut away (Brakspear 1900: 135). A second gallery was erected along the north wall of the nave, blocking earlier windows (ibid. 132). A west gallery at Aconbury was entered through the west range by an upper-storey doorway in the south wall of the church (see Figure 31). A west gallery may be suggested over the nuns' choir at Marrick (N. Yorks.), where joists survive in the east face of the west tower. The exterior east face shows a doorway above an earlier roof line. This may indicate an entrance to a gallery. A large medieval trefoil window (now reset) may have lit the gallery.

The number of groups which required segregated areas within a nunnery church might include nuns, novices, lay-brothers, lay-sisters, women lodgers, secular men and women, and possibly children and servants. The provision of galleries would have afforded ease of segregation. They were commonly used in Bridgettine houses and in German, Scandinavian and Italian nunneries, where the nuns' choirs were positioned in the galleries. A western gallery-choir at the Augustinian nunnery of Asmild (Viborg, Denmark) was entered from the second storey of the west tower (Kristensen 1987: 127). Similar arrangements may be discerned at St Peter's nunnery, Lund (modern Sweden), and the Cistercian nunnery at Roskilde (Denmark), and at the Venetian nunneries of St Maria dei Miracoli and St Alvise, where evidence for western gallery-choirs, or *barca*, survives. Galleries were used to segregate men and women in Byzantine and Italian churches from the sixth century, for example the *matreum*, or women's gallery, at Hagia Sophia, Justinian's church at Constantinople. In England, west galleries were fairly common in the churches of pre-Conquest religious communities such as Deerhurst and Brixworth. They may have been places for secular people, among them women, as illustrated in the tenth-century Benedictional of Æthelwold (Taylor 1975: 166). It appears that English nunneries most often used galleries to accommodate women lodgers at the west or east end of the church, although eastern galleries may have been reserved additionally for novices.

Next to the church was the sacristy, or vestry, where sacred vessels and vestments were stored. Few early twelfth-century nunnery plans included sacristies although some, like Davington (Kent), Polsloe (Devon) and Easebourne (Sussex), were later modified to include one. A sacristy was added at Brewood (Shrops.) between the angle of the presbytery and north transept (Figure 41). Late twelfth-century rebuilding around the south choir aisle at Elstow (Bedfords.) may have been to integrate a sacristy (Figure 44). Some nunneries added sacristies on the side of the church opposite that of the cloister, including Little Marlow (Bucks.) and Kington St Michael (Wilts.) (Figure 45). Late twelfth- and early thirteenth-century foundations, such as Lacock (Wilts.) and St Helen's, Bishopsgate (London), had sacristies integral to their plans, placed between the church and chapter house. Lacock's sacristy was more elaborate than the usual single chamber. It was of three bays, and divided from two chapels at its east end (Figure 14). These were decorated with black five-rayed stars painted onto the vault (Brakspear 1900: 140). A reconstructed plan of the fourteenth-century Minories (London) suggests a sacristy located over the chapter house (Carlin 1987), an arrangement rare for nunneries but not untypical of male houses. Rooms were sometimes provided over the sacristy (for example, at St Radegund's, Cambridge, and St Helen's, Bishopsgate), where a squint allowed sight of the high altar.

The appearance of the sacristy corresponds with increased formalization of liturgy and emphasis on the eucharist, in addition to greater regulation of the separation of male and female religious. Within nunneries the sacristy represented the male liturgical space. As such it was accessible from the nunnery precinct, as at Burnham (Berks.), without ingress to the nuns' cloister (Figure 46). In addition, the male liturgical space of the sacristy

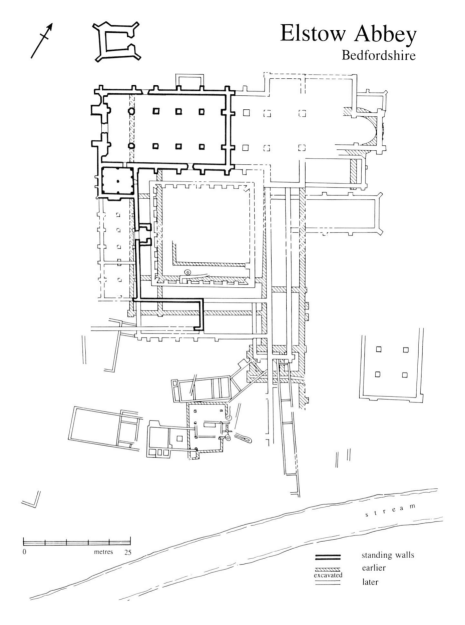

Elstow Abbey
Bedfordshire

standing walls
earlier
excavated
later

0   metres   25

s t r e a m

Figure 44   Elstow (Bedfords.). Excavations suggested a significant interval between the building of the church and cloister ranges. Late twelfth-century rebuilding around the south choir aisle may have involved the addition of the sacristy, an essential part of the nunnery. The original east end of the church was remodelled, and the refectory and dormitory were replanned in the mid-fourteenth century. Plan courtesy of David Baker.

110

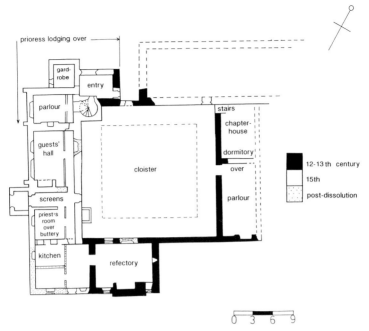

Figure 45 Kington St Michael (Wilts.). The nunnery never possessed a fully developed cloister plan, but rather consisted of discontinuous ranges grouped around a courtyard. After Brakspear 1922–3.

was sometimes the most highly ornamented area of the nunnery. At Carrow the entrance to the sacristy is embellished with refined mouldings and slender shafts; at Lacock the carved corbels supporting the vaulting of the sacristy represent male heads (see Chapter 6, section 2). Male houses were sometimes provided with sacristies, although in contrast to the situation at nunneries, these became redundant as increasing numbers of monks were ordained, and sacristies often eventually served only as a passage through the cloister (Gilyard-Beer 1958: 46). Dissolution surveys of the Yorkshire nunneries suggest that they did not include sacristies. Instead, priests' chambers were provided in the outer court at Thicket, Wilberfoss, Arthington, Baysdale, Wykeham and Swine (W. Brown 1886).

In addition to the sacristy, the ground-floor level of the east range contained the chapter house, and possibly a parlour and warming-room. The chapter house was the focus of the daily meetings of the community. It was normally structurally distinct from the rest of the east range, although in smaller houses (for example, Higham and Little Marlow) it was partitioned by timber screens. Stone benching for the seating of the chapter generally surrounded the interior of the room. The head of the house would occupy a raised seat at the east end. These arrangements survive at Lacock and Cambridge. Excavations at Higham (Kent) revealed a well-defined

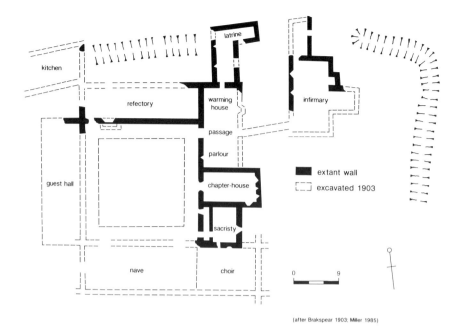

Figure 46 Burnham (Berks.). The precinct was bounded by a moat, with private access for the priest through a doorway in the eastern wall of the sacristy.

rectangular area of chalk rubble that supported the prioress's seat in the east end (Tester 1967: 14). In common with other monasteries, the entrance to the chapter house from the nunnery cloister was generally prominent. At Lacock an entrance of three arches of four members each was decorated with colour. Cambridge boasts a similarly elaborate entrance of three arches. Burnham (Berks.) was entered by a single archway at the west end (Figure 47). Smaller nunneries, such as Higham and possibly Wroxall (Warwicks.), contained the length of the chapter house within the east range. Most extant examples extended the chapter house past the limit of the range, as a single projection breaking forward beyond the outer line of the cloister. Chapter houses were appropriate places of burial for the heads of monastic houses. Coffins were excavated at Lacock; at Burnham slab-covered graves were arranged in pairs down the centre of the chapter house (Brakspear 1900; 1903).

Additional east range components might include a parlour, where daily silence could be broken, and a warming-room, recognized by its fireplace. In smaller nunneries a single chamber may have served both functions, or a slype (passage) next to the chapter house may have sufficed as the parlour (for example, at Davington, Little Marlow and Higham). At Burnham two rooms are apparent, with the warming-room at the north end of the range

112

Figure 47 East range, Burnham (Berks.). Entry to the sacristy from the cloister was through the doorway to the right; the more elaborate central doorway entered the chapter house. A third entrance gave access to the parlour and warming-house at the north end of the range. The nuns' dormitory was positioned over the east range, lit by small windows.

separated from the parlour by a passage through the range to the infirmary. A similar passage survives at Lacock, which provided the only entrance to the warming-house. The length of the east range projected beyond the cloister only in larger houses, such as Elstow, Barking and Nuneaton. The upper floor of the east range generally contained the nuns' dormitory. Access to the church was often by a single stairway for day and night use, contained within the thickness of a wall. At Burnham, Bishopsgate and Lacock these stairs descend near the west entrance to the sacristy. The dormitory was initially an unpartitioned chamber lit by small windows, like the extant example at Burnham (Figure 47).

The end of the range communicated with the latrine block, which frequently resembled a domestic garderobe. At Denney (Cambs.) and Higham (Kent) garderobe pits were sunk into gravel or flagstone floors (Christie and Coad 1980; Tester 1967: 149). At Lacock a two-storey latrine had a row of garderobes perched over the main drain (Brakspear 1900: 149). Modest latrines were flushed by single drains at Little Marlow, Burnham, Polesworth and Elstow (Peers 1902; Brakspear 1903; Mytum 1979; Baker 1971). Only Barking was provided with a more elaborate system of sanitation, where a great culvert was split into two channels

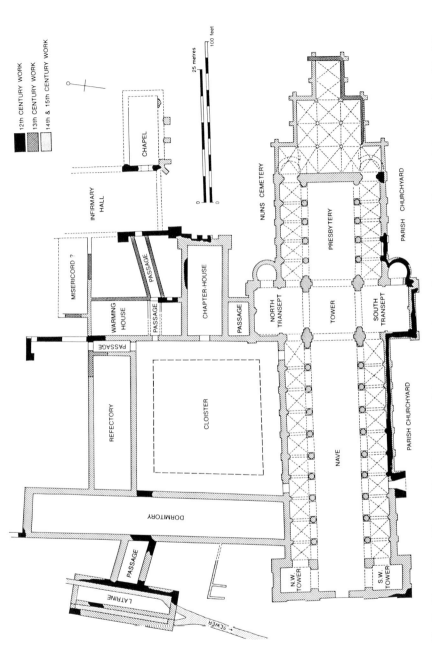

Figure 48 Barking Abbey (Essex). The high status of the nunnery is revealed in the ground plan of the church and buildings, and in the high standard of sanitation, in which the latrine was flushed by a great culvert split into two channels. After Clapham 1913.

beneath the range (Figure 48) (Clapham 1913: 84). In contrast, male houses placed tremendous emphasis on sanitation (C. J. Bond 1989; 1993; Coppack 1990), with provision far superior to most castles and manor houses. At Castle Acre (Norfolk), for example, the latrine block was reached by a bridge from the dormitory, and is nearly the same length as the dormitory itself; the river is tunnelled over and a drain to its south was positioned with lavatory cubicles above. Drinking-water was supplied by a number of possible sources: a separate stream, rainwater collected from roof-eaves, or a well, such as that excavated in a room south of the west range at Polsloe (*Medieval Archaeol.* 23, 1979: 250–1). The siting of urban and suburban nunneries may have demanded better planned water-supplies. Arrangements for Clerkenwell are partially depicted on the fifteenth-century plan of the underground supply to London Charterhouse, showing Clerkenwell's conduit-head, cisterns and piped supply (C. J. Bond 1993: 66).

The range opposite the church contained the refectory. At the entrance into the refectory from the cloister was the *lavatorium*, a ritual washing-place. This normally took the form of a recessed trough, such as the trefoil-headed example at Davington (Kent). The partially extant example at Lacock (Wilts.) is east of the refectory door; a projecting trough and pedestal were set in the surviving recess, which consists of two parallel compartments with paintings above fifteenth-century cornices. Both compartments are decorated with painted abbess figures with croziers. The refectory itself was seldom a simple single-storeyed building, although exceptions were Wilberfoss (Yorks.), Nunkeeling (Humbs.) (W. Brown 1886), Little Marlow (Bucks.) (Peers 1902) and Elstow (Bedfords.) (Baker 1971). Excavations within the extant single-storey refectory at Denney (Cambs.) have provided details of arrangements and decoration (Poster and Sherlock 1987). A drain running north–south across the building may have come from a *lavatorium*. Footings for fixed benching along the north and south walls were paralleled by platformed footrests. The eastern end was raised for the high table. The floor was tiled in a chequer pattern; early drawings suggest lozenge wall-paintings and wooden panelling. Separate doors in the west and east ends of the south wall were for the use of the nuns and abbess (or foundress), respectively. A pulpit projected from the north wall; a similar feature at Elstow was reached by stairs within the thickness of the wall (Baker 1971: 59).

Two-storey refectories are suggested by Dissolution surveys at Wykeham, Kirklees, Thicket and Handale (Yorks.) (W. Brown 1886: 201); eighteenth-century drawings of Clementhorpe, York (Stocker 1984); extant examples at Cambridge (Figure 49), Kington St Michael (Wilts.), Lacock, Easebourne (Sussex), Burnham (Berks.), Chicksands (Bedfords.) and Sinningthwaite (N. Yorks.) (Nichols 1982); and excavations at Goring (Oxfords.) (Stone 1893) and Watton (Humbs.). The upper storey held the refectory, reached by stairs, with the cellarage used for storage. Internally there may have been a

Figure 49 Refectory, St Radegund's, Cambridge (now Jesus College). Like many nunneries, the refectory was located on the upper storey with cellarage beneath.

western gallery and a pulpit projecting externally from the range, for example at Kington St Michael and Lacock, where the arched entrance to the pulpit remains in the north wall. Lacock's ground-floor space was divided into two parts by a crosswall, with the western half possibly used as an inner parlour (Brakspear 1900: 151). The west bay at Easebourne communicated with the kitchen by a slanting hatch, through which food would be served (VCH Sussex 4, 1953: 47).

Double-storey refectories are typical of nunneries, and are frequently associated with orders of canons; occasionally they were constructed for Cistercian monasteries. Peter Fergusson (1986: 173–4) has commented on the iconographic content of this architectural form, postulating an apostolic significance for the upper-storey refectory, which refers to the 'upper room' which contained the Last Supper (Mark 14. 12–16). A more appropriate context for female houses may be the 'upper room' which housed the Apostles, the Virgin Mary, Mary Magdalene and the other Holy Women, after Christ's death (Acts 1.13–14). The *coenaculum* – the upper chapel at St Mary Mount Sion (Palestine), identified with this event – received much attention and rebuilding in the eleventh and twelfth centuries (Pringle 1986: 345). Its restoration may have influenced the building of English nunnery refectories, which appear to have been the only monastic setting in which the participation of women was encouraged, and in which scriptural learning was fostered. Its iconographic archetype, therefore, may refer to the early

116

stages of the Church at Jerusalem, which met in the home of Mary, and acknowledged the participation of women in the Pentecost (Acts 2.1–4; 17–18).

Adjacent to the refectory was the kitchen. This was often sited off the cloister, where incoming supplies could be received from the outer court, and from whence food could be served to both the south and west ranges of the cloister. Excavations at Polsloe revealed a detached kitchen south of the west range, next to a possible garden, later occupied partly by timber structures (see Figure 35) (*Medieval Archaeol.* 23, 1979: 250). Excavations at Little Marlow revealed a kitchen at the junction of the south and west ranges, which also allowed easy access to the infirmary, to the south (see Figure 36). The kitchen's function may be attributed by three excavated hearths and a central fire (Peers 1902). Structural evidence for kitchens seldom survives above ground. Despite the risk of fire, nunnery kitchens may have been partly constructed in timber. Only their entrances may be traced in the stone walls of other ranges, for example at Kington St Michael and Cambridge. Excavations at Kirklees (W. Yorks.) yielded ambiguous results regarding the placing of the kitchen (Armytage 1908). Sir Harold Brakspear and Sir William St John Hope argued that its only possible position was on the upper floor of the west range (1901: 185), and that smaller nunneries would have disregarded monastic planning in favour of ordinary domestic arrangements appropriate to the gentry. The paucity of extant and excavated kitchen remains may support their claim. Equally, double-storey refectories may have been most easily served from kitchens on the upper floor of the adjacent range.

The west range of the nunnery fulfilled a combination of functions which might include: guest-house, prioress's lodge, rooms of the various officers of the house, such as the cellarer, and storage facilities. Its west end was sometimes partitioned for a buttery, for example at Cambridge, where a rotating hatch received food from the kitchen (Figure 50). At Kington St Michael (Wilts.) the remainder of the ground floor was taken up by a guest-hall, screened from the buttery and with its own entrance concealed by a porch (Figure 51) (Brakspear 1922–3). An upper-floor room with a fireplace was considered by the seventeenth-century antiquary John Aubrey to have been the priest's chamber (ibid.). The ground floor of Lacock's west range was divided into three apartments with fireplaces. Brakspear suggested some were chaplains' rooms (1900: 153), although their placing may have been more appropriate to serve corrodians (see Figure 34). The upper floor was the abbess's lodging, with a private stair to the church. Her lodgings in the southern end were partitioned from a guest hall, which was entered by a separate porch. The west ranges of nunneries were often modelled on secular manor houses. Davington (Kent) was arranged like a ground-floor hall, with a private parlour, central hall and domestic offices (Figure 52) (Tester 1980: 210). Likewise, a range of

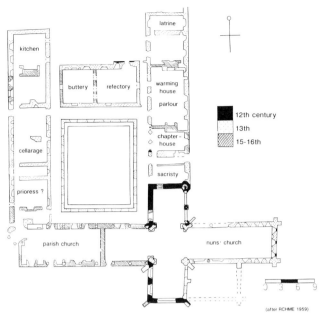

Legend:
- 12th century
- 13th
- 15-16th

(after RCHME 1959)

Figure 50 St Radegund's, Cambridge. The choir of the nuns occupied most of the cruciform church, with the parish church at the west end. The two-storey refectory formed the north range of the cloister. The west range guest-hall was partitioned from a buttery adjacent to the kitchen, which also served the nuns' refectory. After RCHME 1959.

Figure 51 Kington St Michael (Wilts.): the west range. The guest-hall and its buttery occupied the full range, with a private entrance now concealed by the porch. In common with many nunneries, the west range was partially rebuilt in the fifteenth or sixteenth century, here indicated by windows of this date.

118

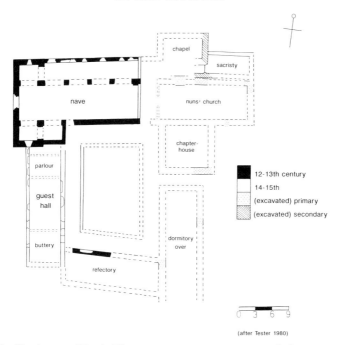

■	12-13th century
□	14-15th
(shaded)	(excavated) primary
(hatched)	(excavated) secondary

(after Tester 1980)

Figure 52 Davington (Kent). The west range guest accommodation was modelled on a secular ground-floor hall, with a private parlour, central hall and domestic offices. After Tester 1980.

c. 1500 built at Pinley (Warwicks.), was originally a three-room hall adjoining the north-west corner of the church (VCH Warwicks 3, 1945: 148). The extant west range at Polsloe is closer in form to secular two-storey halls. It was bisected at ground-floor level by a stone wall (Everett 1934), providing two chambers for the convent's use. The upper floor was divided into three sections. A northern chamber with a fireplace is partitioned from the main stairs of the range by a cob wall. Its proximity to the church suggests it was used by the prioress. A central hall was entered by an external staircase to the west, possibly access for guests. The hall is terminated on the south by a wooden screen, which partitioned the southern chamber and stairway to the kitchen. This last chamber contained the stairway flanked by two chambers: it functioned partly as a buttery to the guest-hall. Nunnery west ranges of all monastic orders acted as guest-houses. The importance placed on hospitality is revealed in the quality of west-range work. Excavations at Little Marlow concluded that this range contained the highest quality masonry in the nunnery (Peers 1902).

Detached prioress's lodges were rare. At Watton (Humbs.) a self-contained prior's lodge included a private chapel and guest quarters (see Figure 30). No such provision was made for the nuns' cloister. A sixteenth-

119

century prioress's lodge survives at Carrow, Norwich, which, as Sir Nikolaus Pevsner quipped 'in its sumptuousness and worldliness almost seems to justify the Dissolution' (1962: 286). However, its positioning, parallel to but not joining the west cloister alley and perpendicular to the church, suggests that this structure was built to replace an earlier west range. Resistivity survey, indeed, has suggested that the earlier west range, on a different alignment, was demolished in a rearrangement of the cloister (Atkin and Gater 1983). A separate entrance led to the guests' hall, and the prioress occupied the northern end, closest to the church. The foundress of Denney (Cambs.) had her own self-contained apartment constructed from the existing nave, upper part of the crossing and south transept of the cruciform church of an earlier community (see Figure 14). A suite of rooms at first-floor level was approached by a private stairway to the west; a watching-chamber in the crossing viewed the nuns' church. The accommodation was used by subsequent abbesses, who modified access by providing a doorway into the nave which connected with a pentice walkway, and a nightstair which communicated with the west end of the nuns' church and the nuns' dormitory (Christie and Coad 1980: 156).

Beyond the cloister, generally to the east, was the infirmary. This positioning facilitated use of the main latrine and drain. A passage sometimes led to the infirmary through the east range, for example at Lacock and Carrow. The infirmary consisted of an open hall with a chapel in the east end, and latrine at the west, such as the extant structure at Burnham (see Figure 46). A *misericorde*, or meat-kitchen, was occasionally provided to administer the supplemented diet of the infirm. Excavations at Barking suggested its position was at the western end of the hall, where a large hearth was screened from the main infirmary (see Figure 48) (Clapham 1913: 85).

Additional features within the inner court might include wells, near the kitchen; free-standing crosses, such as those associated with the churches at Marrick and Kirklees (Armytage 1908: 25); and chapels, for instance the extant example at Godstow (Oxfords.) tucked in the south-east corner of the nunnery's inner court. This may have been the nuns' private chapel, distinct from the shared church to the north of the enclosure (see Figure 53). The chapel was two-storeyed at its west end and abutted a building to the north, from which a view into the chapel could be gained from a squint. To the north, a doorway through the enclosure wall may have admitted priests.

4.3 DEVELOPMENT AND CHANGE

Before taking up residence in the cloister, monastic communities were accommodated in temporary timber structures (for example, those excavated at Norton Priory, Cheshire (Greene 1989)). To date there is no evidence for female communities having been provided with temporary lodgings.

This impression may be a result of the piecemeal nature of most monastic excavations. Excavations at Polsloe suggested fragments of a temporary chapel and structures preceding the nuns' cloister, although these have not been firmly linked to monastic occupation of the site. Refounded nunneries might have used earlier buildings for temporary accommodation. Sir Charles Peers suggested that the sequence adopted in constructing Romsey's (Hants.) Norman church respected existing domestic structures to the south (1901: 320). Nunneries established at existing parish churches, such as St Helen's, Bishopsgate (London), Marrick (N. Yorks.), Wothorpe (Northants.), Swaffham Bulbeck (Cambs.) and Davington (Kent), would have been able to give priority to the construction of domestic quarters.

Elsewhere cloisters developed slowly, according to the predetermined cloister plan. Polsloe, near Exeter, developed around a courtyard from c. 1160, but only received a cloister and walkways c. 1300 (see Figure 35). Excavations at Sopwell (Herts.) were less conclusive, although the developed cloister plan was recognized only in the final structural phase (*Medieval Archaeol.* 10, 1966: 177–8). At Elstow (Bedfords.) excavation suggested a significant interval between the construction of the church and the earliest cloister ranges, the walks of which were probably in timber (see Figure 44) (Baker 1971). Complete cloisters may not always have been achieved. For instance, there was no continuous south range at Kington St Michael (Wilts.) (see Figure 45). Instead, a two-storey refectory was situated towards the west (Brakspear 1922–3). The Elizabethan plan of Chester (see Figure 24) indicates a similar arrangement, with discontinuous west and south ranges. Later foundations may not have adhered strictly to traditional planning. Denney loosely observed an open court plan. Spatial constraints on the Minories (London) resulted in the shifting of components to an upper-storey level, or wherever space could be found. As a result a garderobe was positioned adjacent to the nuns' chancel. To the west of the nuns' buildings were the friars' complex and guest court (Carlin 1987). From his excavations at the Dominican nunnery at Dartford (Kent), Sir Alfred Clapham suggested a church projecting from the east range (1926: 77). The stratigraphic relationship of this structure to the later royal manor house is unclear. However, support for its function as a monastic church comes from parallel arrangements at the French Franciscan nunnery of Provins, and the Irish Augustinian nunnery at Monastirnegalliach (Limerick).

Once established, nunnery plans remained largely static throughout their occupation. This has been indicated by excavations at Davington, Little Marlow and Higham. Even the wealthy house of St Mary's, Winchester, appears to have seen few structural alterations from the twelfth century until the Dissolution (Qualman 1986). Following their initial construction, nuns' churches seldom gained significant new architectural features. Nun Monkton (N. Yorks.), for instance, is essentially a twelfth-century building (see Figure 15), as St Radegund's, Cambridge, is of the thirteenth century (though much restored). Certain features were retained after they had passed out of fashion, such as the ambulatory plan of Romsey's church. The eastern arm of Romsey consists of a square-ended choir with ambulatory carried round it, with chapels projecting east of the ambulatory; apsidal chapels at the ends of the aisles were entered from the ambulatory (Clapham 1934: 45). Similar layouts were, however, remodelled at Barking (Clapham 1913) and Elstow (Baker 1971) (see Figures 48 and 44). Architectural fragments reveal small programmes of rebuilding, such as the excavated thirteenth/fourteenth-century voussoirs from Nun Appleton (N. Yorks.). Existing buildings were sometimes extended in the fourteenth century, for example the east end of the church at Burnham (Brakspear 1903). Chapter houses were extended at Cambridge, Easebourne and Burnham. Major rebuildings were less common, although additions to the cloister and chapter house were made to Malling (Kent) in the late fourteenth century, and a new gatehouse and guest-house were constructed (New 1985: 248–9). Elstow was substantially rebuilt in the mid-fourteenth century, with refectory and dormitory ranges planned simultaneously (Baker 1971) (see Figure 44).

Fifteenth-and sixteenth-century remodellings were rare, although exceptions include the nuns' church at St Helen's, Bishopsgate (London) which received new clerestory windows and a west door (see Figure 40). At many houses the west range guest hall and prioress's lodge continued to be developed. For example, the extant west range at Kington St Michael contains fifteenth-century features (Figure 51). Sixteenth-century ranges sometimes broke with claustral planning, for example the lodge at Carrow which may have overlapped an earlier west range, and the west range at Pinley (Warwicks.) with its axis aligned east–west rather than the usual north–south (VCH Warwicks 3, 1945: 148).

Additions to the initial plan were generally stimulated by secular or parochial interest. In the fourteenth century the parochial south aisle at Ickleton (Cambs.) was widened (Radford 1967: 229) (see Figure 41). The parochial north aisle was extended at Romsey *c.* 1400, where a new doorway joined the enlarged Lady Chapel (*Medieval Archaeol.* 18, 1974: 189). The early fourteenth-century Lady Chapel at Lacock (Brakspear 1900: 132) was built jointly by the convent and John Bluet, who regarded it as his chantry chapel (Cook 1947: 26). Fifteenth-century porches were added to parochial naves at Usk (Gwent) and Bungay (Suffolk), which also received a late west tower to the parish church. Increasingly, new building was dominated by parochial needs – possibly accompanied by the rearrangement of internal space. The wealthy nuns of Shaftesbury (Dorset), for example, were obliged to move their stalls eastward to increase the space available to the parochial congregation (RCHME Dorset 4, 1972: 59).

Perceptions and use of space within monastic cloisters altered over time. In male and female houses communal areas were reduced in favour of private spaces. Hence dormitories were partitioned or rebuilt to house separate cubicles. The fifteenth-century east range at Littlemore (Oxfords.) was divided into two rows of chambers (approximately 2.4 by 3 m each) lit by small windows (Pantin 1970). But the need for individual privacy was not apparently felt at all nunneries. Burnham, for instance, retained a communal dormitory and infirmary.

Instead of individual spaces, nunneries more often splintered into smaller groups within the house. Bishops' visitations reported a gradual neglect of the monastic observance of common *frater* (eating communally in the refectory) in favour of several private messes, much like the private chambers which were replacing great halls in higher status secular settlements. These '*familiae*' developed into distinct households within the nunnery (Power 1922: 317), appearing in injunctions from the late thirteenth century and prevalent by the fifteenth. Such disintegration had architectural implications. A number of possible arrangements have been suggested for the accommodation of Elstow's *familiae*: in converted outbuildings, a partitioned refectory, or timber-framed buildings just outside the precinct (Baker and Baker 1989: 270). More drastic rearrangements were carried out at Godstow (Oxfords.), where the extant walls of the inner court mark an enclosure devoid of claustral buildings. Here, three households replaced the traditional cloister. These were described and drawn in the seventeenth century (Ganz 1972). The households were concentrated in the southern part of the enclosure, towards the chapel. Two parallel ranges were aligned east–west to flank the main conduit running through the south of the enclosure (Figure 53); one survives as a depression to the north of the conduit. A third building, aligned north–south, abutted the outer court, where a single buttress survives to indicate its northern limit.

Cloisters were further compromised by the encroachment of outer court activities. Dissolution surveys reveal that breadhouses, breweries and dairies became commonplace features in the cloisters of small nunneries like Wilberfoss (N. Yorks.); west ranges and refectories were used as granaries at Wykeham, Handale and Thicket (Gilyard-Beer 1958: 46–7). Further departures from monastic planning may have been curtailed by the Dissolution. French nunneries continued to develop new spatial arrangements. At Marcigny (Diocese of Autun), for example, a private church was built communicating with the nuns' chapter house, a configuration which one scholar dismissed as 'une fantaisie feminine' (Monery 1922: 71).

4.4 CONCLUSIONS: CHARACTERISTICS OF NUNNERY PLANNING

Nunneries were distinct from monasteries for men in the placing and internal divisions of the church. It was noted above (see Chapter 4, section 1) that double houses resulted in 'families' of monastic and parochial

Figure 53 Godstow (Oxfords.) from the west. Only the enclosure walls and chapel (top right) remain upstanding. The central conduit may be seen in the centre of the photograph, around which two communal ranges were aligned. This unusual arrangement, in which the standard monastic cloister was replaced with communal halls, seems to have resulted from the fragmentation of the nunnery community into smaller households of women (*familiae*) who lived communally.

churches. Smaller nunneries of all orders shared their churches with rural or urban parishes, so that nunneries were seldom liturgically self-contained. In their tendency to locate alongside parish churches, nunneries resemble secular manor houses and monasteries not dedicated to a regular conventual life, in particular preceptories and alien priories, such as Cogges (Oxfords.) (Blair and Steane 1982). Where Benedictine and Augustinian male monastic churches were shared, it was customary for the parochial element to be contained in the nave or in an aisle. Arrangements within nunneries may have been more diverse, with parishes occasionally occupying the east end. Nunnery churches were predominantly aisleless parallelograms, often divided by a single screen. Secular groups attending the nunnery church were often accommodated in galleries. This method of segregation differed from arrangements preferred in male houses, such as Cistercian Buildwas (Shrops.), where the lay-brothers' nave was screened from the aisles and choir of the monks. The split-level segregation adopted in nunnery churches was closer to that of some manorial chapels, where the family of the manor sat in upper galleries or pews, for example at Newbury Court and Blackmore Farm (both Somerset) (Barley 1986) and Calverley (W. Yorks.).

124

Liturgical prohibitions placed on nuns influenced the design of their churches. Without the increased demand felt in male houses for more altars and side chapels, the parallelograms retained their simplicity. Nunneries were favoured less often with chantries, and the new chapels and sub-divisions with which they were associated. The reliance of nuns on male clerics for the saying of masses resulted in the construction (and retention) of the sacristy as a male presence within the cloister, with evidence in some cases that it was distinguished architecturally as a distinctive space. Male clerics were accommodated in the outer court or in chambers above the gatehouse. Male stewards and bailiffs may have resided in the outer court.

If the church and sacristy signalled the liturgical passivity of nuns, the characteristic double-storey refectory hinted at a more positive role. As an iconographic archetype for twelfth- and thirteenth-century refectories (see Chapter 4, section 2), the *coenaculum* referred to the participation of women in the early Church. Its message was appropriate to this area of nunneries, where scriptural readings by women took place. Indeed at Lacock, wall-paintings of the abbess with her crozier (staff of office) are over the *lavatorium* at the entrance to the refectory, conveying her authority. Excavations in the fourteenth-century refectory at Denney confirmed that while in the refectory the community was spatially delineated according to seniority, with separate entrances and a high table for the abbess. Rank was also observed in the seating of the chapter house, where the head of the house occupied an elevated seat at the east end. While monastic hierarchies were certainly maintained, the female communities appear to have been less stratified than their male counterparts. This is strongly suggested by the paucity of detached prioress's lodges. In contrast to male heads, who often kept distinct households supported by their own portions of the monastic estate (Lawrence 1984: 233), prioresses were admonished to keep common dormitory with their nuns (Power 1922: 62). Only aristocratic abbesses of the wealthiest nunneries, such as St Mary's Winchester and Romsey (Hants.), could expect to command a separate house (Coldicott 1989: 46). In contrast, detached lodges were maintained even at relatively poor male houses of Cistercians (Netley, Hants.; Croxden, Staffs.), Augustinians (Haughmond, Shrops.), Premonstratensians (Easby, N. Yorks.) and Benedictines (Finchale, Co. Durham).

The poverty of nunneries was felt in slow initial building campaigns, limited rebuilding, and departures from standard monastic planning. Some buildings were of timber, or of cob on stone foundations, much like lesser gentry houses (Le Patourel 1973: 68–70). Small nunneries incorporated features more often associated with secular domestic contexts, such as garderobes and possibly upper-storey kitchens. In addition to reflecting lack of resources, the meagre sanitation afforded to most nunneries may have possessed a deeper meaning. Poor sanitation (see Chapter 4, section 2) and relatively lax disposal of domestic refuse (see p. 89) may comment on the different value which male and female religious communities placed on cleanliness. Whereas monasteries outstripped their richest patrons in latrine facilities, nunneries were content with garderobes or single drains. Does this distinction suggest that male houses extended the communality of the dormitory into the latrine, in a 'locker-room culture'? Another possibility may be that religious women embraced poor sanitation as an element of eremitic living, since uncleanness seems to have been valued as a sign of asceticism. The author of the guide for anchoresses, the *Ancrene Wisse*, advised women not to take this aspect of their eremitism to extremes: 'Wash yourselves wherever necessary as often as you wish, and your things as well. Filth was never dear to God, although poverty and plainness of dress are pleasing to him' (Millett and Wogan-Browne (eds) 1992: 141).

West ranges were planned along the models of gentry houses, as double-ended halls. Service wings were added to existing nunnery ranges, such as that which extended from the west range at Kirklees (Figure 42), much as cross-wings were attached to earlier manor houses. Nunneries and gentry complexes shared distinctive features of planning, especially where a courtyard surrounded by discontinuous ranges was contained within a moat. Such features were equally suited to nunneries and manor houses, such as Penhallam (Cornwall) (G. Beresford 1974). Exceptionally wealthy nunneries, such as Shaftesbury, Barking, Elstow and Malling, were planned and comprehensively rebuilt in a manner more closely approximating that of male houses. In such cases the status of the founder and inmates placed the nunnery outside accepted notions of the form and function of female houses.

Sixteenth-century manor houses and nunneries made greater provision for storage than previously. Nunnery ranges were given over to use as granaries (for example at Wykeham, Handale and Thicket, N. Yorks.). Gentry houses placed greater emphasis on provisions for the service end. Likewise at nunneries, domestic and service activity was intensified, with the encroachment of service industries into the cloister. At Kirklees (W. Yorks.) the service wing extending from the west range accommodated the brewhouse and bakehouse, with its excavated oven, and the west range itself contained the breadhouse. At Wilberfoss (N. Yorks.) the ground floor of the west range was taken over by woodstores and butteries; the south range by kitchens, larders and stores; and the east range by the brewhouse, stores and dairy.

Certainly in smaller nunneries much of the cloister began to acquire the service functions which elsewhere are more usually associated with secular or outer court contexts. The proportion of space given over to monastic and service activities may be roughly quantified by considering the surface areas of the ground floor and upper storeys. Both Wilberfoss and Kirklees gave up about 40 per cent of the space within the cloister to domestic services. At Wilberfoss a further 15 per cent was made up by private chambers in the upper storey – communal, monastic space was diminished as a result.

The increasingly domestic personality of nunneries was accompanied by the social and spatial breakdown of the community into households (*familiae*). Smaller groups may have been favoured over the individual space emphasized in male dormitories and infirmaries from the fourteenth and fifteenth centuries. This fragmentation into households forms another aspect of the domestic nature of nunneries, since gentry and aristocratic women often lived segregated lives in the 'inner' household, accompanied by a small number of female companions (see Chapter 6, section 4). At the highest social level these female households were contained in separate dwellings, such as the queen's parlour and chamber within the inner bailey at Corfe Castle and the queen's courtyard complex built at Windsor (Colvin (ed.) 1976: 864–6; 866–88).

Differences between the initial planning of nunneries and monasteries can be traced partly to the social origins of founders and inmates. The patrons and nuns constructed buildings which were akin to their own architectural milieux, or *habitus*. Hence nunneries possessed features of gentry houses, such as moats, discontinuous ranges grouped round court-yards, upper-storey kitchens and garderobes. Certain features resulted from the frequent contact between nunneries and gentry society, brought about through the sharing of nunnery churches with parochial congregations, the close proximity of many nunneries to villages, and the tendency for secular women and children to visit and board within nunneries. This contact resulted in the provision of galleries and west range guest-halls. The increasingly domestic character of nunneries was most strongly felt in the breakdown of the community into households – an identification, perhaps, with the lifestyles of secular women. Gender as a factor in monastic planning determined the prototypes on which buildings were based, in the case of nunneries more strongly linked with gentry forms, and the particular meaning of patterns which diverted from the norm, for example the two-storey refectory and the secular-style garderobe. But in one further respect nunneries invested their architecture with values drawn from traditions of female worship. The next chapter examines the iconographic meaning of one particular aspect of nunnery architecture: the north cloister.

5

THE MEANINGS OF NUNNERY ARCHITECTURE

5.1 THE NORTH CLOISTER

The preceding chapter has shown that a characteristic nunnery architecture was gender-specific, yet within the rules of monastic planning. An aspect of this architectural vocabulary was the high incidence of unorthodox cloister orientation, in which nunnery cloisters were placed to the north of the church in a deviation from the standard monastic plan. Possible meanings of this pattern can be explored according to the iconography of medieval nunnery architecture.

In the context of monastic building the north cloister nunnery may have had a special religious significance. As an architectural image the north cloister may have symbolized an idea. The iconographic analysis of religious architecture deals with the message contained within a structure's design. It presupposes a contemporary familiarity with specific themes or concepts as transmitted through written sources or oral tradition. The cloister orientation may be studied according to Richard Krautheimer's approach to the iconography of medieval architecture (1942), which is based on the premise that geometrical forms were reproduced in order to signal a particular conceptual content. The symbolic subject matter of medieval religious architecture is understood to have operated at two distinct levels (Gem 1983: 1). Original construction of a building would be influenced by the symbolic content intended by the designer – as something which accompanied the particular form chosen for the structure (Krautheimer 1942: 9). After its construction, a level of symbolism would be imposed on the building by its observers. What role did gender play in the iconography of nunnery architecture?

Of the approximately 150 nunneries and 20 double houses known to have existed in England and Wales, the orientation of the nuns' cloister can be identified for 61 (Table 4; Figure 54). Many of these orientations have been verified by excavation, through early maps of the sites or through the accounts of surveys taken at the time of the Dissolution, and others

128

can be inferred from standing remains or the interpretation of earthworks and cropmarks.

Just over one-third of the houses (34.4 per cent sample = 21 N:40 S) were planned with their cloister to the liturgical north of the church. Ideally, cloisters would have been placed to the south of a church. It has generally been assumed that this was to achieve maximum light and warmth (Cook 1961: 59). In male monasteries exceptions to this rule of planning can

Table 4 Orientation of nunnery cloisters.

House	Date of fdn*	Sex of patron	No. of inmates	Dedication	£
North Cloisters					
Benedictine					
Barking	1180	M	37	Ethelburgha	862
Bishopsgate	−1216	M	26	Helen	320
Bungay	c. 1175	F/M	16	Mary & Holy Cross	61
Cambridge	1147	M	11	Radegund & BVM	75
Chatteris	−1016	M/F	15	BVM	97
Hinchingbrooke	1186	M	4	James	17
Ickleton	−1158	?	9	Mary Magdelene	71
Minster, Sheppey	?1130	M	7	Mary & Sexburga	129
Thicket	−1180	M	12	Mary	20
Wilberfoss	−1153	M	20	Mary	21
Augustinian					
Brewood, Shrops.	−1186	?	9	Leonard	17
Burnham	1266	M	20	Mary	51
Clerkenwell	c. 1141	M/F	17	Mary	262
Crabhouse	c. 1181	M	8	BVM & John Ev.	30
Haliwell	−1158	M	17	John Baptist	294
Lacock	1230	F	22	Bernard & BVM	194
Minoresses					
Denney	1342	F	41	James & Leonard	172
Cistercian					
Pinley	−1125	M	7	Mary	23
Cluniac					
Arthington	1150	M	12	Mary	11
Gilbertine					
Shouldham	+1193	M	18	BVM & Holy Cross	240
Watton	1151	M/F	61	Mary	360
South Cloisters					
Benedictine					
Elstow	c. 1078	F	19	Mary & Helen	284
Carrow	c. 1146	M	11	Mary	64
Catesby	c. 1150	M	9	Mary & Edmund	132
Chester	c. 1140	M	13	Mary	66

House	Date of fdn*	Sex of patron	No. of inmates	Dedication	£
Davington	1153	M	14	Mary Magdalene	41
Easebourne	−1248	M	10	Mary	?
Godstow	1133	F	17	Mary & John B.	275
Handale	1133	M	10	Mary	13
Higham	1150	M/F	15	Mary	26
Kington St M.	−1142	M/F	10	Mary	25
Little Marlow	−1194	?	13	Mary	48
Littlemore	−1156	M	7	Mary, Nich., Edm.	33
Malling	c. 1095	M	11	Mary	218
Marrick	1154–8	M	16	Mary	48
Nunkeeling	1153	F	12	Mary & Helen	35
Polsloe	−1160	M	16	Catherine	164
Polesworth	c. 1130	M/F	14	Editha	87
Seton	−1210	M	3	Mary	12
Shaftesbury	c. 1080	M	100	Edward	1166
Sopwell	1140	M	19	Mary	40
Romsey	lt.C11	M	18	Mary & Elfleda	395
Thetford	c. 1160	M	2	George	40
Winchester	c. 1123	M/F	39	Edburgha	179
Wroxall	c. 1135	M/F	9	Leonard	72
Yedingham	−1158	F	13	Mary	21
Augustinian					
Campsey Ash	1195	M	19	Mary	200
Goring	midC12	M	36	BVM	60
Grace Dieu	c. 1239	F	16	Mary & Holy Tr.	92
Cistercian					
Baysdale	c. 1190	M	12	Mary	20
Esholt	−1184	?	11	Mary & Leonard	13
Kirklees	−1138	M	8	BVM	19
Llanllugan	−1236	M	3	?	22
Marham	−1249	F	15	Mary, Barb., Edm.	39
Rosedale	−1158	M	8	Mary & Laurence	37
Swine	−1153	M	9	Mary	82
Wykeham	c. 1153	M	14	Mary & Michael	25
Clunaic					
Delapré	c. 1145	M	8	Mary	119
St John of Jerusalem					
Aconbury	1216	F	15	John B.	67
Gilbertine					
Bullington	c. 1148	M	14	Mary	158
Chicksands	c. 1150	M/F	18	Mary	212

*Sources for dates of foundation are from S. Thompson (1991) and Knowles and Hadcock (1971) for post-Conquest foundations; dates given for refoundations of earlier houses refer to an approximate architectural date for the rebuilding of the cloister. Some nunneries were founded jointly by a man and woman, often a husband and wife, or brother and sister, in such cases sex of patron appears as M/F.

usually be understood according to the functional limitations of the site. Rochester and Waltham, for example, had north cloisters due to the restricted nature of the sites. Tintern and Buildwas adopted north cloisters due to the position of their rivers (Gilyard-Beer 1958: 23). Of the twenty-one nunneries with north cloisters, only Barking may have been planned according to the restricted nature of the site (see Figure 48). The site of Franciscan Denney had been planned by earlier male houses of Benedictines and Knights Templar. Excavation has shown that in the former phase, a north cloister could have existed (Christie and Coad 1980). Nonetheless, in their fourteenth-century reorganization of the site the Minoresses chose to adopt or retain an open court north cloister (see Figure 14).

Frequently it is asserted that the most significant factors in the planning of monastic sites were water-supply and drainage. Running water was needed behind the dormitory for the flushing of the latrine. Hence, the location of the dormitory would probably have determined the position of the cloister. Houses with wealth or influence may have had the resources to adapt a site's condition, for example by diverting watercourses. But poorer, lower-status communities may have been forced to accept the natural limitations of a site.

The lower social and economic level at which nunneries were founded may have been reflected in their inability to alter unsuitable sites – and perhaps also in the likelihood of their receiving them. If a nunnery's water-source was located to the north of the site available, its cloister was more likely to have been positioned to the north of the church. If this were so, the high proportion of north cloisters could be the product of functional planning restrictions precipitated by poverty. However, given that few nunneries possessed latrines flushed by water (see p. 113), it hardly seems likely that this formed the major consideration in the orientation of their cloisters. Nevertheless, in order to test this assumption the water-sources of all of the nunneries in the group of sixty-one were determined where possible (Gilchrist 1990). The results of the mapping were surprising. They indicate that a higher proportion of north cloister nunneries than south cloister ones actually had water-sources to the south of the site. Thus, the position of the cloister was not determined by drainage and source of water-supply. It may be suggested that for approximately one-third of English nunneries the choice of a north cloister was deliberate, and that it possessed meaning which was specific to the architecture of religious women.

The significance of the figure of 34.4 per cent for north cloisters is clearly dependent on the reliability and representativity of the sample. The relative proportion of north/south cloisters will alter as more excavation and research on medieval nunneries is undertaken. However, some indication of the significance of the pattern is given when the total sample of sixty-one is mapped (Figure 23). The south cloisters are evenly distributed across England, whereas the north cloister type cluster into regional groups. Three

Figure 54 Distribution of north and south cloister nunneries. Concentrations of nunneries with their cloisters to the north of the church appear in south-eastern England, East Anglia and the north of England (Yorkshire/Humberside).

discrete clusters can be identified in: (1) the south-east (Barking, St Helen's, Bishopsgate (London), Burnham, St Mary's, Clerkenwell (London), Haliwell (Shoreditch), Minster in Sheppey); (2) East Anglia (Bungay, Cambridge, Chatteris, Crabhouse, Denney, Hinchingbrooke, Ickleton, Shouldham); (3)

Yorkshire and Humberside (Arthington, Thicket, Watton, Wilberfoss). Pinley and Brewood (Shrops.) may form an associated midlands group. Lacock, however, is geographically isolated from other north cloister nunneries. It falls within a group of north cloister monasteries in the Avon Valley of Wiltshire, which includes the male houses of Malmesbury, Stanley and Bradenstoke (see p. 137).

Consideration of the foundation date, or refoundations in certain cases, reveals that the north cloister pattern does not correspond with a particular period; they span the eleventh to fourteenth centuries (Table 4) and correspond with fluctuations of monastic foundation in general (see Figure 7). The north cloisters do not reflect a centrally planned trait specific to a particular order – although it may be suggested that Augustinian nunneries showed a preference for north cloisters and Cistercian nunneries generally chose against them. The tendency for regional clustering lends support to the argument that the north cloister feature was a deliberate choice on the part of planner or patrons. The clusters represent the process of adopting or copying fashions in architecture which conveyed a specific social or iconographic message.

5.2 WOMEN ON THE NORTH: SPATIAL OPPOSITES AND BODY METAPHORS

In what way can the position of the cloister be linked to gender? Is the north cloister nunnery a mirror image of the south cloister male monastery, so that monastic architecture represents a series of binary oppositions? The tenets of structuralism propose that opposites such as north/south comprise the underlying schemes for the organization of material culture, and archaeologists and anthropologists have frequently identified such opposites as reflecting a male/female contradiction. However, this approach assumes that universal rules apply in the relationship between material culture and gender identities. If simple rules of opposition were operating in monastic architecture, their meaning was specific to the practical and cultural knowledge of the masons, patrons and religious inmates, their *habitus*. It is well established that a male/female duality was intrinsic to medieval Christian philosophy (Ruether 1974: 156), in which man represented the spiritual soul and woman represented the corporeal body.

Christian symbolism recognized certain opposites in the attributes of north and south. Generally, the north of a church was associated with the characteristics of night and cold, whereas the south of a church was viewed as the region of warmth and light (Ferguson 1966: 43–4). The north part of a church was given over to symbolism of the Old Testament, in contrast to the New Testament association of the south (ibid.). The observation of opposite attributes included a symbolism of the sun and moon, based on classical representations of pagan sun-gods and personified as male and female respectively (Hall 1974: 86). The associations of classical gods were reproduced in later medieval exegesis and vernacular literature, including the tournament in Chaucer's *Knight's Tale*. Augustine formed the view that the sun and moon symbolized the prefigurative relationship between the Old Testament (moon) and New Testament (sun) (ibid.). An association appears to have developed for north/moon/female/Old Testament and south/sun/male/New Testament.

In addition to the pattern of north cloister nunneries, women seem to have been associated more generally with the north of churches. Margaret Aston has commented on the tendency for women's seating in parish churches to be linked to the north as part of a wider tradition for sexual segregation in church (1990). Representations of the Virgin Mary were consistent in their northern associations (see pp. 140–1), and often female and male saints were linked with the north and south of churches respectively. Rood screens in parish churches sometimes depict a range of female saints on the north and male saints on the south (for example Litcham, Norfolk), a distinction which was also made in the dedications of chapels in monastic churches, such as the London Charterhouse. In some regions this sexual segregation was extended to patterns of burial in parish churchyards, particularly in Sweden, Iceland and the first Christian cemetery in Greenland. Excavations have shown that women were buried to the north of churches at Loddeköpinge and Westerhus (Sweden) (Cinthio and Boldsen 1983). This general pattern of sexual segregation in burial was retained up to the thirteenth century, when burial to the north of Swedish churches ceased entirely. Elsewhere this practice may have been known and discontinued at an earlier date. For example, at the excavated church and cemetery at Raunds (Northants.), zoning of the tenth/eleventh-century cemetery suggested concentrations of women's burials to the west and north of the church (Boddington 1987: 420).

It would seem that the space of any medieval church, parochial or monastic, consisted of an intricate map of gendered spaces. But how did such spaces originate? The earliest references to women's places in the church refer not to the north, but rather to the left. Middle Byzantine sources comment on the arrangements for the early churches of Constantinople, in which the 'women's place' is identified as the left aisle (Mathews 1971: 130–2). This tradition was translated to early Italian churches, such as the sixth-century church of St Apollinare Nuovo, Ravenna, where mosaics on the north of the central nave depict a procession of twenty-two female virgin-martyrs and those on the south depict male figures. This distinction was apparent in British churches from an early date. In Cogitosus's account of the *Life of St Brigit*, dated to the second quarter of the seventh century, the women's half of the church is to the left of the altar, and the men's is to the right (Figure 55; after C. Thomas 1971: 145). To an observer standing in the nave of the church and facing east towards the chancel, the women's place on the left would correspond with the north of the church. Indeed, Alcuin commented on the proper positioning of men and women for the reception of the eucharist as: 'men in the southern part, women in the northern part' (*De Offici Liber* III. 2).

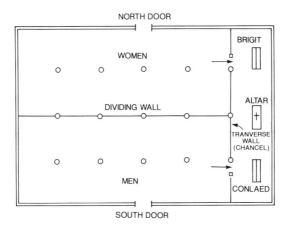

Figure 55 Reconstruction of St Brigit's (Kildare). According to Cogitosus's *Life of Brigit*, dated to the seventh century, the women's half of the church was to the left of the altar (north), and the men's half was to the right (south). A median wall ensured sexual segregation. After C. Thomas 1971: 145.

Yet if observers contemplated the position of God looking down on the church, the women's place on the north would not be to the left, but rather to the right. And if the church itself is seen as a metaphor for the body of Christ, the women's place to the north is at his right hand. This scheme is consistent with representations of the Virgin at the Crucifixion which portray her at the right hand of the cross and John the Evangelist to the left, referring to a passage from John (19. 26–7) 'Jesus saw his mother, with the disciple whom he loved standing beside her'. This scene was present in all medieval churches as the Rood, a cross or crucifix placed over the entry into the chancel and supported by the rood screen beneath. To the observer, the Virgin at Christ's right hand would be positioned to the north of the altar.

The associations of women with the north may be linked to a symbolism of opposites and a series of associations based on the church as a metaphor for the body of Christ. And yet the inconsistency of church imagery, sexual segregation in seating, and the north cloister orientation, representing only one-third of the total sample of nunneries, suggests that a more subtle and specific meaning may have been intended.

5.3 THE DISTRIBUTION OF NORTH CLOISTERS: A SAXON MONASTIC TRADITION?

Explanation may be sought in patterns of north and south cloisters according to a number of factors, among them the sex of a monastery's patron, its number of inmates and financial value. However, in fact, little distinguishes the two groups. Male patrons formed an equal proportion of founders for both north and south cloisters (61.9 per cent and 65.8 per cent) and female patrons showed slightly more interest in the more orthodox south cloisters (18.4 per cent as opposed to 9.5 per cent north cloisters). Both groups are diverse in their representations for number of inmates and value at the Dissolution. The north cloister group, however, appears to have included a higher proportion of wealthier houses.

Given the clustering in the distribution of north cloisters, the key to the pattern may be topographical. In each of the three clusters of north cloister nunneries is at least one originally pre-Conquest foundation which was re-established after a period of abandonment. Within the south-eastern cluster were two Saxon nunneries: Barking and Minster in Sheppey. The best known of all the early houses is Barking, a seventh-century nunnery which was praised by Bede (*HE* iv. 6–10). Within the north-eastern cluster is Watton, thought to be the successor of the seventh-century nunnery '*Wetadun*' where, according to Bede, St John of Beverley wrought a miracle (*HE* v. 3). Although none of the north cloister nunneries in the East Anglian group were reconstructed on the sites of earlier double houses, Chatteris was founded *c.* 1006–16 and Hinchingbrooke was the refoundation of an earlier establishment at Eltisley. Eltisley was a pre-Conquest nunnery associated with the ninth-century saints Pandon and Winfrith, whose burial place of Eltisley was noted in the Chronicle of Hugh Candidus of Peterborough *c.* 1155. From the distribution of their estates made in 1228, it seems that the Benedictine nuns of Eltisley moved to Hinchingbrooke to establish a nunnery, perhaps around an existing church building of *c.* 1100 (Haigh 1988: 41). The standing remains of Hinchingbrooke include the north wall of the church, containing late twelfth- to early thirteenth-century windows, and a semi-circular arch of the chapter house entrance, *c.* 1200 (*Medieval Archaeol.* 12, 1968: 166–7). These remains, in addition to the distribution of Eltisley's estates in 1228, support a refoundation date at Hinchingbrooke of the later twelfth to early thirteenth centuries, contrary to the tradition that Hinchingbrooke was founded *c.* 1087 by William the Conqueror.

Four south cloister nunneries had pre-Conquest origins (Winchester Nunnaminster, Polesworth, Romsey, Shaftesbury). Unlike the refounded middle Saxon houses of the north cloister group, these south cloister houses were all late Saxon foundations with histories of more or less continuous occupation of the same site. These late Saxon nunneries may be distinguished from earlier houses of the seventh to ninth centuries which functioned as double houses. It seems that the north cloister orientation identified with the Saxon tradition of the double house which signified royal female piety.

Saxon double houses which were refounded as north cloister nunneries may have been part of a resurrection of the cult of royal Saxon ladies associated with Bede's *Historia Ecclesiastica*. Susan Ridyard (1988: 241) has suggested that the Norman cults of royal religious women may have been created by the individual house to which an abbess-saint was connected, through the writing of *vitae* and a cult of relics. It appears that Anglo-Saxon cults were not destroyed by the Anglo-Norman ecclesiastical administration. Instead, Ridyard suggests that some monasteries recalled the status of their saint-patrons in order to define themselves and attract endowments (1988: 152). Perhaps nunneries refounded on sites of earlier double houses used a north cloister to invoke associations of the royal Saxon lineage of their abbess-founders, in an attempt to redefine their collective identities and attract continuing patronage.

Support for this argument comes from the double houses which were refounded as monasteries for men. These refoundations were often articulated through a north cloister, for example, at Chester, Repton Priory and Gloucester. The Benedictine grange at Minster in Thanet, in fact a monastery in miniature, had a cloister to the north of its chapel (Platt 1969: 18). The north cloister monastery for men at Malmesbury was refounded on the site of a seventh-century double house. The tradition of this house may have formed the focus of the Avon Valley group of north cloister monasteries (Malmesbury, Stanley, Bradenstoke, Lacock), none of which were planned according to functional restrictions. The Avon Valley group also occurs in a region with a high occurrence of pre-Conquest double houses.

The morphology of the Saxon double house has not yet been elaborated fully by archaeological excavation (see Chapter 2, section 2 and Chapter 4, section 1). It is apparent, however, that these early sites may have had two or three churches, and that separate domestic compounds and cemeteries were provided for the male and female components of the house. This format of multiple churches and segregated domestic quarters was emulated by post-Conquest English double houses. The twelfth-century Gilbertine double houses were planned with the nuns' cloister adjoining the major conventual church. Gilbert's original foundation at Sempringham (I) enclosed the nuns in buildings to the north of his parish church (R. Graham 1903). At Watton, the most fully excavated later medieval double house, the nuns' cloister was to the north of the conventual church. A similar arrangement may be suggested for Shouldham on the basis of cropmarks revealed by aerial photography (Edwards 1989). Later medieval monastic architecture may have translated the early medieval double house tradition into a cloister format, where female religious were symbolized by a cloister orientation alternative to the standard male monastic plan.

Further evidence of this comes from the arrangement of Gilbertine churches, with their parallel aisles for the nuns and canons (see Figure 30). A similar early medieval arrangement is recounted by Cogitosus in his account of the *Life of St Brigit*. He described the timber church at Kildare with its sarcophagi of Bishop Conlaed and Brigit to the right and left of the altar (south and north). A dividing wall bisected the nave into a northern half for the women, associated with Brigit, and a southern half for the men. The median wall met a transverse chancel wall which ensured complete sexual segregation. The men's and women's parts of the church were entered through separate south and north doors (Figure 55).

It seems that early medieval double monasticism associated women with the north part of the church during communal worship. A later medieval attempt to identify with or respect this tradition may have initiated an architecture characterized by north cloisters. The north cloister nunneries occur in the regions with the highest densities of middle Saxon double houses. The earliest house in each cluster was a refoundation or re-establishment of a pre-Conquest double house. Of the south-eastern group, Barking was refounded by Edgar *c*. 965–75, and completely rebuilt *c*. 1180 (see Figure 48; Clapham 1913). Minster was re-edified as a priory in 1130, although its reoccupation may have predated formal recognition. Clerkenwell was founded *c*. 1141, Haliwell before 1158, Bishopsgate before 1216 and Burnham in 1266. The Yorkshire group may have reproduced the pattern set by Gilbertine Watton's nuns' cloister, placed immediately to the north of the church, founded in 1150 and followed by Wilberfoss (–1153), Arthington (1150) and Thicket (–1180). The East Anglian group may have respected Eltisley, located in the centre of a region formed by Chatteris (*c*. 1006–16), Hinchingbrooke (*c*. 1186), Denney (1342), Cambridge (1147), Ickleton (–1158), Bungay (*c*. 1175), Crabhouse (*c*. 1181) and Should-ham (+1193).

The clusters of north cloister nunneries may have aggregated around one pre-Conquest refoundation which was emulated by surrounding houses in an effort to convey social prestige and royal Saxon piety stemming from the Saxon monastic tradition of abbess-saints. The re-establishment was part of a nostalgic movement to identify with Saxon monasticism initiated in the tenth-century monastic reform. It was perpetuated by the Anglo-Norman hagiography of Goscelin which included *vitae* of Wulfhild of Barking and Sexburga of Minster in Sheppey (Millinger 1984: 125 n. 5). These sentiments were fossilized in the later medieval north cloister plans of the refounded houses and their surrounding facsimiles.

5.4 ICONOGRAPHIC ARCHITECTURE: THE VIRGIN AT CHRIST'S RIGHT HAND

Central to the iconography of a medieval religious building was its dedication (Krautheimer 1942: 15). The dedications of the churches associated with the north and south cloister groups can be divided into: single dedications to Mary, single or compound dedications to female saints and single or compound dedications to male saints. Perhaps not surprisingly, about half of each group are single dedications in honour of the Virgin (north cloisters, 38 per cent; south cloisters, 53.8 per cent). Both groups have approximately the same proportion of dedications to male saints (north cloisters, 28.5 per cent; south cloisters, 28.2 per cent), but a larger percentage of the north cloister group were dedicated to female saints (23.8 per cent) than the south cloister churches (17.9 per cent).

Beyond the general associations which the northern regions of churches shared with women and female saints (see pp. 134–5), there were certain liturgical practices which gave the north its feminine connotations. Bynum (1987: 81) noted the iconographic association of female saints with the eucharist, and David Park (1987: 125) has commented on the eucharistic significance of wall-paintings of the Crucifixion, which together with the Resurrection, are associated with the north transept area of churches (1983: 50 n. 105). Easter liturgy, sepulchres and Holy Sepulchre chapels received an appropriate northern location. Moreover, the Easter dramas carried out in the northern parts of churches became juxtaposed with the scene of the Holy Women at the Sepulchre. The *Regularis Concordia* describes how three brethren 'vested in copes and holding thuribles in their hands' assumed the roles of the women: 'Now these things are done in imitation of the angel seated on the tomb and of the women coming with perfumes to anoint the body of Christ' (*RC*: 51–2; cited in Parsons 1989: 16). These associations are demonstrated by the Easter sepulchre at Sibthorpe (Lincs.), which shows the two Marys swinging censers and dressed in male clerical garments (ibid. 18), thus confirming the connections between the north, Easter, and women.

The pertinence of such associations for medieval nunneries is confirmed by a processional associated with the Benedictine nunnery at Chester. This fifteenth-century text gives an account of the nuns' service for Palm Sunday. The priest and chanters begin while the nuns exit the choir. An anthem is said from outside the church door. They proceed singing, with the 'prestes before theym' to the high cross in the churchyard. A deacon reads a gospel while they stand 'on the northe half' of the high cross (Legg 1899: 6). At this nunnery, the Easter liturgy incorporated a location described as north of the crucifixional symbol.

The possible eucharistic and crucifixional associations of the northern areas of churches may relate directly to the most basic level of the iconography of church architecture: the church as a metaphor for the body of Christ crucified. Depictions of the Crucifixion show the wound in Christ's right side, a position which would correspond with the north transept area of a cruciform building. The wound was said to have issued blood and water, so that it came to represent the eucharist and baptism (Hall 1974: 85). It has been noted that the wound became linked to Easter liturgy through a paraphrase of Ezekiel, 'I saw water flowing from the right side of the temple, and all they to whom that water came were saved' (Roberts 1985: 141). Relics associated with the wound came to be housed in areas to the right of the altar. At Westminster Abbey, where the True Blood of Christ was kept, Christ was depicted gesturing to his wound on a central portal of the north transept (ibid.).

According to the iconography of the cruciform building, therefore, the association of the north transept area with the Crucifixion and eucharist must relate to the wound. In the iconography of the Passion Cycle the Virgin Mary was portrayed tending the wound, which itself came to symbolize the birth of the Church, the 'Bride of Christ', from the wounded side of the dying Christ. In late medieval imagery the Virgin came to represent both the Bride of Christ and the personification of the Church (Hall 1974: 75). It is clear that the northern parts of churches were associated not only with female saints and female worship in general, but more specifically with the Virgin Mary at Christ's right hand.

The New Testament yielded little evidence for the life of the Virgin. Old Testament themes were borrowed for Marian devotion as early as the fourth century (Ruether 1974: 178). Israel's personification as the Bride of Yahweh in the Covenant, for example, could be taken to refer to Mary as the Bride of Christ. Equally the image of Sophia was pertinent to Mary (Sir. 14. 20–15. 8; Wis. 8. 2), 'She is the Wisdom of God, the daughter of Yahweh, who sits at his *right hand* and is the mediatrix of all redeeming knowledge.' Iconography associated with the Marian cycle was derived either from the apocryphal texts of pseudo-Melito and pseudo-Matthew (Clayton 1990), or from Old Testament events which were thought to foreshadow Mary's life. This juxtaposition of Old and New Testament, or 'type' and 'anti-type', is particularly relevant to the last scene in the cycle of the Virgin – her Coronation. The Old Testament type for the episode refers to Solomon (I Kings 2. 19): 'And the king rose up to meet her, and bowed himself unto her, and sat down on his throne, and caused a seat to be set for the king's mother, and she sat on his *right hand*'. These types are in keeping with the Old Testament associations of the northern parts of churches in general. The image of Mary on Christ's right hand is consistent with her positioning in Crucifixion and Coronation scenes contemporary to the north cloister constructions. Her association with the north transept area, therefore, might have accompanied the basic iconography of the cruciform plan.

140

It would be difficult to estimate which aspect of Marian symbolism, either the Passion or the Coronation, was most significant to the planners and observers of the north cloister nunneries. The Coronation of the Virgin made an early appearance in English iconographic media. It predated the French 'Triumph' of the Virgin on the Senlis Tympanum (*c.* 1170) and is said to portray Mary in a more passive posture in which she is crowned by Christ instead of being seated in equal majesty (Gold 1985: 53). George Zarnecki (1950: 12) traced the origins of the Coronation in English art to the Winchester illuminations of the Assumption, dated to the late tenth century. The earliest surviving representation in plastic media is the Coronation on a capital from Reading Abbey, *c.* 1130 (ibid. 4); the theme appears in the northern tympanum at Quenington parish church (Gloucs.), *c.* 1150 (see Figure 5), and not long afterwards in the tympanum at Worth Matravers (Dorset) *c.* 1160. During the latter part of the twelfth century the Coronation of the Virgin became an appropriate theme to depict in the northern regions of churches, for example dominating wall-paintings on the north side of the chancel of the small parish church at Sutton Bingham (Somerset) (Figure 56). English devotion to Mary was burgeoning generally at this time with the appearance of Lady Chapels from the late twelfth century onwards, sited towards the east of the church and often adjacent to the north transept, the most celebrated example being the fourteenth-century Lady Chapel to the north of Ely Cathedral.

The iconographic and liturgical implications of the Crucifixion and the popularity and chronological suitability of the Coronation suggest that the patrons and designers of the north cloister nunneries may have been alluding to either theme. The first level of the iconography of medieval nunneries, that of the symbolism intended in their construction, may have referred to a collage of images relating to female worship and Marian devotion. The second level of symbolic subject matter, that imposed on the building by its observers, may be examined through iconography particular to nunneries.

Details of the internal fittings of a north cloister church can be extrapolated from the surviving Dissolution inventory of Minster in Sheppey (Kent) (Walcott 1868). In the upper part of the choir 'a cross of silver and gilt with the Crucifix, Mary and John' was recorded (ibid. 290). Before the Rood over the high altar was a painted cloth of the Resurrection, and in the 'nether part of the quire' were alabaster and painted 'images of our Ladye' (ibid. 291). We have no evidence for the imagery prevalent in the liturgy of twelfth- and thirteenth-century English nunneries, but from the sixteenth-century Bridgettine text, *The Myroure of Our Ladye*, we find that a woodcut of the Coronation of the Virgin accompanies the Masses. Phrases in praise of the Virgin refer to her as 'Thou that syttest at the *righte syde* of the fader', 'the meke mother whose trone is in heuen' and 'quienne of heuen' (Blunt (ed.) 1873: 293, 297, 308). Coronation imagery may have

141

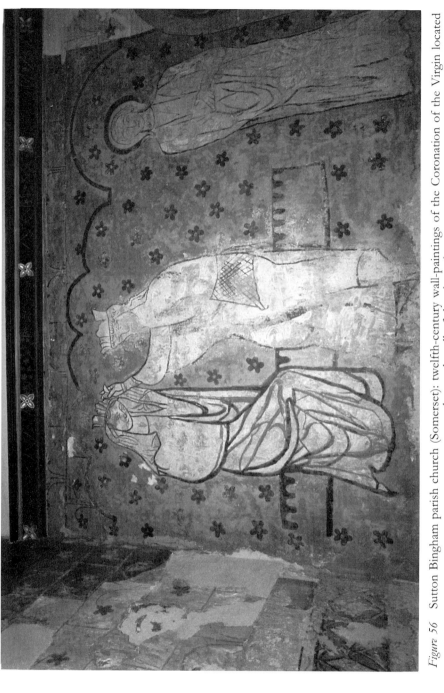

Figure 56 Sutton Bingham parish church (Somerset): twelfth-century wall-paintings of the Coronation of the Virgin located on the north wall of the chancel.

appealed to royal patrons of high status nunneries such as Bridgettine Syon (Middlesex), and a crowned Mary on Christ's right hand may have provided an appropriate scene for royal or highly born novices and nuns to contemplate. But would the symbolism intended by patrons and designers correspond with the nuns' perceptions of the meaning of their architecture?

5.5 COLLECTIVE IDENTITIES: THE NUNNERY SEAL

The imagery prevalent during the life of a nunnery was best reflected in the iconography of its seal. Monastic seals were distinctive marks used by a house in closing and authenticating agreements. Seals in general were never an innovative medium since the image had to be immediately understandable within a pre-existing vocabulary (Heslop 1987: 116). During the twelfth century, historical and allegorical narratives became popular topics for iconographic seals (Heslop 1984: 299). The topic chosen for representation reflected the dedication of the church and the image of authority chosen to represent the house.

From published sources it has been possible to determine the iconography of 136 nunnery seals spanning the twelfth to sixteenth centuries (Table 5). There is some evidence to suggest that the nunneries formed a distinct group in their usage of seals. It seems that allegiances particular to monastic orders were demonstrated on early seals through size rather than design (Heslop 1986: 281) but this may not have been the case with nunneries. In a study of the seals of religious houses in Yorkshire, it was noted that the Cistercian nunneries disregarded official statutes against the use of conventual seals (Ellerton, Esholt, Kirklees, Nun Appleton, Swine) (C. Clay 1928: 7). At the Cistercian nunnery of Catesby (Northants.) an apparently secular seal, depicting a hare within a beaded circle, was used in 1354 and described as the common seal (R. H. Ellis 1986: 20).

Certain regional patterns can be observed in the shape of nunnery seals. The Yorkshire nunneries showed a preference for round seals (Arthington, Ellerton, Esholt, Kirklees, Swine, Yedingham) which is rarely seen in either Yorkshire monasteries for men or in nunneries of other regions. Some neighbouring nunneries shared unusual themes. For example, Benedictine Bungay and nearby Augustinian Flixton, Suffolk, both had seals depicting the *Agnus Dei*; in addition they had the only nunnery seals which represented Christ crucified. The social status and wealth of a nunnery seems to have been reflected in the detail given to its seal. Attention was given to the number of decorative fields on one or two sides of the seal and the complexity of allegorical themes or number of individuals depicted. Houses with the rank of abbey possessed seals with a high degree of ornamentation and complexity of theme represented (Malling, Polesworth, Godstow, Syon, Winchester, Shaftesbury, Barking). In their choice of iconographic themes the nunneries can be understood in terms of chronology and status.

143

Table 5 Iconography of nunnery seals.

Abbess/Prioress
Wilton C13
Winchester 1285
Barking C14
Denney 1400
Nuneaton 1337–45
Aconbury 1447
Amesbury 1337–45
Catesby 1496

Archbishop
Kirklees C12

Church
Chester C13

Christ Enthroned
Markyate mid-C12
Grace Dieu C13

Crowned Virgin standing
Arthington C13
Nun Appleton C12
Yedingham C12

Falcon and Lady
Cook Hill

Hare
Catesby 1354

Seated Virgin
Baysdale 1323
Markyate
Swine C12
Chatteris C12
Studley

Standing Virgin holding Child
Elstow
Tarrant C13
Polesworth C14
Denney C15
Minories 1371
Clerkenwell 1530

Agnus Dei
Esholt C12
Godstow C12; C14
Godstow 1539

Kilburn 1258
Bungay *c.* 1300
Flixton
Ellerton C13
Stamford 1422
Lambley 1323
Nun Cotham 1539

Annunciation
Studley C12–14
Chicksands
Sempringham
Sixhills
Westwood

Christ Crucified
Bungay
Flixton

Coronation of the Virgin
Shaftesbury C13
Denney C14
Amesbury C14
Minories
Delapré
Burnham
Dartford 1422–8
Sopwell

Eagle
Hampole
Crabhouse

Fleur-de-lis
Bullington C13

Patron Saints
Stamford 1371
Whistones C15
Polesworth C12
Arden C12
Moxby C12
Nunkeeling C12

Shrine
Littlemore

Star
Stamford 1527

Throne of Wisdom
Chester C12
Goring C12
Redlingfield C12
Carrow C12–13
Canonsleigh 1539
Flamstead 1296
Stainfield C12–13
Haverholme C12
Bullington C12–16
Bungay *c.* 1200
Wix C13
Holystone 1323
Langley 1284; C13; C15
Grace Dieu C13
Heynings C13
Alvingham C13
Sixhills C13
North Ormsby C13; C16
Orford
Catley C13
Nuneaton C14
Campsey Ash 1352
Fosse C15
Malling C15
Brewood, Staffs. C16
Hampole
Marrick
Swine
Watton
Wykeham
Barking
Chicksands
Easebourne
Catesby

Patron Saints
Cambridge C12
Wroxhall C12
Romsey C12
Godstow C12+
Minster C12
Clementhorpe C12–13
Wilton C13
Henwood C13
Bungay *c.* 1300
Fosse C15
Minories C16

Bishopsgate
Thimbleby
Elstow
Polsloe C16
Stratford at Bow C13
Broomhall 1392
Dartford 1370; 1534
Stamford C13
Wintney *c.* 1330

Tower
Cornworthy

Trinity
Ankerwyke C12

Sources: collated from Victoria County Histories, R. H. Ellis (1986) and C. Clay (1928). The date given is from an associated document or approximately stylistic date.

Relatively few of the seals are devoted to the imagery of Christ (n = 14 or 10.3 per cent). Houses dedicated to patron saints, rather than to the Virgin, frequently depicted the patron on the conventual seal. These are mainly Benedictine houses and make up 18.4 per cent of the sample (n = 25). Over half of the seals relate to the life of the Virgin. To some extent their imagery follows general chronological patterns in the iconography of Mary. Some of the twelfth-century seals depict the Virgin alone, either enthroned (n = 5) or standing (n = 3). By far the largest group (n = 48) display the 'Throne of Wisdom': the crowned Virgin enthroned with the child resting on her (left) knee. A study of French Cistercian seals (Bony 1987) has shown that the seated Virgin and Child was the only image depicted on Cistercian seals. In the thirteenth century, architectural frames and the standing Virgin were added to the repertoire. By the mid-fourteenth century the Cistercians incorporated into their seals the Virgin as 'protectorix', with members of the order kneeling beneath her out-stretched mantle (Bony 1987: 202). The 'Throne of Wisdom', was the most familiar twelfth-century portrayal of the Virgin. This Romanesque treatment was as an hieratic icon – to inspire worship and awe (Gold 1985: 67). From the thirteenth century the Gothic images which dominated Marian iconography were the Virgin standing with the Child in her arms, or the Coronation of the Virgin (Gold 1985: 65).

Wherever possible seals are dated from the earliest documents with which they are associated, so that dates given may sometimes refer to the use of the seal and not its production. Personal seals are dated according to the reign of office of a particular abbess or prioress. The nunnery seals responded to the Romanesque/Gothic transition to a small degree. Six seals, dating from the thirteenth to fifteenth centuries, portray the standing Virgin with Child. The eight Coronation seals all date from the thirteenth to sixteenth centuries (Figure 57). The popularity of the 'Throne of Wisdom', however, never waned. It was maintained as the major symbol of conventual and prioress's seals right up to the sixteenth century. Its usage spanned filiation, status, geographical and temporal space.

Penny Gold (1985: 49) interprets the 'Throne of Wisdom' as a statement of Christ's humanity and divinity through the Incarnation. Mary's role in the scene is as a mother within the context of the Infancy cycle – not within the Marian cycle. Similarly, the five seals depicting the Annunciation illustrate Mary in reference to Christ's birth. Only the Coronation seals indicate devotion to Mary in her own right. Only two of the sample of eight Coronation seals came from north cloister houses. But all of these houses did indeed have royal affiliations, thus confirming the significance of the Coronation image to royal patrons, abbesses and prioresses. The imagery pertinent to this group of houses can be explored further through surviving manuscript illuminations. The Shaftesbury Psalter (c. 1130–40) and the Amesbury Psalter (c. 1250–5) derive from houses which adopted

Figure 57 Burnham (Berks.): a monastic seal showing the Coronation of the Virgin.

Coronation seals. They contain eight and four full-page miniatures, respectively, in which the imagery of the Virgin can be examined (Kauffmann 1975: 82; Morgan 1988: 59). The earlier of the two Psalters, from Shaftesbury, exhibits the familiar Romanesque image of the enthroned Virgin and Child with an abbess kneeling at her feet. The Gothic Amesbury Psalter depicts the seated Virgin feeding the Child with a nun kneeling to her right. In both Psalters, Marian imagery of motherhood predominates. Coronation imagery is absent.

Is it possible to consider in what ways medieval nuns would have related to the various images of Mary, and thus to the meanings of their architecture? Gold (1985: 72) has suggested that the Gothic images of the Coronation and standing Virgin with Child acted as models for female virtue. Religious women would have identified with the attributes of humility and submission embodied by the Coronation and the aspects of tender motherhood demonstrated in the standing figures (ibid.). The Romanesque seated Virgin and Child was a portrayal of Mary's singularity – her perfection that set her apart from all other women. This hieratic image recalled Elizabeth's words to Mary: 'Blessed art thou among women and blessed is the fruit of thy womb' (Luke 1. 42).

The consistent popularity of this image on the nunnery seals, in addition to the maternal imagery of the illuminations, suggests that it was in her unique position as Virgin mother that the nuns celebrated Mary. The seals

147

from north cloister nunneries show little awareness of a Marian iconography linked to the Crucifixion or Coronation. If this symbolism was intended it was by the patrons or designers of nunnery architecture. Its connotations were not maintained throughout the 300–400 years of a nunnery's occupation. Instead nunneries chose the maternal imagery of Mary 'blessed among women' to symbolize their collective identities.

5.6 CONCLUSIONS: AN ICONOGRAPHY OF MANY MEANINGS

The tendency for just over one third of nunneries to place their cloisters to the north of the church appears to be part of a wider series of associations in which women and feminine religious symbolism are connected with the northern regions of churches. These general associations may relate to gendered spaces in all churches which respect the duality between north/south, female/male, moon/sun and Old Testament/New Testament, which resulted in the tendency for women to sit or stand in the north of the church and, at least in early medieval observances, to receive the eucharist in the north. Moreover, the church as a metaphor for the body of Christ crucified linked aspects of the iconography of the Virgin Mary to the north transept area of churches, respecting her position at Christ's right hand at the Crucifixion and Coronation. In addition, by adopting the north cloister, the patrons of certain nunneries may have been invoking a nostalgic tradition of royal Saxon monasticism, which was subsequently emulated by surrounding foundations.

The correlation of female symbolism with the north transept area may have originated in expressions of Christian duality and the practice of segregated worship. It was developed further in reference to themes of Saxon royal female piety and the tradition of double houses. The feminine connotation was retained as the northern region of the church acquired orthodox liturgical associations with the Crucifixion, the Resurrection, Easter liturgies and the eucharist. This imagery was developed as an aspect of Marian iconography which was considered appropriate to nunneries.

Iconographic architecture signalled and constructed a variety of overlapping, multiple meanings. The north cloister orientation may reflect a number of associations linked to female worship, symbolism and Mariology which were interwoven into an imprecise web of meanings. These meanings represented female piety to certain social (or common interest) groups, in particular high-status or royal patrons who sought a link with the royal Saxon monasticism of the past. Nunnery architecture operated as a form of material culture which reflected belief yet also prompted religious women to actively construct and renegotiate their own belief. The nunneries asserted their own choices and collective identities in retaining maternal Marian imagery in their seals and illuminations, which may have contradicted the images of Mary imbedded in the iconographic architecture commissioned as north cloisters and prevalent in the gendered spaces of monastic and parochial churches. The iconography of medieval architecture determined the ways in which monastic spaces were read and interpreted. The social relationships at work in the medieval monastery may be studied through the manner in which various social groups could move physically through these spaces. The following chapter considers gender and space in medieval monasticism according to the embellishment and spatial organization of nunnery architecture.

6

SYMBOLISM AND SECLUSION

6.1 GENDER AND SPACE

Space is a medium through which social relationships are negotiated. Archaeologists have studied space according to the organization of settlements and architecture, and the patterning of artefacts and burials. An analysis of the spaces in which people lived has tremendous potential to comment on gender relations (see pp. 16–18). Space determines how and when men and women meet, work, and mingle. Space becomes a map in which personal identity and boundaries between social groups are expressed.

The relationship between space and gender has formed an important focus of women's studies in sociology, architecture, and geography (for example, MATRIX 1984). It is a useful starting-point in considering the gendered nature of power which, through control over the built environment, determines personal mobility and access to social and economic resources. Often feminist approaches to space have emphasized 'gender domains', in which men and women have separate areas of work and influence (Ardener 1981). These domains have been categorized as a dichotomy between men and women, in which men inhabit a public domain and women are confined to the private domain of the household (Fowler 1984). Early studies of women and space attacked this 'domestic domain' as a material expression of women's subordination, one which helps to determine their isolation, marginalization and lack of status (Hirschon 1985: 15). This negative characterization of space has remained imbedded in the feminist consciousness, exemplified by the comments of the French philosopher Luce Irigaray:

> From the depths of the earth to the vast expanse of heaven, time and time again he robs femininity of the tissue or texture of her spatiality. In exchange, though it never is one, he buys her a house, shuts her up in it, and places limits on her.
>
> (Irigaray 1987: 123).

More recent feminist studies examine the extent to which the 'domestic

150

domain' has been devalued by western attitudes which prioritize the public, and attempt to reassess women's roles through their social, economic and ritual contributions (Hirschon 1984). Such studies have demonstrated the high status attributed to women's activities within their own cultural contexts, for example in maintaining community and kin relations, promoting solidarity between women and encouraging women to act independently from within the domestic domain.

Archaeological approaches to gender and space have concentrated on mapping gender as a way of classifying social relations within households and settlements (Therkorn 1987; H. L. Moore 1987). Archaeological studies of gender domains, like their predecessors in other disciplines, have accepted the subordination of women's domestic domain but have attempted to explain its evolution in the longer term (Yentsch 1991b; Gibb and King 1991); in contrast, some feminist historians have proposed the complementary nature of male and female domains based on the sexual division of labour in the household (Hanawalt 1986).

Certain approaches to space have suggested that spatial arrangements *reflect* social relations, and that the nature of these relations, including gender, can be *predicted* from spatial patterns (for example, Kent 1990). Through the influence of structuralism, methods of formal analysis were developed for reading spatial patterns in architecture like a language (Hillier and Hanson 1984). Specific spatial arrangements were assumed to reflect particular social relations, based on the premise that space directly reflects social structure and complexity. These formal approaches to space are useful in describing the generation of patterns but fail to consider their meaning within specific cultural contexts. Often such studies are characterized by an evolutionary model which implies that current gender relations are inevitable and fixed – a prospect which has been disproven by the dramatic changes in gender roles witnessed during this century.

Space does not merely reflect gender, nor can it be used to predict gender relations. Together gender and space may change meaning over time, according to changing cultural metaphors (H. L. Moore 1987). Space provides more than just a map of social relations, it is primary to the construction of gender identity. Studies of gender and space must ask how space reinforces or transforms one's knowledge of how to proceed as a man or woman in one's society.

Space may be studied as the activity of interpreting spatial orientation, or by observing physical movement through space. In the previous chapter the iconography of nunnery architecture was studied as the activity of interpreting spatial orientation. Here a more formal analysis is made of physical movement through monastic space, participation by medieval religious men and women which informed and reinforced their social actions (after H. L. Moore 1987: 81).

Monastic perceptions of space were informed by boundaries, which in

151

character were both symbolic and actual. Thus the precinct boundary had legal significance, but it also idealized the division between secular and religious domains. Space was used to regulate encounters between groups. The precinct was separated into an outer court, which was accessible to seculars and served non-religious functions, and the inner religious cloister. This inner area was constructed to manage contact between groups of differing social, religious and gender identities. Such control was achieved through the physical manipulation of space through which the inhabitants travelled (see Chapter 6, section 3), and by conceptual spatial divisions inherent to monastic ideals. Attitudes toward space were created through shared knowledge and transmitted through sermons, written liturgy and rules. This codified behaviour informed attitudes toward space, thus reproducing the social order of the nunnery.

Upon entering a nunnery an individual would assimilate both explicit and implicit rules for spatial ordering. Attitudes toward access and movement within a monastic context can be understood through the anthropological study of modern contemplative women's monasticism (for example, D. Williams 1975; Campbell-Jones 1979; Gilchrist 1989b), which emphasizes that monastic space is perceived as being hierarchically ordered. In particular, it can be suggested that space is structured according to seniority within the nunnery, male and female liturgical roles, the distinction between secular and religious, and the dimensions of individual and communal time and space (Gilchrist 1989b). Studies of medieval female monastic enclosure have emphasized the strict, perpetual enclosure of nuns within their cloister (for example, Hunt 1967). Previously, the spatial distinction between seculars and inmates of nunneries has been characterized by rules for 'passive cloister' – that is, regulations against the intrusion of strangers into the nunnery – and 'active cloister', prohibitions placed against nuns leaving their cloisters (Schulenburg 1984: 60). However, a much more subtle categorization of cloister space can be reconstructed, through which individual and group identities were forged.

6.2 RELIGIOUS IMAGERY AND THE DELINEATION OF SPACE

It is likely that hierarchical spatial divisions were reinforced by the embellishment of architectural features. In this way space becomes a matrix constructed by the location and form of images. Iconographic themes are built through sequences of related sculpture, glass, wall-paintings and ceramic tiles. The patterning of such images would help to establish and cement hierarchical relations.

Excavations at nunneries have produced images divorced from their context, such as the stained-glass Old Testament prophet from Denney (Cambs.) (Figure 58) (Christie and Coad 1980). Ceramic tiles often refer to

(scale 2:3)

Figure 58 Stained-glass head from Denney (Cambs.): an Old Testament Prophet or Patriarch, fourteenth-century, from the west range (Christie and Coad 1980). Reproduced by permission of the Royal Archaeological Institute.

the patron saint of the house's dedication, for example the unique Catherine-wheel tiles from Polsloe (Figure 59) (Exeter) (Allan 1984), and those from Campsey Ash (Suffolk) bearing 'BM', *Beata Maria* (see Figure 17) (Sherlock 1970: 133). Occasionally, stone sculpture may signal particularly female religious associations. For instance, a carved sacred heart recovered from Dartford Dominican Nunnery (Kent) (Garrod 1980) may be noted as an early occurrence of an image which achieved widespread attention in the seventeenth century (Figure 60). In addition, the heart may be considered especially appropriate to female devotion, such as that practised by thir-teenth-century German nuns and Flemish holy women (Bynum 1987: 56). Religious women contemplated the heart and blood of Christ in relation to the chalice and wine of the mass – corporate symbols which featured in the visions of women like Hildegard of Bingen (d. 1179) and Mechtild of Hackeborn (d. 1298) (ibid. 62). To the well-educated nuns of Dartford, the carved sacred heart represented a tradition of female worship linked to the eucharist, which predated the image's wider popularity.

Particular meanings are best read within their original spatial context. Despite the paucity of standing structures and modern excavations, certain spatial patterns can be explored in relation to nunneries. Images placed at

(scale 1:4)

Figure 59 A Catherine-wheel tile from Polsloe, near Exeter. The wheel depicted on the ceramic tile alludes to the instrument of torture used in the martyrdom of St Catherine of Alexandria, to whom the nunnery was dedicated. Reproduced courtesy of Exeter Museum Service.

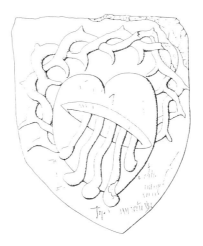

Figure 60 A sacred heart carving from Dartford Dominican Nunnery (Kent) (Garrod 1980). Excavations on the site of the nunnery yielded a carved sacred heart, an image linked to the eucharist, and particularly pertinent to female devotion. Reproduced from *Kent Archaeological Review*, courtesy of the Council for Kentish Archaeology. Drawing by the Kent Archaeological Rescue Unit.

154

main entrances, located at the west end of the church, may have been intended to inform the perceptions of secular guests and parishioners. For example, the west window of Aconbury's church (Herefords.) is marked by a single, veiled female head topping the hood mould. Of the four image-niches at the west end of the church at Nun Monkton (N. Yorks.), two contain remains of their statues. The figure in the extreme southern niche is relatively complete (Figure 61), and appears to depict a female saint. The northern niche contains a smaller fragment of a figure's bare feet. The niches may have contained the four cardinal virtues – justice, prudence, fortitude and temperance – which would have been personified as bare-footed figures. However, perhaps more likely may be Mary Magdalene and the Holy Women, or a group of popular female saints. These sculptures do not appear to have referred to the identity of the nunnery held in its dedication (to the Virgin Mary). Instead these female representations, whether saints or virtues, acted as signifiers in constructing the perceived sexuality – or perhaps asexuality – of the nuns.

Messages to the nuns were apparent inside the cloister. Over the entrance into the extant refectory at Cistercian Sinningthwaite (N. Yorks.) is a twelfth-century stone sculpture of a serpent (Figure 62). This may be read as a reminder to the nuns of the temptation and fall of Eve, which prefigured the redemption of women through the Virgin Mary (Nichols 1982). Alternatively, it may be suggested that the serpent may be the personification of prudence, reminding the nuns to 'be wary as serpents' (Matthew 10. 16), a reading more appropriate to the positive images of female spirituality which may have been suggested by the iconography of the two-storey refectory (see above pp. 116–17).

The sacristy seems to have been associated with eucharistic references to the sacrifice of Christ. The north-east corbel supporting the vaulting of the sacristy at Lacock (Wilts.) depicts the nimbed lamb of God (Figure 63): the *Agnus Dei* with its connotations of eucharistic sacrifice. In a similar spatial context, a wall-painting in the north transept of Marcigny in France (diocese of Autun) shows the lamb (Monery 1922: 66). Rubble infill from the eastern section of the north wall of the church of the Minories (London) included a quatrefoil, possibly the top of a shrine or sedile, which contained a black-line painting of the *Agnus Dei* (Collins 1961: 161). From the same context a painted female sculpture was thought to be Synagogue (Evans and Cook 1956). Either this attribution, or the provenance of the sculpture, may be questioned since depictions of Synagogue generally occur in contexts of particularly high status, such as cathedrals.

Glass in the private chapel of the abbess at Lacock was recorded in 1684 (Brakspear 1900: 156). The saints Bartholomew, Bernard and Chris-topher were depicted, possibly respecting the nunnery's composite dedi-cation to St Bernard and the Blessed Virgin Mary. Bernard was particularly known for his devotion to the Virgin as the mother of Christ (Bynum

Figure 61 A statue of a female saint or virtue survives in an image niche at Nun Monkton (N. Yorks.). Four such images lined the west front of the church, facing the village and marking the entrance into the parish church in the nave of the nunnery.

Figure 62 The Sinningthwaite Serpent. The doorway into the twelfth-century nuns' refectory at Sinningthwaite (N. Yorks.) was marked by a label-stop carved into the head of a serpent, the personification of prudence or wisdom. Illustration by Ted West.

Figure 63 A corbel in the sacristy at Lacock (Wilts.), carved in the form of the *Agnus Dei*, the nimbed lamb of God. This image represents the sacrifice of Christ, and appears to have been common in the sacristies of nunneries. Its theme was appropriate to this room, adjacent to the east end of the church, where sacred vestments and vessels were kept. Illustration by Ted West.

1982); and Christopher repeated the Virgin's role as the bearer of Christ. Wall-paintings in the southern apartment of the west range show St Andrew, the first to follow Christ (John 1. 40–41), and St Christopher, the Christ-bearer. Like nunnery seals (see Chapter 5, section 5), wall-paintings and stained glass referred to devotion to Christ, or the Virgin as mother.

Carvings within cloisters did not always represent scriptural or apocryphal iconography. Capitals and corbels from monasteries and nunneries might also depict animals, foliage and the heads of secular men and women (for example, those excavated from Norton Priory, Greene 1989). Their messages were linked to movement within the cloister, in particular the sensation of travelling from one spatial region to another. At Lacock, the corbels supporting the vaulting survive *in situ* in the sacristy, chapter house and

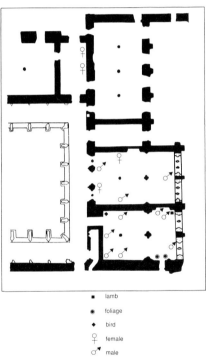

Figure 64 Symbolic architecture: spatial matrix of carved corbels at Lacock. Corbels supporting the vaulting were carved as human heads. Exclusively male representations were used in the sacristy, and some were present in the chapter house, but only female representations figured on carved corbels in the more private spaces of the nunnery.

parlour. Their subjects change as the observer moves from the sacristy, the region of the priest, towards the domain of the nuns (Figure 64). Corbels in the sacristy include the lamb (n = 1), foliage (n = 2), birds (n = 1) and male heads (n = 7). The chapter house corbels show male heads (n = 3)

159

and female heads (n = 2). Within the parlour only two decorated corbels stand at the east end, both female heads. The next room to the north-east, the warming-room, contains no human representations.

The male representations within the cloister at Lacock are most numerous in the sacristy, a room predominantly used by the priest (Figure 65). Male figures occur in smaller numbers in the chapter house, where men would occasionally be admitted (for example, patrons and clergy during the profession of an abbess). The deeper space of the nunnery contains no secular male representations. A similar scheme may be proposed for Marham (Norfolk), where one sculptural figure survives (Figure 66). This figure supports the rib-vaulting of a small room partitioned from the north end of the west range, a likely position for guest accommodation. The half-figure is a bearded man sporting a sword – a secular, male embellishment which would be appropriate only to this least sacred area of the Cistercian nunnery.

When drawn together, the fragmentary evidence for the embellishment of the cloister seems to have reinforced the particular devotional practices of a house and confirmed its identity through reference to its dedication. Group membership and segregation were signalled by a spatial matrix which constructed meaning through the location and content of images.

6.3 FORMAL SPATIAL ANALYSIS OF NUNNERIES AND MONASTERIES FOR MEN

Within the convent, contact between social groups (nuns, novices, priests, corrodians, seculars) was regulated through the manipulation of spatial components according to their placement and routes of access. These mechanisms may be understood through a formal analysis of monastic space. Methods of formal spatial analysis are based in the structuralist premise that space is constructed as a language, following rules which correspond with social categorization. Spatial patterns are thought to be generated, and made subject to decoding, through rules of grammar (for example, Glassie 1975; Hillier and Hanson 1984). Spatial analysis frequently emphasizes the coherence and stability of social space (H. L. Moore 1987: 74). In order to compensate for the static impression given, formal analysis must be made in conjunction with a study of contradiction and change in settlement form (Chapter 4, section 3).

Studies of religious space have often focused on the interface between sacred and profane, locating symbolic and physical progression to a ritual centre, for example in studies of Buddhist monasteries (Khosla 1975; Bandaranayake 1989). However, monasteries were also living spaces which accommodated various religious and secular groups. Encounters between these groups may be studied according to the boundaries and entrances through which social space was categorized. The significance of gender as

Figure 65   A corbel supporting the vaulting of the chapter house at Lacock (Wilts.), carved in the form of a male head. Illustration by Ted West.

Figure 66 Male figure at Marham (Norfolk). A half-figure of a bearded man sporting a sword supported the rib-vaulting of the west range which sprung from his back, a secular image appropriate only to the guest accommodation of the nunnery. Illustration by Ted West.

162

a structuring principle within monastic space can be evaluated through the comparative formal analysis of nunneries and monasteries for men. The method chosen follows syntactic access analysis (after Hillier and Hanson 1984).

While rejecting the interpretative claims of the syntactic model, that spatial form directly reflects social organization, its descriptive properties can nevertheless be harnessed to great effect. Access analysis charts the arrangement of spaces as levels of permeability, measuring relative degrees of depth and shallowness. Each component and entrance is represented as a node connected by lines to other components to which it has access. The resulting network of nodes and lines forms an 'unjustified access map'. This map is 'justified', or calibrated, according to the position of the observer, placed at any single point outside or within the complex. This method has been verified by ethnographic and computer simulated studies (Yiannouli and Mithen 1986) and applied to a number of extant and excavated settlements (for example, Foster 1989; Fairclough 1992).

I have used this method in order to compare plans of monasteries for men and women. Nunneries with the widest possible range of foundation date, status and filiation were chosen, each fulfilling the requirement that entrances and partitions within claustral ranges are known or can be reconstructed. These plans represent a final phase of development, before structures fell into disuse or changed function from that to which they were originally put. Such a state of development may be given a general date between the twelfth to fourteenth centuries. The following nunnery plans were analysed: Watton (Figure 30), Cambridge (Figure 50), Davington (Figure 52), Lacock (Figure 34), Burnham (Figure 46), Little Marlow (Figure 36), Kirklees (Figure 42) and Polsloe (Figure 35). A comparative sample of monasteries for men was chosen in order to represent a range of types, including: a Gilbertine canons' cloister (Watton), a wealthy Cistercian house (Roche Abbey, S. Yorks.), a modest Augustinian monastery (Lanercost Priory, Cumb.), a Benedictine abbey with a north cloister (Chester Abbey, Cheshire), a Benedictine priory which had evolved from a hermitage (Finchale Priory, Durham), a southern Cistercian house (Waverley Abbey, Surrey), a rural mendicant monastery (Walsingham Friary, Norfolk) and a Premonstratensian house (Leiston Abbey, Suffolk) (Gilchrist 1990).

Access analysis was used to determine the relative degrees of monastic enclosure experienced by nuns and monks. 'Justified access maps' (Hillier and Hanson 1984) were prepared using the precinct (the outer, 'carrier space') as the point of departure for routes of access to the cloister. Figures 67 and 68 give examples for male and female monastic plans. These maps revealed the levels of permeability of certain components within nunneries and monasteries. The levels, or stages of access, of the components can be used for two further methods of analysis. An equation measures the degree of integration or segregation of a component from the cloister as a whole

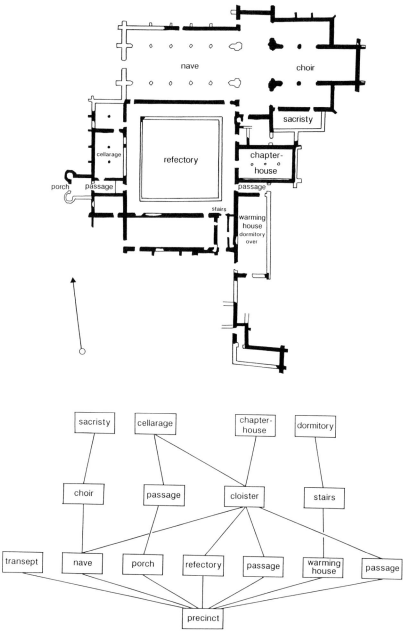

Figure 67 Formal spatial analysis of the monastery for men at Leiston (Suffolk). The rooms were located at three levels of access from the precinct. It was common for the monks' dormitory to be situated in a more shallow space than that of the nuns, and for the deepest space of the monastery to be reserved also for the chapter house and sacristy.

164

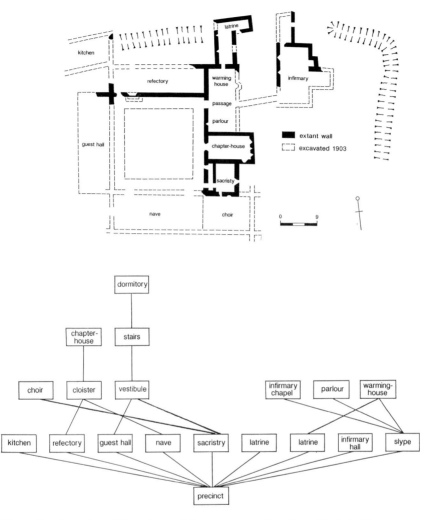

Figure 68   Formal spatial analysis of the nunnery at Burnham (Berks.). The rooms were located at four levels of access from the precinct, with the nuns' dormitory located in the deepest, most inaccessible, space. In contrast to its position in the monastery, the sacristy was situated in the most shallow space.

('relative asymmetry', Hillier and Hanson 1984). In this way it may be determined which components represent the least and most easily accessible parts of nunneries and monasteries. A second equation measures the number of points of access, or points of control, to it ('relative ringiness', Hillier and Hanson 1984).

The access maps showed that the number of levels of permeability (stages of access from the precinct) was higher for nunneries than mon-

165

asteries (Gilchrist 1990). The nunneries also had a higher degree of segregation from their precincts than the monasteries. In other words, it was more difficult to gain access to the nuns' cloisters from their surrounding precincts. The greater enclosure of religious women was guarded by a higher number of physical, as well as ideological, barriers.

Between nunneries and other monasteries the most segregated component of the cloister differed. In nunneries the dormitory was located in the deepest space, whereas male communities were equally, and sometimes more likely to reserve the deepest space for the chapter house – the heart of monastic community and daily routine. Sacristies of nunneries were in shallow space, reflecting their separation from the rest of the cloister, thus limiting the area to which the priest had access (for example, Burnham: Figure 68). Where sacristies occurred in monasteries, they were part of a deeper space, accessible from fewer loci of control and more representative of their function of storing sacred vessels and vestments (for example, Leiston Abbey: Figure 67).

The impermeability of sacristies and chapter houses within monasteries has been suggested elsewhere (Cromwell 1987), in a study which calculated central accessibility (after Hammond 1972). Sacristies and chapter houses were shown to be the least accessible parts of Cistercian monasteries in Yorkshire, where space was used to filter lay-religious from parts of the cloister (Gilchrist 1989b). In Cistercian monasteries, spatial categorization was concerned with maintaining boundaries between groups of differing religious status. Benedictine monasteries for men used spatial divisions to reinforce the structure of authority operating within the community. In these houses, the abbot's lodge forms a discrete area apart from the main complex (for example at Chester and Finchale). In nunneries, emphasis was on the construction of gender identity through the strict enclosure of nuns, and in demarcating male and female liturgical roles. In the Gilbertine double house of Watton, sexual segregation is apparent in the deep level of permeability of the window-house, where the nuns and canons could exchange speech, food and household objects. This component was placed in the deepest space in relation to both the nuns' and canons' cloisters.

Access analysis has been useful in commenting upon the relationships between nuns and secular groups. For example, naves and guest-halls appeared at the first or second level of permeability, that is, they were most easily accessible from outside the cloister. At Little Marlow (Figure 36) and Polsloe (Figure 35), for example, the guest-hall and nave formed discrete areas on the map separate from the central focus, since these areas had no access to the nuns' cloister. Service areas were similarly excluded from the cloister. At Polsloe the kitchen was isolated from other components, in a position suitable for distancing male servants from the nunnery (as suggested above, p. 89), and at Kirklees the ancillary structures were accessible only from the precinct and entry. Space in certain nunneries was used to divide (male or female) servants from religious women, just as the Cistercians segregated lay-brethren into a non-religious area of the precinct (for instance at Rievaulx and Roche (Yorks.), Coppack 1986: 130).

6.4 SEXUAL SEGREGATION AND GENDER DOMAINS

The strict enclosure of female religious, and the partitioning of nunneries into areas of male and female space, may be likened to extreme gender domains. As suggested above, the female domestic domain is not fixed across cultures or time, but is socially constructed, often through the family, within which women assume particular responsibilities linked to motherhood (H. L. Moore 1988: 22). Spatial gender domains are sometimes viewed as a response to hierarchical sexual divisions of labour, which accompany increasing productiveness, specialization and social complexity (Hartmann 1982). Absolute gender domains, in which men and women are fully segregated, are thought to be symptomatic of vigorous social ranking and its legitimation through male lines of inheritance. According to an evolutionary model (Coontz and Henderson 1986), women's identity within the domestic domain becomes absolute and devalued only within state societies, such as medieval England. Women are segregated within the household, thus restricting their mobility and independent access to resources. The spatial confinement of women sometimes becomes a symbol of rank, expressing status through the development of architecture which facilitates segregation, and by demonstrating the surplus labour of women who are alienated from their role in economic production. For example, the architectural seclusion of women within classical Greek society expressed social status (Walker 1983).

Cross-cultural comparisons suggest that absolute gender domains are an expression of male status. Sexual segregation is used to demonstrate the power to release female labour or limit it to the private household. This view of gender and space suggests that architecture is used to reinforce the alienation of women, to confine, control and restrict their social and economic mobility. This approach characterizes gender as the asymmetric power relations of domination, and implies that material culture is employed to force women to conform. Such interpretations give little consideration to the active nature of material culture, or the role of female agency in reinterpreting and transforming material culture in relation to gender. How did high status architecture interact with gender identity in later medieval England? The most appropriate comparison to nunneries may be a consideration of women's space in medieval castles (Gilchrist 1994).

The identification of women's quarters in castles is problematic, since attributing functions can be difficult for any rooms save the hall, chapel, kitchen and latrines. In addition, the form of castles changed continuously from the twelfth to fifteenth centuries. By the thirteenth century, accommodation in enclosure castles had expanded beyond the central keep to include aisled halls and towers protected within fortified perimeter walls. Women in these castles, including the women of the lord's household and a small number of female servants and companions, would have lived in the most private part of the predominantly male household. At Helmsley (N. Yorks.), the women were accommodated in a tower adjoining the hall. This West Tower was rebuilt in the early fourteenth century to provide latrines and fireplaces on each floor of the private suites, where the women lived in isolation from the castle's garrison and administrative offices.

Women of the highest status had their own separate households within castles. An excavated example is the queen's household at Clarendon Palace (Wilts.) (James and Robinson 1988), where the queen's halls, chapels, tower and garden formed, in effect, a private ward of the castle. At Castle Rising (Norfolk) and Pickering (N. Yorks.), women commissioned their own self-contained female households, centred around a hall with private access to a chapel, during the fourteenth century.

Women's quarters were situated in the most segregated parts of castles, and their separate 'inner' household may be likened to the greater segregation of female religious. At public events, such as entertainments and banquets, men and women were often separated, with the men in the hall and the women located in a separate chamber or watching the proceedings from galleries (Girouard 1978: 47). At heraldic funerals, supervised by the College of Arms, the sexes were segregated in the funeral feast and procession, and it was customary for the deceased to be mourned by members of their own sex (Gittings 1984: 174). Protocol required that the chief mourner, the principal mourners in the procession, and even the poor attending the funeral, should be of the same sex as the deceased. Private and public lives were conducted according to a high degree of sexual segregation. But were these 'gender domains' used to control and alienate women?

The tendency for the spatial segregation of women is apparent even where women have been active in commissioning their own quarters, and thus represents an example of the way in which the female subject is both active in interpreting material culture, and complicit in being conditioned by it (see pp. 13–15). At the same time, however, the individual agent possesses the ability to transform social relationships through material culture. This process is apparent for medieval religious women in their rejection of communal dormitory and refectory in favour of separate households, or *familiae* (see p. 123). This pattern was recorded at nunneries of the highest social status, such as Elstow and Godstow, and seems to indicate a choice on the part of high-ranking religious women to identify with the household arrangement familiar to women living in castles. Women in castles and nunneries chose their arrangements of space as *habitus*, an unconscious, practical logic of gender ordered materially through architecture and space.

Both secular and monastic women demonstrated constructions of female sexuality which centred on monogamy and chastity facilitated by spatial segregation. In contrast, peasant women, and those working in towns, participated in a more fluid division of labour, in which sexual and spatial domains were less strictly perceived (Hanawalt 1986; Howell 1986: 10). The strict, perpetual enclosure of medieval nuns may be seen as an extension of the segregation of aristocratic and gentry women within a domestic domain. Despite their religious status, the identity of medieval nuns was constructed primarily with reference to their position as women of a particular class, or estate. The existence of a collective consciousness shared by a common interest group made up of women of certain estates cannot be dismissed. This gender awareness, or construction of femininity, may have been perpetuated by the greater architectural segregation of medieval nuns in comparison to monks, and was actively sought through female agency in the development of households within nunneries (see Chapter 4, section 3). Such enclosure and segregation of women precluded independent access to economic resources and confirmed reliance on the existing institutional structures: a strategy maintained through the placement and economic functions of nunneries (see Chapter 3). In the next chapter, these patterns are contrasted with the opportunities available to medieval religious women through alternative monasticisms: beguinages, hospitals, anchorages and hermitages.

7

AN ARCHAEOLOGY OF ALTERNATIVES

7.1 BEGUINAGES: INFORMAL COMMUNITIES OF URBAN RELIGIOUS WOMEN

And behold, a woman in the city, which was a sinner.

(Luke 7. 37).

The scarcity of women's religious communities in medieval English towns forms a stark contrast with our perceptions of towns of the Low Countries, northern France, and the Rhine valley. Within the walls of Amsterdam, for example, women's houses accounted for fifteen of the eighteen monasteries built in the fourteenth and fifteenth centuries (Carasso 1985: 11). True, these houses are considered to have been only semi-monastic; they were beguinages established by, or for, lay-religious women. This spiritual movement grew from the thirteenth century onwards, when groups of secular women banded together in order to serve the poor and sick (Neel 1989: 322). They established informal communities supported through their own labours and begging for alms (Lawrence 1984). The voluntary poverty embraced by these women represents a female form of the *Vita Apostolica* (Devlin 1984: 184). Even granted the quasi-monastic commitment which the continental beguinages appear to represent, the scale upon which they were established appears, at first sight, to be appreciably larger than anything to be seen in Britain.

Historians have used the term 'beguinage' to describe any informal or spontaneously founded community of religious women, but few were directly associated with the formal order of the Beguines. Informal communities of lay-religious women were described as *béguinage, maison, couvent, hôpital, Beginenhaus* and *begignhuis*; those formally associated with the Beguines were described as *cour de béguinage, grand béguinage, beginenhof* and *begijnhof* (Delmaire 1989: 126). Of the fifteen in Amsterdam, for instance, only the *Begijnhof* was a true beguinage. The lifestyle of the Beguines was between two worlds, *via media*, and combined the secular with the regular religious (McDonnell 1969). The constituency of the Beguines was drawn from the new bourgeoisie or lower aristocracy of the towns; older nobility continued to support traditional monastic institutions (Bynum 1987: 18). Women attracted to this life sought evangelical poverty, self-sufficiency, and a flexible vocation which included active charity. In other words, continental beguinages aimed to be the antithesis of formal nunneries, which remained situated in rural contexts and served the needs of the traditional upper classes.

By the fourteenth century, however, beguinages were enclosed communities which relied on patronage for their subsistence. Efforts were made to enclose the beguines, which culminated in the Council of Vienne (1312). In Belgium the *curtes* were generally built just outside the city walls (McDonnell 1969: 479). There was no standard arrangement for planning, although the central focus was normally the church, around which the community developed. Younger sisters were segregated in special streets, away from the individual houses of the older women (ibid.). These houses were built by widows who joined the order, so that the plan of the *curtis*, *court* or *curia* evolved organically. Arrangements varied from buildings attached directly to a church, such as Anderlecht, to the courtyard layout of St Elizabeth, Bruges. A large beguinage consisted of a church, cemetery, hospital, public square and streets, and possibly a brewery and mill. At Ghent, the Great Beguinage was enclosed by walls and moats (McDonnell 1969: 479); at Bruges the canals were integral to the plan.

Although formal beguinages never developed in England, there is some evidence for similarly informal, spontaneous communities of religious women. These communities have occasionally been recognized through charitable provisions made in the wills of people living in medieval towns. In fifteenth-century Norwich, for example, two separate groups of sisters dedicated to charity lived in tenements within the city (Tanner 1984: 65). Links to the continental tradition are especially strong for the later example, which was established in a tenement in St Laurence's parish owned by a merchant formerly of Bruges (ibid.). These communities received bequests from lord mayors, their wives and the clergy. They were short-lived and situated in ordinary urban houses.

A third group of semi-religious women has been noted in medieval Norwich: those living in a house in the churchyard of St Peter Hungate (ibid.). Similar communities were known elsewhere, for example in the churchyard of St Andrewgate, York, and are generally assumed to be *maisons dieu*, small houses of charity (Cullum 1992: 199). But to what extent did the form and functions of *maisons dieu* and informal beguinages (*maisons*) overlap? *Maisons dieu*, established to relieve the poor, were often set up in the founder's house; early beguines, who were devoted to active charity, lived in their own houses. Poor women living in *maisons dieu* were provided for in return for their prayers, just as bequests were made to poor women in French beguinages, referred to as '*pauvres béguines puses dans les convents du*

171

beguinages' or *'béguines sans rente'* (Delmaire 1989: 139). Where urban charity has been studied, it appears that provision for poor women increased from the fourteenth century, for example in York at St Andrewgate, St Nicholas (from 1380), All Saints Pavement and Ousebridge *maisons dieu* (1433–5) (Cullum 1992). It may be asked whether these urban women engaged, to any degree, in voluntary poverty, thus rendering English *maisons dieu* for women closely cognate with beguinages of the Low Countries and northern France, informal German communities, in which women resided in small groups within ordinary houses (McDonnell 1969: 480), and Italian *penitente* or *pinzochere*, households of women living pious domestic lives as *Humilati* either at home or in small communities (Bolton 1973: 81; M. M. McLaughlin 1989: 298). If so, the numbers of women in English medieval towns who conducted semi-religious lives of voluntary poverty or charity may have been seriously underestimated by historians of medieval piety.

Informal beguinages were not characterized by particular forms which might be easily recognized archaeologically. However, beguinages and *maisons dieu* for poor women should figure within the range of functions to be considered for structures excavated in urban churchyards (for instance, at Barton on Humber (Rodwell and Rodwell 1982); St Mary in Tanner Street, Winchester (*Antiquaries Journal* 55, 1975); and St Helen, York (Magilton 1980)).

7.2 HOSPITALS: A LIFE OF CHARITY

Now when Jesus was in Bethany, in the house of Simon the leper, there came unto him a woman having an alabaster box of very precious ointment.

(Matthew 26. 6–8).

Pious women resided informally in *maisons dieu* established in ordinary houses or churchyards, but English women seeking a more regular life were attracted to hospitals. There, a semi-religious life could be found which closely approximated the *via media* of the Beguines. An unknown number of smaller hospitals was established, such as the house recognized at Stow (Cambs.), where young women in habits of russet garments lived around a chapel from *c.*1250 ministering to the poor (Rubin 1987: 136). This particular house survived for at least one hundred years, and like others documented in Lincolnshire, served a variety of charitable functions (Owen 1981: 55–6).

Like monasteries, hospitals were founded in response to a variety of motives. The act of founding such an institution brought benefactors a degree of public recognition, while the prayers of the inmates were viewed as a form of religious intercession on behalf of the founders' souls. As altruistic gestures, hospitals for the poor, sick and aged met a real urban need – they represented welfare as well as religious provision. The social position of a hospital's founders varied according to its function. Leper hospitals might be established by municipal corporations; hospices by the military orders; houses for the poor by individuals, guilds and fraternities. Rotha Mary Clay (1909: 71-9) noted the particular concern shown by royal women and queens for founding hospitals and *leprosariae*. Patricia Cullum has commented upon the special responsibilities assumed by women in administering charity (1992).

The term hospital encompasses several distinct types of charitable institution. Medieval canonists divided hospitals between those which provided physical relief and those which provided a religious element through the mass, confession and facilities for burial (Rubin 1987: 104). In practice, all hospitals were at least semi-religious due to the believed connection between spiritual and physical disease. Some were properly monastic, and frequently followed the Rule of St Augustine. These hospitals were often established or run by monastic houses. Several nunneries actually evolved from hospitals, including St Mary de Pré (Herts.), Ilchester (Somerset), Thanington (Kent), and possibly Mary Magdalene, Bristol (S. Thompson 1991: 46). Aconbury (Herefords.), originally allied to the Hospitallers, may have acted as a hospital (ibid. 50), and nunneries maintained hospitals in or near the precincts of Grace Dieu (Leics.), Barking (Essex), Castle Hedingham (Essex) and Nunkeeling (N. Humbs.). Many nunneries established hospitals elsewhere for male inmates, including Wimborne (Dorset), Wilton (Wilts.), Romsey (Hants.) and Marrick (at Rerecross, N. Yorks.); Shaftesbury (Dorset) and Barking (at Ilford, Essex). Two Gilbertine double houses outside Lincoln evolved into charitable institutions. Infirmaries and pilgrims' hospices run by the Hospitallers and Trinitarians were serviced by sisters or lay-sisters, for example at Thelsford (Warwicks.) sisters were mentioned in 1300 and 1473 (Margaret Gray, pers. comm.).

Autonomous, semi-monastic hospitals were founded between 1100 and 1250. Miri Rubin (1987: 1) has estimated that a minimum of 220 hospitals were established in twelfth-century England, and 310 in the thirteenth century. From the fourteenth century, smaller hospitals were founded by rich merchants, lay-fraternities and guilds. At the Dissolution, approximately 800 hospitals were documented, and perhaps a further 300 are known to have previously fallen into disuse (R. M. Clay 1909; Knowles and Hadcock 1971). Most examples are assumed to have been mixed communities of male and female inmates, although 119 are recorded as being for men only, and 37 for women only (ibid.). The greater number of male institutions may reflect their dual purpose as hospitals and chantries, since many later foundations were private chantries which were combined with relief of the poor.

The earlier group of semi-monastic hospitals provided an alternative vocation for religious women. Mixed, or double, hospitals were presided over by a master and staffed by lay-brothers and sisters who cared for male and female inmates. The male and female staff were assisted by servants of both sexes. Occasionally a hospital was made up predominantly of sisters, with only a few brothers among the inmates, for instance the Sustren Spital, Winchester (Keene 1985: 979). In some hospitals there were hierarchies for both sexes which observed differences in religious vocation and social background. In some mixed hospitals, such as St Laurence, Canterbury, a prioress ruled over the female section of the house (Rubin 1987: 168). The sisters divided into those who wore habits and made regular religious observances, and those who worked in the hospital (R. M. Clay 1909: 152). The will of the poet Gower distinguished between two groups of sisters at St Thomas's, London: 'professed' and 'nurses of the sick' (ibid. 154). The professed women possessed a more contemplative vocation, such as those described at St John's, Reading: 'certyn relygyous women, wydowes in chast lyvngg in God's servyce praying nygt and day' (ibid. 26). Women of lower birth appear to have assisted with nursing, for example at Bridgwater (Somerset) (ibid. 153). A possible third category, that of serving woman, or 'sister-huswiff', was referred to at Heytesbury (Wilts.) (ibid. 156). Occasionally, female administrators were differentiated according to their task, much like the female officials who presided over German hospitals (Wiesner 1986: 39). At Northallerton (N. Yorks.), for example, two sisters cared for the sick, and a third looked after household affairs (R. M. Clay 1909: 153). Mixed hospitals were able to provide a greater range of services than male-run houses; in particular they cared for pregnant women and ran orphanages (Rubin 1987: 158).

In smaller, mixed hospitals, like St John the Baptist, Winchester, the dividing line between the brothers and sisters and their supporting servants was not always clear (Keene 1985: 816). It seems, however, that the permanent residents of the hospital undertook 'an act of religious or contemplative devotion as well as simple acceptance of charity' (ibid.). They received their food, accommodation and clothing in return for caring for the short-term patients.

Hospitals offered medieval English women a more flexible religious life than did nunneries. Their observances were less formal, more actively charitable, and available to a wider social spectrum of women. The differing roles and relationships between nunneries and hospitals may be glimpsed from the patterns of distribution of the two types of institution. Hospitals, in contrast to nunneries, were normally located near, or in, towns, and thus provided a religious life for urban women.

Like the monasteries to which they were akin, hospitals were laid out to fairly standard ordinances. The degree of formality engaged varied according to the function of the hospital, and the number of social groups which required segregation. The largest regular hospitals consisted of several cloisters serving specific groups within the community. For example, the sisters of St Leonard, York, had their own lodgings and refectory by 1364 (Cullum 1993). Hospitals of this size may have had a number of chapels, and a larger conventual church reserved for the monastic community. At St Leonard's the western part of the conventual church was reserved for the sisters (ibid. 15).

Where remains of hospitals survive, they are generally represented by the infirmary hall which housed the inmates. The hall had a chapel at its eastern end, so that in plan the two buildings were similar to the nave and chancel of a parish church. The inmates' beds were placed in the aisles of the building with the central space left clear for the movement of the staff. At Ospringe and Strood (Kent) the hall was divided into two aisles by a central arcade; the aisles were further subdivided into bed-recesses, or cubicles, possibly by partitions supported by a slot and post, as excavations at Cirencester (Gloucs.) suggested (Leech and McWhirr 1982).

A number of double or twin hospitals survive which were arranged to segregate male and female inmates (Godfrey 1955). At St John's, Canterbury, a long hall was divided into two equal parts, with access from both parts into a double chapel joined at right angles to the hall. The chapel was centrally partitioned to correspond with inmates coming from the two halls. To the north were separate latrine blocks serving the men's and women's sides of the hall (Tatton-Brown 1984). Strood's hall was centrally divided, with double doors entering a shared chapel (A. C. Harrison 1970). Alternative means of segregation were provided by parallel infirmary halls. At St John's, Winchester, two halls separated by a spinal wall shared a common chapel (*Medieval Archaeol.* 26, 1982: 185) (Figure 69). St Nicholas, Salisbury, retains evidence for twin halls and chapels arranged in parallel (Godfrey 1955: 34) (Figure 69). The infirmary hall(s) generally formed one side of a quadrangle, close, or cloister. At Salisbury the halls were to the south of the quadrangle, and an extant north range may have accommodated staff. Excavations at Ospringe (Kent) showed that the main buildings were arranged around a close (Smith 1980). The western range was made up by a common hall with chapel; to the south were the church and private chapel attached to a hall and gatehouse. To the north of the close is a four-bayed hall over an undercroft. To the west a separate close contained service buildings.

Variations on the mixed and double hospital plans included two-storey hospitals. These are later infirmary halls, of the fifteenth and sixteenth centuries, which segregated male and female inmates on two floors which communicated with the same chapel. This arrangement may be suggested for Saints John the Baptist and John the Evangelist, Sherborne (Dorset), Leicester Hospital, and All Saints, Stamford (Lincs.).

Arrangements at mixed rural hospices are suggested by excavations at St Giles, Brough (N. Yorks.). In the late thirteenth century St Giles was

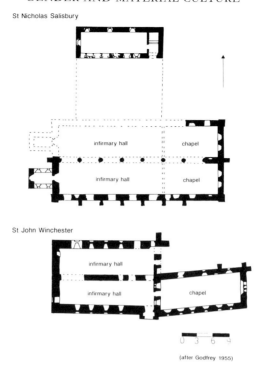

St Nicholas Salisbury

St John Winchester

(after Godfrey 1955)

Figure 69 Sexual segregation in medieval hospitals: St Nicholas, Salisbury and St John the Baptist, Winchester. At Salisbury twin halls and chapels were provided. At Winchester a median wall segregated male and female inmates. After Godfrey 1955.

transformed from a male to a mixed community. This change was roughly contemporary with a reorganization of the hospital, with a stone-built detached chapel positioned in relative isolation from the timber or half-timber domestic halls (Cardwell 1990).

From extant documents, architecture and excavated remains, it seems that mixed hospitals segregated male and female staff and inmates in separate closes or halls. In common with nunneries and double houses, efforts to separate the sexes during worship involved delineation of vertical and horizontal space. The much larger number of hospitals in comparison to nunneries, and their greater variation in function and status, provided an alternative outlet for practical religious (or semi-religious) commitment on the part of medieval English women.

176

7.3 ANCHORAGES: THE SOLITARY RELIGIOUS WOMAN

Mary has chosen the better part and it shall not be taken from her.
(Luke 10. 42).

Large numbers of religious women lived solitary lives as anchoresses attached to monastic or parish churches. Male and female anchorites were common from the twelfth century. They can be seen as part of a larger eremitic movement which encouraged individual religious experience. Anchorites chose to live on the margins of society – in emulation of the desert tradition. Thus their cells were positioned in liminal places. Many chose cemeteries, or the north sides of churches.

Anchoritic solitude was reinforced by a vow of permanent enclosure. To be immured in a cell represented a separation from the world and a symbolic death. Indeed, the author of the *Ancrene Wisse* commented, 'Looking at her own white hands does harm to many an anchoress whose hands are too beautiful because they are idle. They should scrape up earth every day out of the grave in which they shall rot' (Salu 1990: 51). But many anchorites appear to have combined a contemplative, solitary life with an intercessory role. From their cells some attracted local reputations for counselling, healing and prophesying. Others observed more formal isolation attached to nunneries, monasteries, hospitals and friaries. To some extent anchorages were regarded as monastic; their inmates followed a daily monastic timetable and cells were dissolved at the Reformation. Rarely, nunneries may have evolved from anchorages; at Fosse (Lincs.) the townspeople seem to have formalized an anchorage on the north side of the parish churchyard into a nunnery (S. Thompson 1991: 30).

By tabulating references to anchorites, Ann Warren (1985: 20) has demonstrated that English recluses were predominantly women. This trend is particularly strong for the thirteenth to fifteenth centuries, the ratio of female to male in each century being 4:1, 5:2 and 5:3, respectively. The social backgrounds of these women are only rarely apparent, since the anchoress was seldom referred to by her former identity. Nevertheless, from what is known about the social groups from which they were drawn, these appear to have been diverse. Some of the women were previously nuns, although this, too, can be difficult to ascertain (Warren 1984). Others were vowesses – widows who took vows of chastity upon their husband's death. It seems, however, that most vowesses were not expected to be permanently enclosed.

Warren has also shown that anchoritism began as a rural phenomenon, which became increasingly urban from the thirteenth century (1985: 38). She suggests that large numbers of women were drawn to anchoritism because the more unorthodox alternatives, such as beguinages, were unavailable to English women (ibid. 22). It has also been postulated that recluses were ethnically Anglo-Saxon, and that their piety appealed to those who did not wish to support the Anglo-Norman religious establishment (Holdsworth 1978: 203). However, female recluses were not specific to medieval England. Thirteenth-century beguines of northern France, who lived alone or in small groups, have been likened to recluses living in their own homes and supported by servants or companions (Delmaire 1989: 127). Female anchoritism was not peculiarly English, nor was it comparable to the actively charitable vocation of the Beguines. Only in England, however, did the movement for independent ascetic life remain formalized, and widespread, into the sixteenth century.

The enclosure of an anchoress was supervised and confirmed by the bishop in each diocese. Her spiritual and physical well-being were tested; guarantees were sought for financial support and the suitability of the cell (Warren 1985: 53). Patrons provided the recluse with her anchorage, and with food, clothes, fuel, servants and confessors for the period of enclosure. Benefactors might be royal, aristocratic or of the gentry, but urban anchoresses appear to have been supported by smaller bequests from individuals or trade guilds (Tanner 1984; Warren 1985).

From the few surviving anchorholds of solitary men and women, it seems that scale varied from a single room (for example Leatherhead, Surrey), possibly with an upper storey (such as Compton, Surrey), to the two-storey, four-room structure at Chester-le-Street (Durham) (R. M. Clay 1914: 83–4). Occasionally group anchorages were recorded, such as the trio of women at Tarrant Crawford (Dorset), each of whom in the fourteenth century occupied her own cell, and shared a male servant (Warren 1985: 33). Anchorages have not been subject to modern archaeological excavation; as a result the standards maintained for anchorages are not yet clear, in particular whether servants' accommodation was expected, and whether cooking and privy facilities were usual. The cell's basic requirement was a window or squint from which to observe the mass, and a grilled or shuttered window through which the confessor communicated. Anchorites' squints sometimes survive, for instance the cross-shaped opening on the north side of St John the Baptist, Newcastle upon Tyne, through which Christina Umfred (*c.* 1260) may have viewed the high altar (R. M. Clay 1914: 82). The fourteenth-century cell of Christina Carpenter stood in the angle between the chancel and the north transept at Shere, Surrey.

Churches with anchorages may have emphasized the delineation of sacred space even more strongly. At Lindsell (Essex), for example, an anchorite's window survives to the north of the chancel, and a Latin inscription survives over the south entrance to the nave which warned of spatial prohibitions placed on laymen, translated as, 'The scripture forbids laymen to sit in the chancel. Anyone who read, sings or speaks must go out' (Pritchard 1967: 74). The placing of the cell in relation to the church may have varied according to the sex and clerical status of the anchorite. This pattern is suggested by the rules observed in a twelfth-century enclosure ceremony. The position at which the postulant lies prostrate varied from mid-choir for clerics, entrance to the choir for unordained men, to west end of the church for women (Wilson 1910: 243–4). This orientation was sometimes maintained in the placing of cells. While many cells were to the north of the chancel, some women's anchorholds were located to the west. For example, the opening to Celia Moys' cell at Marhamchurch (Cornwall) (1403–5) can still be identified in the west wall of St Marwenna's, where a window with cusped head and transom has a lower part divided by a mullion (Pevsner 1970: 114). Emma de Raughtone's (c. 1430) cell at All Saints North Street, York, was built at the southern limit of the west end of the church. At the ground-floor level is a small oblong opening with chamfered reveals and remains of the original wrought-iron grill; above this is an an archway. Earlier this century, a third opening was unblocked at the upper-storey level, positioned to observe the high altar (RCHME York 3, 1972: 6).

Churches which supported anchoresses may have developed particular concerns for the female piety and mysticism with which the tradition was connected. These concerns would have been translated into the material culture of the church or cell. For instance, an antiquary's description of remains at Hampole (W. Yorks.) in 1831, may relate to the cell of the well-known mystic Richard Rolle (d. 1349), or anchoress Margaret de Kirkeby (d. 1401–5), both of whom resided at the nunnery. Wall-paintings were described of the emblems of the Passion and the Five Wounds with the heart in the centre (Whiting 1938). These were appropriate symbols for mystical contemplation which concentrated on Christ's suffering. The mystic tradition may have been fostered where anchoresses were attached to parish churches. Roughly contemporary with the cell at All Saints North Street, York, was the commissioning of the unique stained-glass window, 'The Pricke of Conscience'. This was a visualization of the most popular poem of the fifteenth century, at which time it was ascribed to Richard Rolle, who is cited as author in the majority of extant fifteenth-century manuscript editions (Allen 1927: 387). The parishioners who maintained the anchoress may have held the renowned mystic Rolle in special regard, due to his authorship of a rule for anchoresses, 'The Form of Living' (c. 1348).

An early copy of another rule, the *Ancrene Wisse*, was translated by Bishop Simon of Ghent (1297–1315) for his sisters, who were anchoresses at Tarrant Crawford (Dorset) (R. M. Clay 1914: 98). Their group anchorage appears to have adjoined the parish church on the south wall of the thirteenth-century nave, where an absence of windows suggests a former structure abutted. The nave retains an unusual group of fourteenth-century wall-paintings (Figure 70). Thirteen panels depict scenes from the life of St Margaret of Antioch (Tristram 1955: 255). This iconography may have sounded particular resonance for female religious, an idea confirmed by the liturgy of the nearby Cistercian nunnery at Tarrant, which included the

Figure 70 Tarrant Crawford parish church (Dorset): wall-paintings of the Life of St Margaret of Antioch adorn the upper register of the south wall of the nave, against the external wall of which stood the anchorage. Thirteen scenes are depicted; here scenes three to seven are shown: the provost Olybrius approaches; Margaret appears before him; she is imprisoned; she refuses to worship idols; the saint is scourged; she continues to defy the provost. Her torture continues until she is swallowed by the dragon and emerges from its belly unharmed.

Passio of St Margaret of Antioch, more appropriate to parochial than monastic liturgies (Chadd 1986: 309). Margaret was a saint favoured by women in childbirth, a juxtaposition resulting from her own legendary escape from the belly of the dragon. Her relevance to celibate women may appear remote. However, maternal imagery is prevalent in writings associated with anchoresses, such as Julian of Norwich's 'Revelations of Divine Love' and the *vita* of Christina of Markyate.

One version of the life of Margaret seems to have been particularly aimed at celibate women. This was contained in the Katherine Group, associated with the *Ancrene Wisse*, and included an additional speech by the dragon regarding the dangers of sexual temptation (Elkins 1988: 159). Margaret's struggle with the dragon was paralleled by the story of St George. It may be significant that wall-paintings of St George at Hardham (Sussex) were roughly contemporary to an anchorite (of unknown sex) recorded in 1253. Margaret's life was sometimes interchanged with that of Pelagia (the actress of Antioch), the desert recluse who disguised herself as a monk and lived a penitential life in a solitary cell (B. Ward 1987: 60). Margaret's iconography may have referred to the desert tradition of the female recluse, in which Pelagia, Mary of Egypt and the Virgin of Jerusalem assumed male identities in order to undertake the anchoritic life. The English recluse Christina of Markyate donned male clothing in her struggle to protect her virginity.

Wall-paintings in the parish church at Faversham (Kent) repeat the themes of motherhood and the potential swapping of male and female religious identities. Anchoresses were recorded as living on the north side of the church at Faversham from the fifteenth century, although others may have been in place contemporary to the fourteenth-century execution of the wall-paintings. These are located on the south-east column of the north transept, and consist of three tiers of scenes. The lower and middle tiers deal with Christ's birth and childhood: the Annunciation, the Visitation, the Adoration of the Magi, the Nativity, the Annunciation to the Shepherds, and the Presentation in the Temple. The top tier is concerned with Christ's death: the Crucifixion and the Marys at the Tomb (Tristram 1955: 171–2). This iconographic scheme of Christ's birth and death takes on the connotations of Easter, which may be expected in the north transept area of churches (see p. 139). The position of the Holy Women in the Easter drama has already been discussed (see p. 139), with the implications for cross-dressing which are apparent for priests participating in the drama, and for representations of the Marys at the Tomb. Iconography in the setting of an anchoress's cell observed general patterns for female associations, and the mystics' predilection for maternal imagery and the suffering of Christ. In addition, references to Margaret and the Marys may have signalled cross-dressing to some observers – a reminder of the male identity assumed by anchoresses of the desert tradition, and of the self-renunciation demanded by the anchoritic vow.

7.4 HERMITAGES: RELIGIOUS WOMEN BEYOND THE PALE?

[Martha] had a sister called Mary, which also sat at Jesus's feet, and heard his word.

(Luke 10. 39).

Although informal communities of female hermits were quickly regularized into nunneries (see pp. 90–1), and women did not figure among the large number of unenclosed solitary hermits, some communal hermitages may have accommodated women. Hermitages for men were often independent institutions which eventually adopted a monastic rule, or were absorbed into one of the reformed monastic orders (for example, the male houses of Nostell, Fountains, Kirkstall (Yorks.) and Llanthony (Gwent). Other communal hermitages continued to be founded, either as ascetic private monasteries supported by secular patrons, or as retreat houses of more orthodox monasteries. Privately founded hermitages attracted the patronage of women, demonstrated, for instance, by the benefactress's effigy in the tomb chapel at Warkworth cave hermitage (Northumb.). The informality of privately founded hermitages may have encouraged the participation of religious women as inmates. Glimpses of previously unrecognized double, or predominantly female, hermitages can sometimes be found in documents and place-names associated with excavated sites.

Grafton Regis (Northants.) is the only excavated example of a private, communal hermitage (*Medieval Archaeol.* 10, 1966: 202–4). Documents associated with the site indicate that Grafton was a double hermitage, occupied by 'brothers, sisters and other ministers of the house' (Lincoln Record Office, Bishop's register 2, fo. 125v; Parker 1982: 250). Its unorthodoxy resulted from continued private patronage by the Woodville family, who retained the right to elect the master (ibid.). Excavations showed that Grafton was arranged similarly to a small nunnery, with a small thirteenth-century cloister to the north of the church (Figure 71). The church contained burials in the east end, and was screened into a short chancel and a long aisleless nave. It was joined to the south by a square cell which also contained burials, and a wider rectangular projection parallel with the nave. The resulting arrangement somewhat resembles the parallel aisle churches of double houses and twin-hospitals. Two domestic ranges flanked the north and east sides of the cloister. A staircase in the east cloister walk led to upper storeys, and a square external projection appears to have been a latrine with drain.

To the west of the cloister, a domestic complex was added in the fourteenth or fifteenth centuries, possibly arranged around a close or outer cloister. This contained ovens, hearths, a vat and kiln. Its separation from the main cloister is suggested by the alignment of the precinct wall, which bisected the complex into religious and service areas. Positioned on the

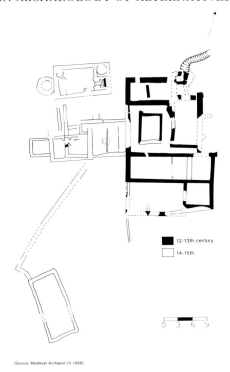

(Source: Medieval Archaeol 10 1966)

Figure 71   A double hermitage: Grafton Regis (Northants.). After *Medieval Archaeology* 10, 1966: 202–4.

precinct wall, to the south-west of the cloister, was another range. This building was placed to allow access to the proposed 'parallel aisle' of the church, and to the dovecote and service buildings. Such a combination of religious observances and domestic duties may have been appropriate to sisters or lay-sisters of the house. Leyser (1984: 49) has described the sexual division of labour in continental hermitages, where men administered the sacraments and provided protection, but women did a great deal of manual labour. Arrangements at Grafton, in common with all mixed monasteries, emphasized the spatial segregation of groups within the community.

A second hermitage site is suggested by its place-name, and antiquaries' descriptions. At Chew Valley (Somerset) there were earthworks known as Nunnery Fields, and medieval ruins known as St Cross Nunnery (Rahtz and Greenfield 1977: 124). Sir William Dugdale's *Monasticon* (1655–73) recorded a nunnery at Chewstoke (Somerset), which was described as a cell for four nuns. Excavations at the site were interpreted as revealing structures appropriate for a secular manor or grange (Rahtz and Greenfield 1977: 125). However, the excavated features at Chew were equally characteristic of a small nunnery (see Chapter 4, section 4). St Cross was sited

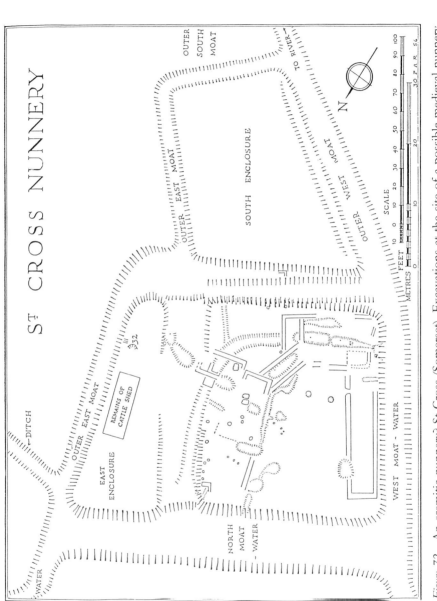

Figure 72 An eremitic nunnery? St Cross (Somerset). Excavations at the site of a possible medieval nunnery (Rahtz and Greenfield 1977). Reproduced with permission of Philip Rahtz.

on a sandy prominence, where three enclosures were formed by moats, one of which contained a series of twelfth-century timber structures on stone foundations, with an associated drainage system (Figure 72). Later stone buildings formed eleven units, or rooms, not necessarily joined into ranges (ibid. 127). The form and construction of the buildings, the siting of the settlement, and the use of moats, are all features in keeping with smaller nunneries. The later stone-built rooms would be consistent with the *familiae* recognized in nunneries from the fourteenth century, or with the self-contained huts present in communal hermitages of the south-west (for example, St Helen's, Scilly, O'Neill 1964). An unstratified artefact associated with the site was interpreted as a medieval nun's finger-ring (Figure 73) (Rahtz and Greenfield 1977: 326).

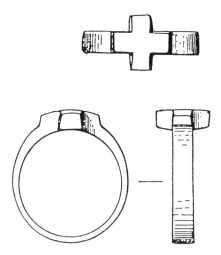

Figure 73 Nun's finger ring found near the site of St Cross (Somerset) (scale 2:3). From Rahtz and Greenfield 1977. Reproduced with permission of Philip Rahtz. Scale 2:3.

Ownership of the site at Chewstoke has been linked to the Sancta Cruce family, who may have played a role similar to that of the Woodvilles at Grafton Regis. In 1325, Agnes de Sancta Cruce was prioress at Barrow Gurney (also known as Minchin Barrow, Somerset) (ibid. 122). Indeed, a relationship may be postulated between Barrow and Chewstoke, in which the latter served as a hermitage and retreat house to the former nunnery.

In his *Itinerary*, Leland listed three further nunneries for which no definite records survive: Mangotsfield (Gloucs.), Marshfield (Gloucs.) and Sandwich (Kent). These too may have been double or female hermitages, supported by private sponsorship. R. M. Clay's survey of medieval hermitages listed forty-two sites as private foundations, including at least one mixed community at Stratford Saye (Loddon, Hants.) of *'inclusus et heremita'* and brethren (Clay 1914: 219).

The private, elusive nature of these sites is reminiscent of the family monasteries of the sub-Roman and early medieval periods. Like them, the hermitages of Grafton Regis and Chewstoke were family concerns which easily reverted to secular occupation. Excavations at both have suggested the cessation of monastic activity by or during the fifteenth century. It is precisely this flexibility of observances and fluidity between secular and religious, which provided an alternative lifestyle for religious women.

7.5 CONCLUSIONS: THE 'SINFUL WOMAN'

To some extent religious women arrived in beguinages, hospitals, anchorages and hermitages as a result of the opportunities open to them. Certainly beguinages and hospitals accepted a greater social range of women than nunneries, and hospitals offered a greater number of places. The largely urban siting of beguinages, hospitals and anchorages was in contrast to the rural character of nunneries, and provided openings in centres of densest population.

The enclosed, contemplative life of the nunnery is in contrast to the active charity of the beguinages and hospitals. The opportunity – or choice – of vocation in Leah over Rachel, or Martha over Mary, created an alternative religious role for women. Hermitages and anchorages served women more ascetic in their outlooks than those in nunneries. These eremitic women chose strict enclosure and a form of contemplation more closely linked to spiritual learning. Anchoresses were strongly linked to mysticism, both in the books that they owned (R. M. Clay 1953), and in their own visionary writings. Devotional meditations were a natural form of worship for religious women, who were excluded from the formal Latin offices of the church (Petroff 1986: 9). Their mystic and ecstatic experiences may have resulted from their physical isolation as ascetics, and their pyschological alienation from mainstream secular and religious concerns.

The four differing lifestyles are drawn together by their penitential strand. Women in beguinages, hermitages, and possibly some *maisons dieu*, chose the voluntary poverty of the *Vita Apostolica*. Twelfth-century hermits were particularly concerned with private sin and its expiation. Their emphasis on penance and contrition gave a central place to Mary Magdalene (Leyser 1984: 64), a sinful woman 'healed of evil spirits and infirmities ... out of whom went seven devils' (Luke 8. 2). Churches linked to traditions of female eremiticism may have given special prominence to Mary Magdalene, for instance wall-paintings at St Pega, Peakirk (Cambs.), associated with Pega's eighth-century hermitage, include a Passion cycle culminating with the *Noli me tangere*, Christ's appearance to Mary Magdalene (Rouse 1953: 140).

186

Women administering to the poor and sick in hospitals were expected to encourage physical and spiritual healing. While sickness continued to be linked with sin, hospitals were places of prayer and penance (Rubin 1987: 151). Mary Magdalene was linked to healing through the episodes of anointing, her special place at the Resurrection, and the association of Mary of Bethany with the house of Simon the leper and the illness of Lazarus. Through a conflation of the Biblical Marys, Mary Magdalene became a popular saint for the dedications of hospitals, particularly leper hospitals. Representations of Mary Magdalene formed the subject of wall-paintings commissioned for hospitals, for example at Durham (R. M. Clay 1909: 163). In contrast, dedications to Mary Magdalene were rare for nunneries, which were most frequently dedicated to the Virgin Mary.

The anchoress identified with early Desert ascetics, whose caves represented penitential prisons. Lives of the Desert Fathers and Harlots emphasized sequences of repentance and conversion. The women were generally reformed prostitutes, who achieved sanctity through the acceptance of mercy (B. Ward 1987: 7). The main role model was, of course, Mary Magdalene. In her apocryphal life she lived the penitential existence of a solitary recluse in the caves at Baume (Provence). Similarly much of the *Ancrene Wisse* concentrated on penance; and the enclosure ceremony for anchoresses included a gospel reading of Luke 10, referring to the better part of Mary over Martha (Elkins 1988: 151–2).

The four alternative vocations for religious women are outwardly diverse, but bound together by their emphasis on penitence – a religious theme embodied by Mary Magdalene. Such imagery is in sharp contrast with that observed by cloistered nuns, religious women who celebrated the unique status of the Virgin Mary as mother of Christ and Queen of Heaven (see pp. 140–8). This contrast is in keeping with the semi-religious nature of the alternative vocations, lifestyles which may have offered greater expression and intensity of devotion, through the asceticism of the anchoress or eremitic, or the active charity of the beguine or hospital sister.

8

CONCLUSIONS: GENDER AND MEDIEVAL MONASTICISM

8.1 PATTERNS IN THE ARCHAEOLOGY OF RELIGIOUS WOMEN

This book began by defining gender as the social construction of difference between men and women. Gender as a comparative and analytical category has thrown up patterns of similarity and difference in the monasticism of medieval men and women.

Differences can be seen in the provision of monasteries for men and women and their institutional characteristics. Early medieval monasticism encouraged a greater fluidity between male and female communities, and a degree of informality which was not tolerated in later medieval monasticism (see pp. 25–36). Later medieval nunneries were less common than religious houses for men; there were approximately 150 nunneries in medieval England and six times that number of monasteries for men and friaries (see pp. 36–41). Nunneries affiliated to particular monastic orders were founded later than their male counterparts, and at lower economic scales. These factors reflect the different social level at which the majority of post-Conquest nunneries were founded, and the social group to which they were predominantly linked: the local gentry.

The contrasting expectations placed on medieval religious men and women is suggested by the landscape settings of their settlements and the economic levels at which they operated. Like the more ascetic male houses, nunneries were set in liminal surroundings, with regard to both the natural landscape and the topography of towns (see pp. 63–9). However, in contrast to their male counterparts, nunneries were not endowed in order to achieve their self-sufficiency. Nunneries seldom altered landscapes or initiated industrial activities; indeed their outer courts took on a more domestic function (see pp 74, 83–5). It seems that the majority of post-Conquest nunneries were never established in order to fulfil a major tenet of monasticism: to be self-sufficient in all things.

To a great extent, the architecture of nunneries was based on standard monastic forms. But the forms varied from male houses in their arrangement, construction and development. Nunnery cloisters developed slowly, and often consisted of little more than a penticed walkway. It was not unusual for the buildings around the cloister, with the exception of the church, to be built in timber or cob, rather than the usual stone (see p. 95). Nunnery churches were also simple, housing the minimum number of altars, and often remaining aisleless parallelograms. Nunneries shared their churches with parochial congregations, so that rather incongruous arrangements developed in contrast to those known in male houses. In particular, they developed 'parallel aisles' to separate the church of the convent from that of the parish, and galleries to segregate the various social groups entering the church (see pp. 99–109). Because nunneries were frequently established in association with villages, and they shared their churches with parochial congregations, the number of secular people visiting their precincts must have been significant.

In many ways the smaller nunneries resembled manor houses more than standard monasteries. In addition to their more modest construction, they sometimes had discontinuous ranges flanking a courtyard, rather than the fully developed monastic plan (see p. 121). Many used moats as precinct boundaries, features which were more usual as a symbol of gentry aspirations associated with manors (Dyer 1989). In contrast to the lavish provision known at male monasteries, nunneries possessed only basic sanitary require-ments, generally consisting of garderobes or small latrines flushed by a single drain (see p. 113). The west ranges of nunneries were reserved for guest-houses, and were often arranged as double-ended halls in keeping with gentry houses (see pp. 117–19). Some, like Kirklees (W. Yorks.) developed service wings resembling the cross-wings attached to manor houses (see pp. 74, 107, 126), and many possessed the church galleries which were at this time common to manorial chapels.

By the fifteenth or sixteenth centuries nunneries were taking on an increasingly domestic character. Storage, baking and brewing were con-ducted within the main cloisters of several of the Yorkshire nunneries (see p. 123), and excavations in outer court areas at St Mary's, Clerkenwell (London), and Elstow (Bedfords.) have indicated that these areas were used for domestic occupation (see pp. 83–5). The monastic space of the cloister broke down in many of the wealthier houses from the fourteenth century, with the community splintering into smaller households of women (*familiae*) (see p. 123). Yet at the vast majority of nunneries, the abbess or prioress never adopted a separate lodge (see pp. 119–20). In contrast to male houses, communal space appears to have been better guarded against the encroachment by the desire for privacy.

Space within the nunnery reproduced divisions created through the ecclesiastical hierarchy, for instance in patterns of seating in the choir and refectory (for example, at Denney, Cambs.). In addition, space was used to separate male and female groups and to delineate liturgical roles, particularly in the positioning of the sacristy as the male presence within the nunnery. The sacristy was sometimes the most highly ornamented room within the cloister (see pp. 109–11), and was situated in order to allow access to the priest without entering the more private parts of the nunnery. The male and female areas of the cloister seem to have been accentuated by architectural embellishments, so that male representations were common in the sacristy or guest house but not within the deeper space of the nunnery (see pp. 159–60). A formal analysis of monastic space has shown that monasteries and nunneries reserved their most sequestered spaces for different rooms. In monasteries the chapter house and sacristy were most secluded, whereas in nunneries it was more likely to be the dormitory of the nuns. In addition, the nuns were guarded by a greater physical degree of enclosure (see pp. 164–6).

Segregation of religious men and women was felt equally in hospitals (see pp. 175–6) and mixed hermitages (see p. 183), and gender determined the positioning of the anchorite during the enclosure ceremony and the location of the cell in relation to the church (see pp. 178–9). In parish churches, patterns of seating and iconographic schemes were linked to rules of gender and space (see pp. 134–5, and also Aston 1990). Occasionally in secular contexts the sexes were allowed to mingle in their religious observances. For instance, fraternities encouraged mixed celebrations, such as the Corpus Christi feast in which brothers and sisters processed, attended mass, feasted at mixed tables and finally dispersed in couples to distribute food to the poor (Rubin 1986: 107).

There is no doubt that when gender is adopted as a comparative category of analysis it is possible to identify previously unrecognized differences between men's and women's monasteries. These distinctions are less apparent for the wealthier nunneries, mainly those established as pre-Conquest houses in Wessex, but this contrast within the range of female houses only stresses the extent to which gender and class are interconnected. Some may argue that the divergences between male and female houses are not a product of gender, but rather of the greater poverty of the nuns. To the contrary, I would suggest that nunneries were established for different purposes than monasteries by a different social group, largely the gentry, and were modelled on different prototypes, particularly those drawn from gentry settlement. If nunneries looked different from monasteries, were placed in different landscape situations, and were never endowed in order to achieve self-sufficiency, this is because medieval patrons had a different purpose in mind for medieval religious women.

Previously historians have suggested that nunneries were poor because their piety was less valued by their medieval contemporaries (C. N. L. Brooke 1974; Burton 1979; Butler 1989; S. Thompson 1991). However, this assumption has been disproven by Oliva in a study of 4,000 medieval wills from the Diocese of Norwich (1994). Oliva has shown that the wills of local gentry and merchants continued to bequeath gifts and money to the nuns even after monks had lost favour with benefactors. The nuns and friars continued to be supported by lower- and middle-ranking local people, precisely the social group from which the founders and inmates of nunneries were drawn and with whom the nuns would have had frequent contact. These people valued and respected the prayers of their local religious women. The founders of nunneries must have anticipated this local network of support, and endowed their nunneries accordingly. Perhaps nunneries never achieved economic prosperity because they were not intended to do so? Certainly the purpose of nunneries is clear. From the nature of their archaeology and the evidence of medieval wills, it seems that nunneries were founded in order to interact closely with the local community.

It would seem then that medieval female religious experience was *different* from that of men, not *less successful*. It has previously been misunderstood because it has been judged according to standards defined by male monasticism (see pp. 24–5). Indeed, the less orthodox female vocations have frequently been overlooked by historians and archaeologists. These alternative vocations, the beguine, sister in a hospital, anchoress and female hermit, were constructed according to different cultural and iconographic metaphors from that of the cloistered nun. Material culture associated with nunneries has suggested that nuns celebrated devotion to Christ, and to the Virgin Mary as Mother of Christ (see pp. 141–8). Women participating in the alternative religious roles, however, seem to have identified more strongly with the figure of Mary Magdalene (see pp. 186–7). These oppositions were at the root of their spirituality: repentance *versus* the purity of the nun; penitence *versus* the contemplation of the cloister. Patterns in the archaeology of religious women comment on the diversity of gender roles and expectations ascribed to medieval monastic men and women.

8.2 GENDER AND MATERIAL CULTURE: *HABITUS*, AGENCY AND IDENTITY

It certain respects nunnery architecture demonstrates the active nature of material culture, and the multiple meanings to which it is subject. The architecture of the nunnery was active in constructing images of female spirituality. Observers would have been drawn into a process of interpretation, in which a building's form or spatial orientation was given meaning. The primary meaning engaged by the patron or convent may have referred to an archetype, or particular iconographic message. For example, nunneries tended to have two-storey refectories, the iconography of which suggests the *coenaculum*, the upper storey of the home of Mary, where women participated in the early Church at Jerusalem (see pp. 116–17). The perceived meaning of an architectural form may have altered over time, and certainly differed according to the social identity of the observer. An example is the iconography of the north cloister, which may have represented the Virgin Mary at Christ's right hand, or may have referred to more ancient associations of women on the north of churches (see pp. 133–40). The particular message intended may have been reinterpreted and transformed by subsequent generations of inmates of nunneries, who commissioned seals which expressed a distinctive collective identity linked to the Virgin Mary as Mother (see pp. 143–8). A building's iconography signalled overlapping, multiple meanings. The message intended at any time, or directed towards any specific group, can sometimes be better understood in conjunction with other media, such as manuscript illumination, stained glass, wall-painting and sculpture. The ambiguity of the iconography of medieval architecture highlights the need for such multi-disciplinary studies.

Monastic architecture was central to the social construction of difference between medieval religious men and women. Religious identities, personal mobility and perceptions of sexuality were maintained through space, boundaries and architectural embellishment. A sense of masculinity or femininity, a gender identity, was constructed in relation to other factors, such as patronage, filiation (associations to a monastic order), and class. Material culture was used to construct the *habitus* which linked common interest groups. Nunneries were connected to the gentry through their material culture, to particular families through choices in siting and architecture (see pp. 53–6), and to some extent to particular monastic orders by similarities in architectural form (see pp. 52–3). However, the strongest pull was in the *habitus* of gentry and aristocratic women. Sexual segregation in monasteries and the greater enclosure of monastic women was in keeping with the lives which secular women of the 'inner household' lived in manor houses and castles (see pp. 167–9). Gender and class combined to construct a *habitus* for women, a common-sense knowledge constructed with reference to the material world, which connected monastic and secular gender roles.

The seclusion of women was sometimes a product of their own agency. Where religious women chose to transform monastic space they divided the community into 'households' much like those which predominated in upper-status secular contexts (see p. 123). These transformations demonstrate the ability of female agents to act upon material culture to bring about change, yet they illustrate the extent to which women could be complicit in reproducing gender relations which appear to render them subordinate.

8.3 GENDER AS AN ANALYTICAL CATEGORY: NEW PERSPECTIVES FOR MEDIEVAL ARCHAEOLOGY?

What new perspectives have been gained by adopting gender as an analytical category? By prioritizing debates surrounding material culture and gender it has been possible to liberate at least one aspect of medieval archaeology, 'the handmaid', from the agenda defined by documentary history (see pp. 8–13). In this study, documents have been used to expand or corroborate rather than to provide explanation. By stepping outside the bounds of traditional monastic history, it has been possible to enrich our definition of monasticism. For the first time it has been possible to see the archaeological variance between monasteries for men and women, and to demonstrate that these incongruities were linked to gender.

Adopting gender as an analytical category provides a new way of looking at medieval monasticism. Moreover, it challenges previous interpretations and methods as being incomplete and incorrect. Like other case studies in gender archaeology (Gero and Conkey (eds) 1991), this new perspective reveals that the male-biased approach constitutes 'bad science' which is neither rigorous nor complete (Wylie 1991: 38). Moreover, that the archaeology of religious women remained for so long 'hidden from history' comments on the androcentrism of previous interpretations and the structural sexism of the discipline of archaeology.

Gender as an analytical category requires us to re-examine our own values, to confront the preconceptions which we project onto our interpretations, and the assumptions which we make in our analyses and working environments. Gender archaeology not only brings us new perspectives on the past, it should encourage us to re-evaluate our lives in the present and to consider the possibility for change in the future. The contribution of gender to archaeology is to enable a more comprehensive, humanistic, and sensitive study of the lives of men and women in the past.

BIBLIOGRAPHY

Allan, J. P. (1984) *Medieval and Post-medieval Finds from Exeter* (Exeter Archaeological Reports 3) Exeter.

Allen, H. E. (1927; 1966) *Writings Ascribed to Richard Rolle, Hermit of Hampole*. New York: Modern Language Association of America.

Andrén, A. (1985) *Den Urbana Scenen*, (Acta Archaeologica Lundensia 13) Malmö, Sweden.

Andrews, D., Cook, A., Quant, V. and Veasey, E. A. (1981) 'The archaeology and topography of Nuneaton Priory', *Transactions of the Birmingham and Warwickshire Archaeological Society* 91: 55–81.

Ardener, S. (1981) 'Ground rules and social maps for women: an introduction', in S. Ardener (ed.) *Women and Space*. London: Croom Helm.

Armstrong, K. (1986) *The Gospel According to Woman*. London: Pan.

Armytage, G. (1908) 'Kirklees Priory', *Yorkshire Archaeological Journal* 20: 24–32.

Astill, G. and Grant, A. (eds) (1988) *The Countryside of Medieval England*. Oxford: Blackwell.

—— (1988a) 'The medieval countryside: approaches and perceptions', in G. Astill and A. Grant (eds) *The Countryside of Medieval England*, 1–11. Oxford: Blackwell.

—— (1988b) 'The medieval countryside: efficiency, progress and change', in G. Astill and A. Grant (eds), *The Countryside of Medieval England*, 213–34. Oxford: Blackwell.

Aston, Margaret (1990) 'Segregation in church', in W. J. Shiels and D. Wood (eds) *Women in the Church*. Studies in Church History 27: 237–94. Oxford: Blackwell.

Aston, Mick and Munton, A. (1976) 'A survey of Bordesley Abbey and its water control system', in P. A. Rahtz and S. Hirst (eds) *Bordesley Abbey* (BAR 23), 24–37. Oxford: British Archaeological Reports.

Atkin, M. W. and Gater, J. A. (1983; unpubl.) 'Carrow Priory, Norwich, resistivity survey', Norfolk Museums Service Archive.

Atwood, M. (1985; 1987) *The Handmaid's Tale*, London: Virago.

Austin, D. (1990) 'The "proper study" of medieval archaeology', in D. Austin and L. Alcock (eds) *From the Baltic to the Black Sea: Studies in Medieval Archaeology*, 9–42. London: Unwin Hyman.

—— and Thomas, J. (1990) 'The "proper study" of medieval archaeology: a case study', in D. Austin and L. Alcock (eds) *From the Baltic to the Black Sea: Studies in Medieval Archaeology*, 43–78. London: Unwin Hyman.

Avril, J. (1989) 'Les fondations, l'organisation et l'évolution des établissements de moniales dans le diocèse d'Angers (du XI au XIII siècle)', in M. Parisse (ed.) *Les Religieuses en France au XIIIe siècle*, 27–67. Nancy: Presses Universitaires de Nancy.

Bailey, R. (n. d., unpubl.) 'The Hovingham Slab'.

Baker, D. (1971) 'Excavations at Elstow Abbey, Bedfords, 1968–70', *Bedfordshire Archaeological Journal* 6: 55–64.

—— and Baker, E. (1989) 'Research designs: timber phases and outbuildings with special reference to Elstow Abbey and Grove Priory', in R. Gilchrist and H. Mytum (eds) *The Archaeology of Rural Monasteries* (BAR 203), 261–76. Oxford: British Archaeological Reports.

Bandaranayake, S. (1989) 'Monastery plan and social formation: the spatial organization of the Buddhist monastery complexes of the Early and Middle Historical period in Sri Lanka and changing patterns of political power', in D. Miller, M. Rowlands and C. Tilley (eds) *Domination and Resistance*, 179–95. London: Unwin and Hyman.

Barley, M. W. (1964) 'The medieval borough of Torksey: excavations 1960–2', *Antiquaries Journal* 44: 164–87.

—— (1986) *Houses and History*, London: Faber.

Barlow, F. (1979) *The English Church*, 1000–1066. London: Longman.

Barrett, J. (1988) 'Fields of discourse: reconstituting a social archaeology', *Critique of Anthropology* 7.3: 5–16.

Barrière, B. (1984) 'Corrize: Aubazine, Monastère de Coyroux', *Archéologie médiévale* 17: 188–9.

Bascombe, K. (1987) 'Two charters of King Suebred of Essex', in K. Neale (ed.), *An Essex Tribute to F. G. Emmison*, 85–95. London: Leopard Head Press.

Bateson, M. (1899) 'The origin and early history of early double monasteries', *Transactions of the Royal Historical Society* 13: 137–98.

Beaudry, M. C., Cook, L. J., and Mrozowski, S. A. (1991) 'Artifacts and active voices: material culture as social discourse', in R. H. McGuire and R. Paynter (eds) *The Archaeology of Inequality*, 150–91. Oxford: Blackwell.

Beaussart, P. and Maliet, V. (1983) 'Les pavements de l'abbatiale de Fontenelle à Maing', *Revue du Nord* 65: 123–47.

Becquet, J. (1989) 'Les religieuses dans le diocèse de Limôges au XIII siècle', in M. Parisse (ed.) *Les Religieuses en France au XIIIe siècle*, 69–74. Nancy: Presses Universitaires de Nancy.

Bede (*HE = Historia Ecclesiastica*): Colgrave, B. and Mynors, R. A. B. (eds) (1969) *Bede's Ecclesiastical History of the English People*. Oxford: Oxford University Press.

Bender, B. (1989) 'The roots of inequality', in D. Miller, M. Rowlands and C. Tilley (eds) *Domination and Resistance*, 83–95. London: Unwin Hyman.

Beresford, G. (1974) 'The medieval manor of Penhallam, Jacobstow, Cornwall', *Medieval Archaeology* 18: 90–127.

Beresford, M. and St Joseph, J. K. S. (1979) *Medieval England: An Aerial Survey*. Cambridge: Cambridge University Press.

Berman, C. H. (1988) 'Men's houses, women's houses: the relationship between the sexes in twelfth-century monasticism', in A. MacLeish (ed.) *The Medieval Monastery*, 43–52. St Cloud, Minn.: North Star Press.

Biddick, K. (1989) *The Other Economy: Pastoral Husbandry on a Medieval Estate*. Berkeley: University of California Press.

Binford, L. (1989) *Debating Archaeology*. London: Academic Books.

Blair, J. (1985) 'Saint Leonard's Chapel, Clanfield', *Oxoniensia* 50: 209–14.

—— (1986) 'The foundation of Goring Priory', *Oxoniensia* 51: 194–7.

—— (1987) 'Saint Frideswide reconsidered', *Oxoniensia* 52: 71–127.

—— (1988) 'Thornbury, Binsey: a probable defensive enclosure associated with Saint Frideswide', *Oxoniensia* 53: 3–20.

—— and Steane, J. M. (1982) 'Investigations at Cogges, Oxfords, 1978–81: the priory and the parish church', *Oxoniensia* 47: 37–125.

Blunt, J. (ed.) (1873) *The Myroure of Oure Ladye* (Early English Text Society Extra Series 19).

Boase, T. S. R. (1971) 'Fontevrault and the Plantagenets', *Journal of the British Archaeological Association* 34: 1–10.

Boddington, A. (1987) 'Raunds, Northamptonshire: analysis of a country church-yard', *World Archaeology* 18.3: 411–25.

Bolton, B. (1973) 'Mulieres Sanctae', in D. Baker (ed.) *Sanctity and Secularity: The Church and the World* (Studies in Church History 10), 77–95. Oxford: Blackwell.

—— (1983) *The Medieval Reformation*. London: Edward Arnold.

Bond, C. J. (1989) 'Water management in the rural monastery', in R. Gilchrist and H. Mytum (eds) *The Archaeology of Rural Monasteries* (BAR 203), 83–111. Oxford: British Archaeological Reports.

—— (1993) 'Water management in the urban monastery', in R. Gilchrist and H. Mytum (eds) *Advances in Monastic Archaeology* (BAR 227), 43–78. Oxford: British Archaeological Reports.

Bond, S. and Maines, C. (1988) 'The archaeology of monasticism: a survey of recent work in France', *Speculum* 63: 794–825.

Bony, P. (1987) 'An introduction to the study of Cistercian seals: the Virgin as mediatrix, then protectorix on the seals of Cistercian abbeys', in M. P. Lillich (ed.), *Studies in Cistercian Art and Architecture*, vol. 3: 201–40. Kalamazoo: Cistercian Publications.

Bourdieu, P. (1977) *Outline of a Theory of Practice*. Cambridge: Cambridge University Press.

Bourdillon, A. F. C. (1926; 1965) *The Order of Minoresses in England*, Manchester: Manchester University Press.

Braithwaite, M. (1982) 'Decoration as ritual symbol: a theoretical proposal and an ethnographic study in southern Sudan', in I. Hodder (ed.) *Symbolic and Structural Archaeology*, 80–8. Cambridge: Cambridge University Press.

Brakspear, H. (1900) 'Lacock Abbey, Wilts,' *Archaeologia* 57: 125–58.

—— (1903) 'Burnham Abbey', *Records of Buckinghamshire* 8: 517–40.

—— (1922–3) 'Excavations at some Wiltshire monasteries', *Archaeologia* 73: 225–52.

—— and St John Hope, W. (1907) 'Plan of Kirklees', *Proceedings of the Society of Antiquaries of London* 21: 184–7.

Brooke, C. N. L. (1974) *The Monastic World 1000–1300*, London: Elek.

—— (1986) 'St Bernard, the patrons and monastic planning', in C. Norton and D. Park (eds) *Cistercian Art and Architecture in the British Isles*, 11–23. Cambridge: Cambridge University Press.

Brooke, R. B. and Brooke, C. N. L. (1978) 'St Clare', in D. Baker (ed.) *Medieval Women* (Studies in Church History, Subsidia 1), 275–88. Oxford: Blackwell.

Brown, P. (1987) 'Late antiquity', in P. Veyne (ed.) *A History of Private Life: From Pagan Rome to Byzantium*, 235–311. London: Harvard University Press.

Brown, S. (1986 unpubl.) 'Report on the human bone from St Mary's, Winchester, Hants' (Excavations at St Mary's Abbey, Winchester: Excavations since 1972).

Brown, W. (1886) 'Descriptions of the buildings of twelve small Yorkshire priories at the Reformation', *Yorkshire Archaeological Journal* 9: 197–215.

Brumfiel, E. M. (1991) 'Weaving and cooking: women's production in Aztec Mexico', in J. Gero and M. Conkey (eds) *Engendering Archaeology*, 224–51. Oxford: Blackwell.

Brush, K. (1988) 'Gender and mortuary analysis in pagan Anglo-Saxon archaeology', *Archaeological Review from Cambridge* 7.1: 76–89.

Burrow, I. (1985) 'Mynchin Buckland Priory: topographical notes', *Somerset Archaeology and Natural History* 129: 110–13.

Burton, J. (1979) *The Yorkshire Nunneries in the Twelfth and Thirteenth Centuries* (Borthwick Paper 56). York: University of York.

—— (1986) 'The foundation of the British Cistercian houses', in C. Norton and D. Park (eds) *Cistercian Art and Architecture in the British Isles*, 24–39. Cambridge: Cambridge University Press.

Butler, L. A. S. (1982) 'The Cistercians in Wales: factors in the choice of sites', in B. Chauvin (ed.) *Mélanges Anselme Dimier* (Architecture Cistercienne 3), 35–8. Arbois: Pupillin.

—— (1987) 'Medieval urban religious houses', in J. Schofield and R. Leech (eds) *Urban Archaeology in Britain*, 167–76 (CBA Research Report 61). London: Council for British Archaeology.

—— (1989) 'The archaeology of rural monasteries in England and Wales', in R. Gilchrist and H. Mytum (eds) *The Archaeology of Rural Monasteries* (BAR 203), 1–27. Oxford: British Archaeological Reports.

Bynum, C. W. (1982) *Jesus as Mother: Studies in the Spirituality of the High Middle Ages.* Berkeley: University of California Press.

—— (1987) *Holy Feast and Holy Fast: The Religious Significance of Food to Medieval Women*, Berkeley: University of California Press.

Cahill, S. E. (1987) 'Directions for an interactionist study of gender development', in M. J. Deegan and M. Hill (eds) *Women and Symbolic Interaction*, 81–98. Boston: Allen & Unwin.

Campbell-Jones, S. (1979) *In Habit: An Anthropological Study of Working Nuns*, London: Faber.

Carasso, D. (1985) *A Short History of Amsterdam.* Amsterdam: Historical Museum.

Cardwell, P. (1990 unpubl.) 'Excavations at St Giles Hospital, Brough, North Yorkshire', Interim Report 1989.

Carlin, M. (1987 unpubl.) 'Holy Trinity Minories: Abbey of St Clare 1293/4–1539', St Botolph Aldgate Gazetteer (The Social and Economic Study of Medieval London). Archive of the Institute of Historical Research, London.

Carr, R. D., Tester, A. and Murphy, P. (1988) 'The middle Saxon settlement at Staunch Meadow, Brandon', *Antiquity* 62: 371–80.

Cave-Brown, Revd. J. (1897) 'Minster in Sheppey', *Archaeologia Cantiana* 22: 144–68.

Chadd, D. F. L. (1986) 'Liturgy and liturgical music: the limits of uniformity', in C. Norton and D. Park (eds) *Cistercian Art and Architecture in the British Isles*, 299–314. Cambridge: Cambridge University Press.

Champion, T. (1991) 'Theoretical archaeology in Britain', in I. Hodder (ed.) *Archaeological Theory in Europe: The Last Three Decades*, 129–60. London: Routledge.

Christie, P. M. and Coad, J. G. (1980) 'Excavations at Denny Abbey', *Archaeological Journal* 137: 138–279.

Cinthio, H. and Boldsen, J. (1983) 'Patterns of distribution in the early medieval cemetery at Loddeköpinge', *Papers of the Archaeological Institute, University of Lund* 5: 116–27.

Clapham, A. W. (1913) 'The Benedictine abbey of Barking', *Essex Archaeological Transactions* 12: 69–89.

—— (1926) 'The priory and manor house of Dartford', *Archaeological Journal* 83: 67–85.

—— (1934) *English Romanesque Architecture after the Conquest*, Oxford: Clarendon Press.

Clark, A. (1905) *The English Register of Godstow Nunnery*, part i (Early English Text Society, vol. 129). London.

Clarke, D. (1972) 'A provisional model of an iron age society and its settlement system', in D. Clarke (ed.) *Models in Archaeology*, 801–69. London: Methuen.

Clarke, H. (1984) *The Archaeology of Medieval England*, London: British Museum.

Clay, C. (1928) 'The seals of the religious houses of Yorkshire', *Archaeologia* 78: 1–36.

Clay, R. M. (1909) *The Medieval Hospitals of England*. London: Methuen.

—— (1914) *The Hermits and Anchorites of England*. London: Methuen.

—— (1953) 'Further studies on medieval recluses', *Journal of the British Archaeological Association* 16: 74–86.

Clayton, M. (1990) *The Cult of the Virgin Mary in Anglo-Saxon England*. Cambridge: Cambridge University Press.

Coldicott, D. K. (1989) *Hampshire Nunneries*. Chichester: Phillimore.

Coldstream, N. (1986) 'Cistercian architecture from Beaulieu to the Dissolution', in C. Norton and D. Park (eds) *Cistercian Art and Architecture in the British Isles*, 139–59. Cambridge: Cambridge University Press.

Colgrave, B. (ed. and trans.) (1985) *Felix's Life of Guthlac*. Cambridge: Cambridge University Press.

Collins, F. J. (1961) 'Notes on the church of Holy Trinity, Minories', *Transactions of the London and Middlesex Archaeological Society* 20.4: 160–5.

Colvin, H. M. (ed.) (1963) *The History of the King's Works*, vol. 2. London: HMSO.

Conkey, M. W. (1991) 'Contexts of action, contexts for power: material culture and gender in the Magdalenian', in J. Gero and M. Conkey (eds), *Engendering Archaeology*, 57–92. Oxford: Blackwell.

—— and Spector, J. (1984) 'Archaeology and the study of gender', in M. Schiffer (ed.) *Advances in Archaeological Method and Theory* 7: 1–38. New York: Academic Press.

Cook, G. H. (1947) *Medieval Chantries and Chantry Chapels*. London: Phoenix House.

—— (1961) *English Monasteries in the Middle Ages*. London: Phoenix House.

Coontz, S. and Henderson, P. (1986) 'Property forms, political power and female labour in the origins of class and state societies', in S. Coontz and P. Henderson (eds) *Women's Work, Men's Property*, 108–55. London: Verso.

Coppack, G. (1986), 'Some descriptions of Rievaulx Abbey in 1538–9', *Journal of the British Archaeological Association* 139: 100–33.

—— (1989) 'Thornholme Priory: the development of a monastic outer court landscape', in R. Gilchrist and H. Mytum (eds) *The Archaeology of Rural Monasteries* (BAR 203), 185–222. Oxford: British Archaeological Reports.

—— (1990) *Abbeys and Priories*, London: Batsford/English Heritage.

Coulson, C. (1982) 'Hierarchism in conventual crenellation', *Medieval Archaeology* 26: 69–100.

Cowan, I. B. and Easson, D. E. (1976) *Medieval Religious Houses of Scotland*. London: Longman.

Cra'aster, M. D. (1966) 'Waterbeach Abbey', *Proceedings of the Cambridgeshire Antiquarian Society* 59: 75–95.

Cramp, R. (1976) 'Monastic sites', in D. Wilson (ed.) *The Archaeology of Anglo-Saxon England*, 201–52. Cambridge: Cambridge University Press.

Cromwell, T. (1987 unpubl.) 'A brief investigation into the viability of networks and other techniques of spatial analysis, through examination of a known data set', MA dissertation deposited at the Dept. of Archaeology, University of York

Cullum, P. H. (1992) '"And hir name was Charite": charitable giving by and for women in late medieval Yorkshire', in P. J. P. Goldberg (ed.) *Woman is a Worthy Wight: Women in English Society, c.1200–1500*, 182–211. Stroud: Alan Sutton.

—— (1993) 'St Leonard's York: the spatial and social topography of an Augustinian

198

hospital', in R. Gilchrist and H. Mytum (eds) *Advances in Monastic Archaeology* (BAR 227), 11–18. Oxford: British Archaeological Reports.

Cunliffe, B. (1984) 'Saxon Bath', in J. Haslam (ed.) *Anglo-Saxon Towns in Southern England* (BAR 227), 11–18,: 345–58. Chichester: Phillimore.

Daniels, R. (1989) 'The Anglo-Saxon monastery at Church Close, Hartlepool, Cleveland', *Archaeological Journal* 145: 158–210.

Dashwood, G. H. (1859) 'Notes of deeds and survey of Crabhouse Priory, Norfolk', *Norfolk Archaeology* 5: 257–62.

Davis, K. (1991) 'Critical sociology and gender relations', in K. Davis, M. Leijenaar and J. Oldersma (eds) *The Gender of Power*, 65–86. London: Sage.

——, Leijenaar, M., and Oldersma, J. (eds) (1991) *The Gender of Power*. London: Sage.

Dawes, J. D. (n. d., unpubl.) 'Clementhorpe Nunnery: the human bones', York Archaeological Trust Archive.

Deegan, M. J. (1987) 'Symbolic interaction and the study of women: an introduction', in M. J. Deegan and M. Hill (eds) *Women and Symbolic Interaction*, 3–15. Boston: Allen & Unwin.

Delmaire, B. (1989) 'Les béguines dans le nord de la France au première siècle de leur histoire (vers 1230–vers 1350)', in M. Parisse (ed.) *Les Religieuses en France au XIIIe siècle*, 121–62. Nancy: Presses Universitaires de Nancy.

Devlin, P. (1984) 'Feminine lay piety in the high middle ages: the Beguines', in J. A. Nichols and L. T. Shank (eds) *Medieval Religious Women*, 1: *Distant Echoes*, 183–95. Kalamazoo: Cistercian Publications.

Dobson, R. B. and Donaghey, S. (1984) *The History of Clementhorpe Nunnery* (The Archaeology of York 2.1). London: Council for British Archaeology.

Dommasnes, L. H. (1991) 'Women, kinship, and the basis of power in the Norwegian Viking age', in R. Samson (ed.) *Social Approaches to Viking Studies*, 65–74. Glasgow: Cruithne.

Driscoll, S. T. and Nieke, M. R. (eds) (1988) *Power and Politics in Early Medieval Britain*. Edinburgh: Edinburgh University Press.

Dümmler, E. (ed.) (1895) *Alcuini Epistolae,* in *Monumenta Germaniae Historica, Epistolarum* 4, 1–481.

Dugdale, W. (1655–73; 1846 edn) *Monasticon Anglicanum*, London: Bohn.

Dyer, C. C. (1983) 'English diet in the later Middle Ages', in T. H. Aston, P. R. Cross, C. C. Dyer and J. Thirsk (eds) *Social Relations and Ideas: Essays in Honour of R. H. Hilton*, 191–214. Cambridge: Cambridge University Press.

—— (1988a) 'Changes in diet in the late Middle Ages: the case of the harvest workers', *Agricultural History Review* 36.1: 21–37.

—— (1988b) 'Documentary evidence: problems and enquiries', in G. Astill and A. Grant (eds) *The Medieval Countryside*, 12–35. Oxford: Blackwell.

—— (1989) *Standards of Living in the Later Middle Ages*. Cambridge: Cambridge University Press.

Eckenstein, L. (1896) *Women under Monasticism*. Cambridge: Cambridge University Press.

Edwards, D. A. (1989) 'Norfolk churches and air photography', *Bulletin of the CBA Churches Committee* 26: 4–8.

Ehrenberg, M. (1989) *Women in Prehistory*. London: British Museum.

Ekwall, E. (1960) *The Concise Oxford Dictionary of English Place-names*. Oxford: Clarendon Press.

Elkins, S. K. (1988) *Holy Women of Twelfth-century England*. Chapel Hill, NC: University of North Carolina Press.

Ellis, R. (1985) 'Excavations at 9 St Clare Street', *London Archaeologist* 5.5: 115–21.

Ellis, R. H. (1986) *Catalogue of Seals in the Public Record Office: Monastic Seals*, vol. 1. London: HMSO.

Evans, J. and Cook, N. (1956) 'A statue from the Minories', *Archaeological Journal* 113: 102–7.

Everett, A. W. (1934) 'St Katherine's Priory, Exeter', *Devon Archaeological Explorations Association Proceedings* 2: 110–19.

Everson, P. (1989) 'Rural monasteries within the secular landscape', in R. Gilchrist and H. Mytum (eds) *The Archaeology of Rural Monasteries* (BAR 203), 141–6. Oxford: British Archaeological Reports.

Fairclough, G. (1992) 'Meaningful constructions: spatial and functional analysis of medieval buildings', *Antiquity* 66: 348–66.

Fehring, G. (1991) *The Archaeology of Medieval Germany: An Introduction*, London: Routledge.

Fell, C. (1984) *Women in Anglo-Saxon England*. London: Blackwell.

Ferguson, G. (1966) *Signs and Symbols in Christian Art*. Oxford: Oxford University Press.

Fergusson, P. (1986) 'The twelfth century refectories at Rievaulx and Byland Abbeys', in C. Norton and D. Park (eds) *Cistercian Art and Architecture in the British Isles*, 160–80. Cambridge: Cambridge University Press.

Ferrante, J. M. (1975) *Woman as Image in Medieval Literature*. Durham, NC: Labryinth Press.

Flannery, K. V. and Winter, M. C. (1976) 'Analysing household activities', in K. V. Flannery (ed.) *The Early Mesoamerican Village*, 34–47. New York: Academic Press.

Foreville, R. and Keir, G. (1987) *The Book of St Gilbert*. Oxford: Oxford University Press.

Foster, S. (1989) 'Analysis of spatial patterns in buildings (access analysis) as an insight into social structure: examples from the Scottish Atlantic Iron Age', *Antiquity* 63: 40–50.

Foucault, M. (1979) *Discipline and Punish*. Harmondsworth: Penguin.

Fowler, P. (1984) 'The public and private in architecture: a feminist critique', *Women's Studies International Forum* 7.6: 449–54.

Ganz, D. (1972) 'The buildings of Godstow Nunnery', *Oxoniensia* 37: 150–7.

Garmonsway, G. N. (ed. and trans) (1972) *The Anglo-Saxon Chronicle*. London: Burns & Oates.

Garrod, D. (1980) 'Important find from Dartford,' *Kent Archaeological Review* 61: 19–20.

Gem, R. (1978) 'Church architecture in the reign of king Æthelred', in D. Hill (ed.) *Æthelred the Unready* (BAR 59), 105–14. Oxford: British Archaeological Reports.

—— (1983) 'Towards an iconography of Anglo-Saxon architecture', *Journal of the Warburg and Courtauld Institutes* 46: 1–18.

Gero, J. and Conkey, M. (eds) (1991) *Engendering Archaeology. Women and Prehistory*. Oxford: Blackwell.

—— (1991) 'Tensions, pluralities, and engendering archaeology: an introduction to women and prehistory', in J. Gero and M. Conkey (eds), *Engendering Archaeology: Women and Prehistory*, 3–30. Oxford: Blackwell.

Gibb, J. G. and King, J. A. (1991) 'Gender, activity areas, and homelots in the seventeenth-century Chesapeake region', in D. Seifert (ed.) *Gender in Historical Archaeology*, (Historical Archaeology 25.4), 109–31.

Gibbs, L. (1987) 'Identifying gender representation in the archaeological record: a contextual study', in I. Hodder (ed.) *The Archaeology of Contextual Meanings*, 79–89. Cambridge: Cambridge University Press.

Giddens, A. (1984) *The Constitution of Society*, Cambridge: Polity Press.

Gilchrist, R. (1988) 'The spatial archaeology of gender domains: a case study of medieval English nunneries', *Archaeological Review from Cambridge* 7.1: 21–8.

—— (1989 Ancient Monuments Laboratory Report) 'Excavations at the Dominican priory, Beverley, Humbs., 1986: The animal bones'.

—— (1989b) 'Community and self: perceptions and use of space in medieval monasteries', *Scottish Archaeological Review* 6: 55–64.

—— (1990) 'Gender, ideology and material culture: the archaeology of female piety', Ph.D. thesis, Dept. of Archaeology, University of York.

—— (1991) 'Women's archaeology? Political feminism, gender theory and historical revision', *Antiquity* 65: 495–501.

—— (1994) 'Medieval bodies in the material world: gender, stigma and the body', in S. Key and M. Rubin (eds) *Framing Medieval Bodies*, 43–61. Manchester: Manchester University Press.

Gilyard-Beer, R. (1958) *Abbeys*. London: HMSO.

Girouard, M. (1978) *Life in the English Country House*. London: Yale University Press.

Gittings, C. (1984) *Death, Burial and the Individual in Early Modern England*. London: Routledge.

Glassie, H. (1975) *Folk Housing in Middle Virginia: A Structural Analysis of Historic Artifacts*. Tennessee: Tennessee University Press.

Godfrey, W. H. (1955) *The English Almshouse*. London: Faber.

Gold, P. S. (1985) *The Lady and the Virgin: Image, Attitude and Experience in Twelfth Century France*. Chicago: Chicago University Press.

Goody, J. (1986) *The Development of the Family and Marriage in Europe*. Cambridge: Cambridge University Press.

Graham, H. (1992) ' "A woman's work…": labour and gender in the late medieval countryside', in P. J. P. Goldberg (ed.) *Woman is a Worthy Wight: Women in English Society c. 1200–1500*, 126–48. Stroud: Alan Sutton.

Graham, R. (1903) *St Gilbert of Sempringham and the Gilbertines*. London: Elliot Stock.

—— and Clapham, A. W. (1924) 'The order of Grandmont and its houses in England', *Archaeologia* 75: 159–210.

Gramsci, A. (1929-35; 1971) *Selections from the Prison Notebooks*. London: Lawrence & Wishart.

Graves, C. V. (1984) 'Stixwould in the market place', in J. A. Nichols and L. T. Shank (eds) *Medieval Religious Women, 1: Distant Echoes*, 213–35. Kalamazoo: Cistercian Publications.

Gray, A. (1898) *The Priory of St Radegund, Cambridge*. London: George Bell & Sons.

Greene, P. (1989) *Norton Priory: The Archaeology of a Medieval Religious House*. Cambridge: Cambridge University Press.

Grierson, P. (1959) 'Commerce in the Dark Ages: a critique of the evidence,' *Transactions of the Royal Historical Society* 9: 123–40.

Gwynn, A. and Hadcock, R. N. (1970) *Medieval Religious Houses of Ireland*. London: Longman.

Hadcock, R. N. (1937) 'Bullington Priory, Lincs', *Antiquity* 11: 213–17.

Haddan, A. W. and Stubbs, W. (eds) (1871; repr. 1964) *Councils and Synods*, vol. 3. Oxford: Clarendon Press.

Haigh, D. (1988) *The Religious Houses of Cambridgeshire*. Cambridge: Cambridgeshire County Council.

Hall, J. (1974) *A Dictionary of Subjects and Symbols in Christian Art*. London: Murray.

Hammond, H. D. C. (1972) 'Locational models and the site of Lubaantun: a classic Maya center', in D. Clarke (ed.) *Models in Archaeology*, 757–800. London: Methuen.

Hanawalt, B. A. (1986) *The Ties that Bound: Peasant Families in Medieval England*. Oxford: Oxford University Press.

Harding, S. (1983) 'Why has the sex/gender system become visible only now?', in S. Harding and M. B. Hintikka (eds) *Discovering Reality: Feminist Perspectives on Epistemology, Metaphysics, Methodology and Philosophy of Science*, 311–25. Dordrecht: Reidel.

—— (1986) *The Science Question in Feminism*. Ithaca, NY: Cornell University Press.

Härke, H. (1989) 'Knives in early Saxon burials: blade length and age at death', *Medieval Archaeology* 33: 144–8.

Harris, K. (1984) *Sex, Ideology and Religion*. New Jersey: Barnes & Noble.

Harrison, A. C. (1970) 'Excavations at the site of St Mary's Hospital, Strood', *Archaeologia Cantiana* 84: 139–60.

Harrison, K. (1968) 'Vitruvius and acoustic jars in England during the Middle Ages', *Transactions of the Ancient Monuments Society* 15: 49–54.

Hartley, R. F. (1987) *The Medieval Earthworks of North-east Leicestershire* (Leicester Museums and Art Gallery Archaeological Reports 9). Leicester: Leicester Museums and Art Gallery.

Hartmann, H. (1982) 'Capitalism, patriarchy, and job segregation by sex', in A. Giddens and D. Held (eds) *Classes, Power and Conflict*, 446–69. London: Macmillan.

Hastorf, C. (1991) 'Gender, space and food in prehistory', in J. Gero and M. Conkey (eds), *Engendering Archaeology*, 132–59. Oxford: Blackwell.

Hatcher, J. (1986) 'Mortality in the fifteenth century: some new evidence', *Economic History Review* 39: 19–38.

Hazlewood, F. (1894) 'Inventories of monasteries suppressed in 1536', *Proceedings of the Suffolk Institute of Archaeology* 8: 83–116.

Heslop, T. A. (1984) 'Seals', in G. Zarnecki, J. Holt and T. Holland (eds) *English Romanesque Art 1066–1200*, 298–319. London: Weidenfeld & Nicholson.

—— (1986) 'Cistercian seals in England and Wales', in C. Norton and D. Park (eds) *Cistercian Art and Architecture in the British Isles*, 266–83. Cambridge: Cambridge University Press.

—— (1987) 'English seals in the thirteenth and fourteenth Centuries', in J. Alexander and P. Binski (eds) *Age of Chivalry: Art in Plantagenet England 1200–1400*, 114–17. London: Weidenfeld & Nicholson.

Hillier, B. and Hanson, J. (1984) *The Social Logic of Space*. Cambridge: Cambridge University Press.

Hirschon, R. (1984) 'Introduction: power, property and gender relations', in R. Hirschon (ed.) *Women and Property – Women as Property*, 1-22. London: Croom Helm.

—— (1985) 'The woman–environment relationship: Greek cultural values in an urban community', *Ekistics* 52: 15–21.

Hirst, S. and Wright, S. (1983) *Bordesley Abbey II* (BAR 111), Oxford: British Archaeological Reports.

Hodder, I. (ed.) (1987a) *The Archaeology of Contextual Meanings*, Cambridge: Cambridge University Press.

—— (ed.) (1987b) *Archaeology as Long-term History*. Cambridge: Cambridge University Press.

—— (1990) *The Domestication of Europe*. Oxford: Blackwell.

Hodges, R. (1982) *Dark Age Economics*. London: Duckworth.

——(1983) 'New approaches to medieval archaeology, part 2', in D. A. Hinton (ed.) *Twenty-five Years of Medieval Archaeology*. Sheffield: Department of Prehistory and Archaeology, University of Sheffield.

Holdsworth, C. J. (1978) 'Christina of Markyate', in D. Baker (ed.) *Medieval Women*:

(Studies in Church History Subsidia 1.), 185–204. Oxford: Blackwell.

Horn, W. and Born, E. (1979) *The Plan of St Gall* vol. 2. Berkeley: University of California Press.

Howell, M. C. (1986) *Women, Production and Patriarchy in Late Medieval Cities.* Chicago: Chicago University Press.

Huggins, P. J. (1978) 'Excavation of a Belgic and Romano-British farm with Middle Saxon cemetery and churches at Nazeingbury, Essex, 1975–6', *Essex Archaeology and History* 10: 29–117.

Hugo, T. (1867) *The Medieval Nunneries of the County of Somerset and the Diocese of Bath and Wells.* London: privately printed.

Hunt, N. (1967) *Cluny under St Hugh 1049–1109.* London: Edward Arnold.

Irigaray, L. (1987) 'Sexual difference', in T. Moi (ed.) *French Feminist Thought*, 118–30. Oxford: Blackwell.

James, T. B. and Robinson, A. M. (1988) *Clarendon Palace: The History and Archaeology of a Medieval Hunting Lodge near Salisbury, Wilts.* (Society of Antiquaries Report 45). London: Society of Antiquaries.

Jones, M. U. (1963 unpubl.). 'An interim report on Haverholme Priory, near Sleaford, Lincolnshire'.

Kauffmann, C. M. (1975) *Romanesque Manuscripts 1066–1200*, London: Harvey Miller.

Keene, D. (1985) *Survey of Medieval Winchester I and II* (Winchester Studies 2). Oxford: Clarendon Press.

Kent, S. (1990) 'A cross-cultural study of segmentation, architecture, and the use of space', in S. Kent (ed.) *Domestic Architecture and the Use of Space*, 127–52. Cambridge: Cambridge University Press.

Khosla, K. (1975) 'Architecture and symbolism in Tibetan monasteries' in P. Oliver (ed.) *Shelter, Sign and Symbol*, 71–83. London: Barrie & Jenkins.

Knowles, D. (1955) *The Religious Orders in England*, vol. 2: *The End of the Middle Ages.* Cambridge: Cambridge University Press.

—— and Hadcock, R. N. (1953; 1971) *Medieval Religious Houses: England and Wales.* London: Longman.

—— and St Joseph, J. K. S. (1952) *Monastic Sites from the Air.* Cambridge: Cambridge University Press.

Komter, A. (1991) 'Gender, power and feminist theory', in K. Davis, M. Leijenaar and J. Oldersma (eds) *The Gender of Power*, 42–64. London: Sage.

Krautheimer, R. (1942) 'Introduction to an iconography of medieval architecture', *Journal of the Warburg and Courtauld Institutes* 5: 1–33.

Kristensen, H. K. (1987) *Middelalderbyen Viborg.* Denmark (place not stated): Centrum.

Lambrick, G. (1985) 'Further excavations of the second site of the Dominican priory, Oxford', *Oxoniensia* 50: 131–208.

Larking, L. B. (ed.) (1857) *The Knights Hospitaller in England* (Camden Society, vol. 65). London.

Latham, R. E. (1965) *Revised Medieval Latin Word-list.* Oxford: Oxford University Press.

Lawless, G. P. (1987) *Augustine of Hippo and his Monastic Rule.* Oxford: Clarendon Press.

Lawrence, C. H. (1984) *Medieval Monasticism.* London: Longman.

Leclercq OSB., J. (1984) 'Does St Bernard have a specific message for Nuns?', in J. A. Nichols and L. T. Shank (eds) *Medieval Religious Women*, 1: *Distant Echoes*, 269–78. Kalamazoo: Cistercian Publications.

Leech, R. H. and McWhirr, A. D. (1982) 'Excavations at St John's Hospital,

Cirencester, 1971 and 1976', *Transactions of the Bristol and Gloucestershire Archaeology Society* 100: 191–209.

Legg, J. W. (1899) *The Processional of the Nuns of Chester* (Henry Bradshaw Society, vol. 18). London.

Leland, J. (1535–43; 1964) *Itinerary of John Leland* (ed. and trans. L. Toulmin). London: Centaur.

Le Patourel, H. E. J. (1973) *The Moated Sites of Yorkshire* (Society for Medieval Archaeology Monographs 5). London.

—— and Roberts, B. K. (1978) 'The significance of moated sites', in A. Aberg (ed.) *Medieval Moated Sites* (CBA Research Report 17), 46–55. London: Council for British Archaeology.

Levitan, B. (1987) 'Medieval animal husbandry in southwest England: a selective review and suggested approach', in N. D. Balaam, B. Levitan and V. Straker (eds) *Studies in Palaeoeconomy and Environment* (BAR 181), 51–80. Oxford: British Archaeological Reports.

—— (1989) 'Bone analysis and urban economy: examples of selectivity and a case for comparison', in D. Serjeantson and T. Waldron (eds) *Diet and Crafts in Towns* (BAR 199), 161–88. Oxford: British Archaeological Reports.

Leyser, H. (1984) *Hermits and the New Monasticism*. London: Macmillan.

MOLAS (1986 archive) Museum of London Archaeology Service Archive Report: 'The building at 13 Haydon Street and its relevance to the Minories Abbey'.

—— (1987 archive) Museum of London Archaeology Service Archive Report: 'Reconstruction plan of Clerkenwell Nunnery'.

—— (1990) *Current sites: January 1990* (Current work by the Department of Urban Archaeology of the Museum of London). London: Museum of London.

McCann, J. (1952) *The Rule of St Benedict*. London: Sheed & Ward.

McDonnell, E. W. (1969) *The Beguines and Beghards in Medieval Culture*. New York: Octagon.

McEwan, B. G. (1991) 'The archaeology of women in the Spanish New World', *Historical Archaeology* 25.4: 17–32.

MacGowan, K. (1987) 'Saxon timber structures from the Barking Abbey excavations', *Essex Journal* 22: 35–8.

McGuire, R. H. and Paynter, R. (1991) *The Archaeology of Inequality*. Oxford: Blackwell.

MacKay, D. and Swan, V. (1989) 'Earthworks at Marton and Moxby Priories', *Yorkshire Archaeological Journal* 61: 71–84.

McLaughlin, E. C. (1974) 'Equality of souls, inequality of sexes: woman in medieval theology', in R. R. Ruether (ed.) *Images of Women in the Jewish and Christian Traditions*, 213–66. New York: Simon & Schuster.

McLaughlin, M. M. (1989) 'Creating and recreating communities of women: the case of Corpus Domini Ferrara, 1406-52', *Signs* 14.2: 293–320.

McNamara, J. and Wemple, S. F. (1977) 'Sanctity and power: the dual pursuit of medieval women', in R. Bridenthal and C. Koonz (eds) *Becoming Visible: Women in European History*, 90–118. London: Houghton Mifflen.

Magilton, J. R. (1980) *The Church of St Helen-on-the-walls, Aldwalk* (The Archaeology of York 10.1). London: Council for British Archaeology.

Martin, A. R. (1937) *Franciscan Architecture in England*. Manchester: Manchester University Press.

Mathews, T. F. (1971) *The Early Churches of Constantinople: Architecture and Liturgy*. Pennsylvania: Pennsylvania State University Press.

MATRIX (1984) *Making Space: Women and the Man-made Environment*. London: Pluto.

Mellor, J. E. and Pearce, T. (1981) *The Austin Friars, Leicester* (CBA Research Report 35). London: Council for British Archaeology.

Meyer, M. A. (1977) 'Women and the tenth century English monastic reform', *Revue Bénédictine* 87: 34–61.

Miller, D. D., Miller, D. M. and Sister Jane Mary, SPB (1985) 'The manor and abbey of Burnham', *Records of Bucks* 27: 94–100.

Millett, B. and Wogan-Browne, J. (eds) (1992), *Medieval English Prose for Women: the Katherine Group and the Ancrene Wisse*, Oxford: Oxford University Press.

Millinger, S. (1984) 'Humility and power: Anglo-Saxon nuns in Anglo-Norman hagiography', in J. A. Nichols and L. T. Shank (eds) *Medieval Religious Women*, 1: *Distant Echoes*, 115–29. Kalamazoo: Cistercian Publications.

Moessner, V. J. (1987) 'The medieval embroideries of convent Wienhausen', in M. P. Lillich (ed.) *Studies in Cistercian Art and Architecture*, 13: 161–77. Kalamazoo: Cistercian Publications.

Moi, T. (ed.) (1987) *French Feminist Thought: A Reader*. Oxford: Blackwell.

Monery, M. (1922) 'L'église du prieuré de Marcigny, Saône-et-Loire', *Bulletin de La Diana* 19 (1913–14) [1922]: 60-73.

Moore, H. L. (1982) 'The interpretation of spatial patterning in settlement residues', in I. Hodder (ed.) *Symbolic and Structural Archaeology*, 74–9. Cambridge: Cambridge University Press.

—— (1987) *Space, Text and Gender*. Cambridge: Cambridge University Press.

—— (1988) *Feminism and Anthropology*. London: Polity Press.

—— (1990) 'Paul Ricoeur: action, meaning and text', in C. Tilley (ed.) *Reading Material Culture*, 85–120. Oxford: Blackwell.

Moore, J. S. (1982) *Domesday Book: Gloucestershire*. Chichester: Phillimore.

Moorhouse, S. (1981) 'Iron production', in M. L. Faull and S. Moorhouse (eds) *West Yorkshire: An Archaeological Survey to AD 1500*, 783–6. Wakefield: W. Yorks. Metropolitan County Council.

—— (1989) 'Monastic estates: their composition and development', in R. Gilchrist and H. Mytum (eds) *The Archaeology of Rural Monasteries* (BAR 203), 29–82. Oxford: British Archaeological Reports.

—— (1993) 'Pottery and glass in the medieval monastery', in R. Gilchrist and H. Mytum (eds) *Advances in Monastic Archaeology* (BAR 227), 127–49. Oxford: British Archaeological Reports.

Morgan, N. (1988) *Early Gothic Manuscripts*, vol. 2: 1250–85. London: Harvey Miller.

Morris, M. C. F. (1907) *Nunburnholme: Its History and Antiquities*. York: Sampson.

Morris, R. K. (1979) *Cathedrals and Abbeys of England and Wales 600–1540*. London: J. M. Dent & Sons.

—— (1989) *Churches in the Landscape*. London: J. M. Dent & Sons.

Mytum, H. C. (1979) 'Excavations at Polesworth', *Transactions of the the Birmingham and Warwickshire Archaeological Society* 89: 79–90.

—— (1992) *The Origins of Early Christian Ireland*. London: Routledge.

Nash-Williams, V. E. (1950) *The Early Christian Monuments of Wales*. Cardiff: University of Wales Press.

Neel, C. (1989) 'The origins of the Beguines', *Signs* 14.2: 321–41.

New, A. (1985) *A Guide to the Abbeys of England and Wales*. London: Constable.

Newman, J. (1969) *The Buildings of England: West Kent and the Weald*. Harmondsworth: Penguin.

Nichols, J. A. (1982) 'Sinningthwaite Nunnery', in M. P. Lillich (ed.) *Studies in Cistercian Art and Architecture*, 1: 49–52. Kalamazoo: Cistercian Publications.

—— (1984) 'Medieval Cistercian nunneries and English bishops', in J. A. Nichols and L. T. Shank (eds) *Medieval Religious Women*, 1: *Distant Echoes*, 237–49. Kalamazoo: Cistercian Publications.

Nyberg, T. (1965) *Birgittinische Klostergründungen des Mittelalters* (Bibliotheca Historica Lundensis 15). Lund, Sweden.

O'Connor, T. P. (1993) 'Bone assemblages from monastic sites: many questions but few data', in R. Gilchrist and H. Mytum (eds) *Advances in Monastic Archaeology* (BAR 227), 107–11. Oxford: British Archaeological Reports.

Oliva, M. (1990) 'Aristocracy or meritocracy? Office-holding patterns in late medieval English nunneries', in W. J. Sheils and D. Wood (eds) *Women in the Church* (Studies in Church History 27), 197–208. Oxford: Blackwell.

—— (1992 unpubl.) 'Gender and history: medieval religious women in the diocese of Norwich'. Women's History Seminar paper, Institute of Historical Research, London.

—— (1994) *The Convent and the Community in the Diocese of Norwich from 1350 to 1540*. Woodbridge: Boydell & Brewer.

O'Neill, H. E. (1964) 'Excavations of a celtic hermitage on St Helen's, Isles of Scilly, 1956–8', *Archaeological Journal* 121: 40–69.

Owen, D. M. (1981) *Church and Society in Medieval Lincolnshire* (History of Lincoln 5). Lincoln: History of Lincolnshire Committee.

Owen-Crocker, G. R. (1986) *Dress in Anglo-Saxon England*. Manchester: Manchester University Press.

Pader, E. (1982) *Symbolism, Social Relations and the Interpretation of Mortuary Remains* (BAR international series 130). Oxford: British Archaeological Reports.

Pantin, W. A. (1970) 'Minchery Farm, Littlemore', *Oxoniensia* 35: 19–26.

Park, D. (1983) 'The wall paintings of the Holy Sepulchre Chapel', in *Medieval Art and Architecture at Winchester Cathedral* (British Archaeological Association Conference Proceedings 6), 38–62.

—— (1987) 'Wall painting', in J. Alexander and P. Binski (eds) *Age of Chivalry. Art in Plantagenet England 1200–1400*, 125–30. London: Weidenfeld & Nicolson.

Parker, G. (1982) 'The medieval hermitage of Grafton Regis', *Northants Past and Present* 4.5: 247–52.

Parsons, D. (1989) *Liturgy and Architecture in the Middle Ages* (The Third Deerhurst Lecture, 1986). Leicester: Friends of Deerhurst Church.

Patlagean, E. (1987) 'Byzantium in the tenth and eleventh centuries', in P. Veyne (ed.) *A History of Private Life: From Pagan Rome to Byzantium*, 551–641. London: Harvard University Press.

Peers, C. R. (1901) 'Recent discoveries in Romsey Abbey Church', *Archaeologia* 57: 317–20.

—— (1902) 'The Benedictine nunnery of Little Marlow', *Archaeological Journal* 59: 307–25.

Petroff, E. A. (1986) *Medieval Women's Visionary Literature*. Oxford: Oxford University Press.

Pevsner, N. (series ed.) (1951–76) *The Buildings of England* (volumes published by county). Harmondsworth: Penguin.

—— (1962) *The Buildings of North-east Norfolk and Norwich*. Harmondsworth: Penguin.

—— (1970) *The Buildings of England: Cornwall*. Harmondsworth: Penguin.

Platt, C. (1969) *The Monastic Grange in Medieval England*. London: Macmillan.

Poster, J. and Sherlock, D. (1987) 'Denny Abbey: the nuns' refectory', *Proceedings of the Cambridgeshire Antiquarian Society* 76: 67–82.

Poulson, G. (1840) *The History and Antiquities of the Seignory of Holderness*. London: Pickering.

Power, E. (1922) *Medieval English Nunneries*. Cambridge: Cambridge University Press.

Pringle, D. (1986) 'The planning of some pilgrimage churches in Crusader Palestine', *World Archaeology* 18. 3: 341–62.

Pritchard, V. (1967) *English Medieval Graffiti*. Cambridge: Cambridge University Press.

Purser, M. (1991) ' "Several Paradise Ladies are visiting in town": gender strategies in the early industrial West', *Historical Archaeology* 25.4: 6–16.

Qualman, K. G. (1986) 'Winchester Nunnaminster', *Current Archaeology* 102: 204–7.

Radford, C. A. R. (1967) 'Ickleton Church', *Archaeological Journal* 124: 228–9.

Rahtz, P. A. (1976) 'The building plan of the Anglo-Saxon monastery of Whitby Abbey', in D. Wilson (ed.) *The Archaeology of Anglo-Saxon England*, 459–62. Cambridge: Cambridge University Press.

—— (1981) *The New Medieval Archaeology*. York: University of York.

—— (1983) 'New approaches to medieval archaeology, part 1', in D. A. Hinton (ed.) *Twenty-five Years of Medieval Archaeology*. Sheffield: Dept. of Prehistory and Archaeology, University of Sheffield.

—— (1987) 'The Nuer archaeology: theory vs history – comment on Driscoll', *Scottish Archaeological Review* 3.2: 109–12.

—— and Hirst, S. (1976) *Bordesley Abbey* (BAR 23). Oxford: British Archaeological Reports.

—— and Greenfield, E. (1977) *Excavations at Chew Valley Lake, Somerset* (DoE Archaeol. Reports 8). London: HMSO.

Reddan, M. and Clapham, A. W. (1924) *The Parish of St Helen, Bishopsgate: Part 1* (Survey of London, vol. 9). London: London County Council.

Reece, R. (1987) 'Sequence is all: or archaeology in an historical period', *Scottish Archaeological Review* 3.2: 113–15.

Reid, A. G. and Lye, D. M. (1988) *Pitmiddle Village and Elcho Nunnery* (Perthshire Society of Natural History). Dundee: Stevenson.

Richards, J. D. (1987) *The Significance of Form and Decoration of Anglo-Saxon Cremation Urns* (BAR 83). Oxford: British Archaeological Reports.

Richardson, J. S. (1928) 'A thirteenth century tile kiln at North Berwick, East Lothian, and Scottish medieval ornamental floor tiles', *Proceedings of the Society of Antiquaries of Scotland* 63: 281–310.

Ricoeur, P. (1981) *Hermeneutics and the Human Sciences*. Cambridge: Cambridge University Press.

Ridyard, S. J. (1988) *The Royal Saints of Anglo-Saxon England*. Cambridge: Cambridge University Press.

Rigold, S. E. (1968) 'The double minsters of Kent and their analogues', *Journal of the British Archaeological Association* 31: 27–37.

Roberts, M. E. (1985) 'The relic of the Holy Blood and the iconography of the thirteenth century north transept portal of Westminster Abbey', in W. M. Omrod (ed.) *England in the Thirteenth Century*, (Proceedings of the Harlaxton Symposium 1984), 129–42. Grantham: Harlaxton.

Robinson, D. M. (1980) *The Geography of Augustinian Settlement in Medieval England and Wales, Parts I and II* (BAR 80. 1–2). Oxford: British Archaeological Reports.

Rodwell, W.J. (1989) *Church Archaeology*. London: English Heritage/Batsford.

—— and Rodwell K. (1982) 'St Peter's Church, Barton-upon-Humber: excavation and structural study, 1978–81', *Antiquaries Journal* 62: 283–315.

Rollason, D. W. (1986) 'The shrines of saints in later Anglo-Saxon England: distribution and significance', in L. A. S. Butler and R. Morris (eds) *The Anglo-Saxon Church*, 32–43 (CBA Research Report 60). London: Council for British Archaeology.

Rouse, E. C. (1953) 'Wall-paintings in the Church of St Pega, Peakirk', *Archaeological Journal* 110: 135–49.

RCHM(E) (1937) *Royal Commission on Historical Monuments: Middlesex.* London: HMSO.

RCHM(E) (1959) *Royal Commission on Historical Monuments: Cambridge 1.* London: HMSO.

RCHM(E) (1972) *Royal Commission on Historical Monuments: Dorset 4.* London: HMSO.

RCHM(E) (1972) *Royal Commission on Historical Monuments: North-east Cambridgeshire 2.* London: HMSO.

RCHM(E) (1972) *Royal Commission on Historical Monuments: York 3.* London: HMSO.

RCHM(E) (1987) *Churches of South-east Wiltshire.* London: HMSO.

Rubin, M. (1986) 'Corpus Christi fraternities and late medieval piety', in W. J. Sheils and D. Wood (eds) *Voluntary Religion* (Studies in Church History 23), 97–109. Oxford: Blackwell.

—— (1987) *Charity and Community in Medieval Cambridge.* Cambridge: Cambridge University Press.

Ruether, R. R. (1974) 'Misogynism and virginal feminism in the fathers of the Church', in R. R. Ruether (ed.) *Images of Women in the Jewish and Christian Traditions*, 150–83. New York: Simon & Schuster.

Rushton, J. H. (1965) 'Keldholme Priory: the early years', *The Ryedale Historian* 1: 15–23.

Rutland, S. M. (1965) 'St Mary's Nunnery, Chester', *Chester and North Wales Archaeological Society Journal* 52: 26–32.

St John Hope, W. H. (1901) 'The ground plan of Watton in the East Riding of Yorkshire', *Yorkshire Archaeological Journal* 58: 1–34.

Salu, M. (trans.) (1990) *Ancrene Wisse.* Exeter: Exeter University Press.

Samson, R. (ed.) (1991) *Social Approaches to Viking Studies.* Glasgow: Cruithne.

Sawyer, P. (ed.) (1968) *Anglo-Saxon Charters.* London: Royal Historical Society.

Schulenburg, J. T. (1984) 'Strict active enclosure and its effect on the female monastic experience', in J. A. Nichols and L. T. Shank (eds) *Medieval Religious Women*, 1: *Distant Echoes*, 51–86. Kalamazoo: Cistercian Publications.

—— (1989) 'Women's monastic communities 500–1100: patterns of expansion and decline', *Signs* 14.2: 261–92.

Searle, E. (1974) *Lordship and Community: Battle Abbey and its Banlieu 1066–1538.* Toronto: Pontifical Institute for Mediaeval Studies.

Segal, L. (1990) *Slow Motion: Changing Masculinities, Changing Men.* London: Virago.

Seifert, D. (ed.) (1991) *Gender in Historical Archaeology (Historical Archaeology* 25.4).

—— (1991) 'Within sight of the White House: the archaeology of working women', *Historical Archaeology* 25.4: 82–108.

Senior, J. R. (1989) 'The selection of dimensional and ornamental stone types used in some northern monasteries', in R. Gilchrist and H. Mytum (eds) *The Archaeology of Rural Monasteries* (BAR 203), 223–50. Oxford: British Archaeological Reports.

Shanks, M. (1992) *Experiencing the Past: On the Character of Archaeology*, London: Routledge.

—— and Tilley, C. (1987a) *Re-constructing Archaeology.* Cambridge: Cambridge University Press.

—— (1987b) *Social Theory and Archaeology.* Oxford: Polity Press.

Sharpe, J. (1985) 'Osney Abbey, Oxford: archaeological investigations, 1975–83', *Oxoniensia* 50: 95–130.

Sherlock, D. (1970) 'Excavation at Campsea Ash Priory', *Proceedings of the Suffolk Institute of Archaeology* 32.2: 121–39.

Sloane, B. (1991 unpubl.) 'St Mary's Clerkenwell: a research design'. Museum of London Archaeology Service.

Smallwood, J. (1978) 'A medieval tile kiln at Abbey Farm, Shouldham', *East Anglian Archaeology* 8: 45–54.

Smith, G. H. (1980) 'The excavation of the Hospital of St Mary of Ospringe, commonly called Maison Dieu', *Archaeologia Cantiana* 95: 81–184.

Sørensen, M. L. S. (1987) 'Material order and cultural classification: the role of bronze objects in the transition from bronze age to iron age Scandinavia', in I. Hodder (ed.) *The Archaeology of Contextual Meanings*, 90–101. Cambridge: Cambridge University Press.

—— (1988) 'Is there a feminist contribution to Archaeology?', *Archaeological Review from Cambridge* 7.1: 9–20.

South, S. (1977) *Method and Theory in Historical Archaeology*. New York: Academic Press.

Spector, J. (1991) 'What this awl means: toward a feminist archaeology', in J. Gero and M. Conkey (eds), *Engendering Archaeology*, 388–406. Oxford: Blackwell.

Stalley, R. (1986) 'Cistercian churches of Ireland, 1142–1272', in C. Norton and D. Park (eds) *Cistercian Art and Architecture in Britain*, 117–38. Cambridge: Cambridge University Press.

—— (1987) *The Cistercian Monasteries of Ireland*. London: Yale University Press.

Stalsberg, A. (1991) 'Women as actors in North European Viking age trade', in R. Samson (ed.) *Social Approaches to Viking Studies*, 75–86. Glasgow: Cruithne.

Steane, J. M. (1985) *The Archaeology of Medieval England and Wales*. London: Croom Helm.

Stenton, F. M. (1943) 'The historical bearing of place-name studies: the place of women in Anglo-Saxon society', *Transactions of the Royal Historical Society* 25: 1–13.

Stocker, D. A. (1984) 'Four views of Clementhorpe Priory', in R. B. Dobson and S. Donaghey *The History of Clementhorpe Nunnery* (The Archaeology of York 2.1), 31–4. London: Council for British Archaeology.

Stone, P. G. (1893) *An Exact Account of the Church and Priory at Goring in the County of Oxford* (2nd edn). Goring: Henry L. Smith.

Talbot, C. H. (ed. and trans.) (1959) *The Life of Christina of Markyate*. Oxford: Oxford University Press.

Tanner, N. P. (1984) *The Church in Late Medieval Norwich 1370–1532*, Toronto: Pontifical Institute for Mediaeval Studies.

Tatton-Brown, T. (1984) *St John's Hospital, Canterbury 1084–1984*. Canterbury: Canterbury Archaeological Trust.

Taylor, H. M. (1975) 'Tenth-century church building in England and on the Continent', in D. Parsons (ed.) *Tenth Century Studies*, 141–68. London: Phillimore.

—— (1978) *Anglo-Saxon Architecture*, vol. 3. Cambridge: Cambridge University Press.

—— and Taylor, J. (1965) *Anglo-Saxon Architecture*, vols 1–2. Cambridge: Cambridge University Press.

Tester, P. J. (1967) 'Excavations on the site of Higham Priory', *Archaeologia Cantiana* 82: 143-61.

—— (1980) 'A plan and architectural description of the medieval remains of Davington Priory', *Archaeologia Cantiana* 95: 205–12.

Therkorn, L. (1987) 'The inter-relationships of materialist meanings: some suggestions on housing concerns within iron age Noord-Holland', in I. Hodder (ed.) *The Archaeology of Contextual Meanings*, 102–10. Cambridge: Cambridge University Press.

Thomas, C. (1971) *The Early Christian Archaeology of North Britain*, Oxford: Oxford University Press.

Thomas, J. (1991) *Rethinking the Neolithic.* Cambridge: Cambridge University Press.

Thompson, M. W. (1991) *The Rise of the Castle.* Cambridge: Cambridge University Press.

Thompson, S. (1978) 'The problem of the Cistercian nuns in the twelfth and early thirteenth centuries', in D. Baker (ed.) *Medieval Women* (Studies in Church History, Subsidia 1), 227–52. Oxford: Blackwell.

—— (1984) 'Why English nunneries had no history: a study of English nunneries founded after the Conquest', in J. A. Nichols and L. T. Shank (eds) *Medieval Religious Women*, 1: *Distant Echoes*, 131–49. Kalamazoo: Cistercian Publications.

—— (1991) *Women Religious: The Founding of English Nunneries after the Conquest.* Oxford: Clarendon Press.

Thorn, C. F. (1980) *Domesday Book: Somerset.* Chichester: Phillimore.

Tillotson, J. H. (1988) *Monastery and Society in the Late Middle Ages: Selected Account Rolls from Selby Abbey, Yorks., 1398–1537.* Woodbridge: Boydell & Brewer.

—— (1989) *Marrick Priory: A Nunnery in Late Medieval Yorkshire* (Borthwick Paper 75). York: University of York.

Tristram, E. W. (1955) *English Wall Painting of the Fourteenth Century.* London: Routledge.

Varley, W. J. (1973) 'Giants Hill, Swine: the excavations of 1960–1', *Yorkshire Archaeological Journal* 45: 142–8.

VCH (1906) *The Victoria History of the County of Norfolk 2.* London: HMSO.

VCH (1907) *The Victoria History of the County of Sussex 2.* London: HMSO.

VCH (1945) *The Victoria History of the County of Warwickshire 3.* London: HMSO.

VCH (1948) *The Victoria History of the County of Cambridgeshire 2.* London: HMSO.

VCH (1953) *The Victoria History of the County of Sussex 4.* London: HMSO.

Walcott, E. C. (1868) 'The priory of Minster in Sheppey', *Archaeologia Cantiana* 7: 287–306.

Walde, D. and Willows, N. (eds) (1991) *The Archaeology of Gender* (Proceedings of the 22nd Annual Chacmool Conference). Calgary: Archaeological Association of the University of Calgary.

Walker, S. (1983) 'Women and housing in classical Greece: the archaeological evidence', in A. Cameron and A. Kuhrt (eds) *Images of Women in Antiquity*, 81–91. London: Croom Helm.

Wall, D. D. (1991) 'Sacred dinners and secular teas: constructing domesticity in mid-nineteenth-century New York', in D. Seifert (ed.) *Gender in Historical Archaeology* (*Historical Archaeology* 25.4), 69–81.

Walsh, J. (trans.) (1961) *Revelations of Divine Love of Julian of Norwich.* London: Burns & Oates.

Walton, J. (1931) 'Medieval ironstone working in Bradley Wood, Huddersfield, W. Yorks.', *Naturalist*, 333–4.

Ward, SLG, B., (1987) *Harlots of the Desert.* London: Mowbray.

Ward, S. W. (1990) *Excavations at Chester. The Lesser Medieval Religious Houses: Sites Investigated 1964–1983.* Chester: Chester City Council.

Warner, M. (1976) *Alone of All Her Sex.* London: Picador.

Warner, S. T. (1948) *The Corner that Held Them.* London: Chatto & Windus.

Warren, A. K. (1984) 'The nun as anchoress: England 1100–1500', in J. A. Nichols and L. T. Shank (eds) *Medieval Religious Women*, 1: *Distant Echoes*, 197–211. Kalamazoo: Cistercian Publications.

—— (1985) *Medieval English Anchorites and Their Patrons.* Berkeley: University of California Press.

Watson, P. and Kennedy, M. C. (1991) 'The development of horticulture in the eastern woodlands of North America: women's role', in J. Gero and

M. Conkey (eds), *Engendering Archaeology: Women and Prehistory*, 255–75. Oxford: Blackwell.

Weaver, O. J. (1987) *Boscobel House and White Ladies Priory*. London: English Heritage.

Weedon, C. (1987) *Feminist Practice and Poststructuralist Theory*. Oxford: Blackwell.

West Yorks. Archaeology Service (1988 unpubl.) 'Nun Appleton House, N. Yorks.: excavations 1988, preliminary summary'.

Whelan, M. K. (1991) 'Gender and historical archaeology: eastern Dakota patterns in the nineteenth century' in D. Seifert (ed.) *Gender and Historical Archaeology* (*Historical Archaeology* 25.4), 17–32.

Whitelock, D. (ed.) (1979) *English Historical Documents*, 1: *500–1042* (2nd edn). London: Methuen.

—— Brett, M., and Brooke, C. N. L. (eds) (1981) *Councils and Synods*, vol. 1. Oxford: Clarendon Press.

Whiting, C. E. (1938) 'Excavations at Hampole Priory, 1937', *Yorkshire Archaeological Journal* 34: 204–12.

Whitwell, B. (1991) 'Flixborough', *Current Archaeology* 126: 244–7.

Wiesner, M. E. (1986) *Working Women in Renaissance Germany*. New Jersey: Rutgers University Press.

Wiessner, P. (1989) 'Style and changing relations between the individual and society', in I. Hodder (ed.) *The Meaning of Things: Material Culture and Symbolic Expression*, 56–63. London: Unwin Hyman.

Williams, D. (1975) 'The brides of Christ', in S. Ardener (ed.) *Perceiving Women*, 105–12. London: Malaby Press.

Williams, David H. (1975) 'Cistercian nunneries in medieval Wales', *Cîteaux* 26: 155–74.

Wilson, H. A. (1910) *The Pontifical of Magdalen College* (Henry Bradshaw Society, vol. 39). London.

Wood, I. (1987) 'Anglo-Saxon Otley: an archiepiscopal estate and its crosses in a Northumbrian context', *Northern History* 23: 20–38.

Wylie, A. (1991) 'Gender theory and the archaeological record: why is there no archaeology of gender?', in J. Gero and M. Conkey (eds), *Engendering Archaeology: Women and Prehistory*, 31–54. Oxford: Blackwell.

—— (1992 forthcoming) 'The interplay of evidential constraints and political interests: recent archaeological research on gender', *American Antiquity*.

Yentsch, A. (1991a) 'Engendering visible and invisible ceramic artifacts, especially dairy vessels', in D. Seifert (ed.), *Gender and Historical Archaeology* (*Historical Archaeology* 25.4), 132–55.

—— (1991b) 'The symbolic divisions of pottery: sex-related attributes of English and Anglo-American household pots', in R. H. McGuire and R. Paynter (eds) *The Archaeology of Inequality*, 192–230. Oxford: Blackwell.

Yiannouli, E. and Mithen, S. J. (1986) 'The real and random architecture of Siphnos: analysing house plans using simulation', *Archaeological Review from Cambridge* 5.2: 167–80.

Yorke, B. (1989) ' "Sisters under the Skin"? Anglo-Saxon nuns and nunneries in southern England', *Reading Medieval Studies* 15: 96–117.

Zarnecki, G. (1950) 'The Coronation of the Virgin on a capital from Reading Abbey', *Journal of the Warburg and Courtauld Institutes* 13: 1–12.

INDEX

Bascombe, Kenneth 30
Bath 65
Battle Abbey 89
Baume (Provence) 187
Baysdale (N. Yorks.) 66, 111
Beauchamp family 51
Beauvale Charterhouse 73
Beauvoir, Simone de 16
Bede 32, 136; *Epistola ad Ecgbertum* 29;
    Penitential 34; Historia Ecclesiastica Table
    1, 137
beguinages 170–2, 177, 186, 191
Beguines 170–1, 172, 177–8
behaviour, non-verbal 19
Belgium 171
bell-casting 83
Belton 72
Benedict, St, Rule of 18, 39
Benedictines 23, 24, 36, 38, 39, 40–4, 47,
    52, 53, 61, 68, 72, 74, 124, 125, 131, 136,
    137, 139, 143, 146, 163, 166, Figs 8, 9,
    14, 38
berdache 6
Berkeley (Gloucs.) 32
Berkshire 33
Bernard of Clairvaux, St 39, 155–6
Berwick 48
Bethany (Palestine) 101
Beverley 88, 89
biblical exegesis 15
Biddle, Martin 52, Fig. 13
Bigod, Roger 52
Blackborough (Norfolk) 38, 74
Blackmore Farm (Somerset) 124
Blair, John 39–40
Blanche, Queen of Navarre 51, 53
Blithbury (Staffs.) 38
Bluet, John 122
Bolton Abbey (Yorks.) 72
bone-working 83
Bordesley Abbey 59, 83
boundaries 151–2, 189
Bourdieu, Pierre 13, 14
Bradenstoke (male monastery) 137
Bradford-on-Avon (Wilts.) 32–3, 72
Brakspear, Sir Harold 23, 53, 117
Brandon (Suffolk) 31, 32
brasses 59, Figs 19, 20
Bretford (Warwicks.) 90
brewing 83, 123, 189
Brewood (Shrops.) 58, 66, 95, 109, 133,
    Fig. 41
Bridgettines 38, 94, 103, 108, 141

Bridgwater (Somerset) 174
Brigit, St 138
Bristol 64
Brixworth 109
Broadholme (Notts.) 38
Brooke, Christopher 24
Brown, Peter 18
Bruisyard (Suffolk) 51, 66, 77, 80
Buddhism 160
Buildwas (Shrops.) (male monastery) 124,
    131
Bullington (Lincs.) 50, 77, 82, 85
Bungay (Suffolk) 63, 122, 132, 138, 143
burial 7–8, 56–61, 95, 112, 134, 182, *see also*
    grave goods
Burnham (Berks.) 23, 56, 66, 99, 108, 109,
    112, 113, 115, 120, 122, 123, 132, 138,
    163, Figs 43, 46, 47, 68
Bury St Edmunds 33, 44
butchering 89
Butler, Lawrence 39
Byland (Yorks.) 73
Bynum, Caroline Walker 89, 139
Byzantium 6, 109, 134

Caesarius of Arles 65, 86
Calverley (W. Yorks.) 124
Cambridge 64, 90, 108, 111, 112, 115, 117,
    122, 132, 138, 163; *see also* St Radegund
Cambridgeshire 72
Campsey Ash (Suffolk) 20, 23, 38, 49, 56,
    95, 97, 153, Figs 17, 18
canonica 27
canons 38, 44, 82, 93, 94, 103, 104, 116,
    163, Fig. 30
Canonsleigh (Devon) 73
Carbrook Magna and Parva (Norfolk) 68
Carpenter, Christina 178
Carrow (Norfolk) 58, 59, 64, 97, 105, 111,
    120, 122
Carthusians 41
carvings *see* sculpture
Castle Acre (Norfolk) 115
Castle Hedingham (Essex) 63, 74, 173
Castle Rising (Norfolk) 168
castles 63, 64; women's quarters in 167–8
Catesby (Northants.) 38, 66, 71, 85, 143
Catherine of Alexandria, St 154
Catherine wheel 153, Fig. 59
Catley (Lincs.) 77
celibacy 18–19, 30
ceremony 18, 19
Chaldese, Joan 39

213